The Unity of Perception

The Unity of Perception

Content, Consciousness, Evidence

Susanna Schellenberg

OXFORD
UNIVERSITY PRESS

OXFORD
UNIVERSITY PRESS

Great Clarendon Street, Oxford, OX2 6DP,
United Kingdom

Oxford University Press is a department of the University of Oxford.
It furthers the University's objective of excellence in research, scholarship,
and education by publishing worldwide. Oxford is a registered trade mark of
Oxford University Press in the UK and in certain other countries

Published in the United States of America by Oxford University Press
198 Madison Avenue, New York, NY 10016, United States of America

British Library Cataloguing in Publication Data
Data available

Library of Congress Control Number: 2018941573

ISBN 978-0-19-882770-2

To Ezra

Preface

The ideas in this book developed over many years. I first became interested in perception as an undergraduate, but my focus was redirected towards issues in philosophy of language, especially Frege's philosophy of language. As a graduate student, I spent many years thinking primarily about the nature of semantic content, inferences, and modes of presentation before finding my way back to perception. The view of singular content and gappy modes of presentations that I develop in Chapter 4 of this book builds on ideas I worked on during those years. The rest of the ideas in this book have been developed in subsequent years.

I was lucky to get my first academic job at the Research School for Social Studies at the Australian National University. In that stimulating environment and in hours of discussions at the daily teas and the many social gatherings, I started seeing connections between my ideas about content and ways of analyzing perceptual consciousness. I owe a lot to conversations with David Chalmers and Daniel Stoljar, as well as with Alex Byrne, Tim Crane, and Fiona Macpherson who visited the department for extended periods. These conversations have continued and I am grateful for all that I have learned from them over the years as well as for their friendship and support. In the last two years of my time at the ANU, John Bengson and John Maier were there as postdocs. Our many and long discussions about capacities allowed me to see connections between my earlier work on the role of capacities in spatial perception and my interest in perceptual content and consciousness. Those discussions led me to recognize perceptual capacities as the foundational element in developing a unified account of the epistemological, phenomenological, and cognitive role of perception; a unified account that is sensitive to empirical data from cognitive psychology and neuroscience. Towards the end of my time at the ANU, I developed my ideas about capacities to advance an account of the epistemic force of perception and the nature of evidence and knowledge.

Conversations with epistemologists at Rutgers allowed these ideas to crystallize into the view of evidence and knowledge in this book. I am grateful in particular to Ernie Sosa for many long discussions, for his unwavering support, and for being a paragon of how to be a philosopher. In my first year at Rutgers, I taught a graduate seminar on perceptual particularity that helped shape the form and structure of this book. I thank all the participants for their contributions to the seminar and for the many discussions we have had since. They include Tony Cheng, Will Fleisher, Georgi Gardiner, Richard Garzón, Simon Goldstein, David Anton Johnston, Jeff King, Brian McLaughlin, and Lisa Miracchi. I am grateful especially to Jeff King for his support and friendship over the years and for several helpful conversations about the nature of propositions. That same semester, I sat in on Jerry Fodor and Zenon Pylyshyn's seminar on the semantics of mental representation. Each week Jerry Fodor and I got coffee before his seminar. The conversations we had over coffee helped me formulate some key ideas in a way that I hope makes them more understandable to those critical of my approach. I am privileged to be associated with RuCCS, the stellar cognitive science program at Rutgers. In particular the work of Jacob Feldman, Randy Gallistel, Rochel Gelman, and Zenon Pylyshyn has been critical in developing my thinking about perception, object tracking, representational capacities in humans and other animals, the psychophysics of perceptual systems, and the development of neurophysiologically plausible computational models.

In the Spring of 2015, I had the honor of being a visiting professor at the Department of Philosophy, Universitat de Barcelona. During this visit, I co-taught a two-week seminar with Manuel García-Carpintero in which we worked through the very first version of this book. I am grateful to the participants in that workshop and especially to Manuel García-Carpintero, Pepa Toribio, and Marc Artiga for many stimulating conversations and helpful suggestions. A later version of the book was the topic of a workshop at TMU, Taipei in December 2015. Many thanks to Hei-Man Chan, Paul C. W. Chen, Yi-Hsin Chuang, Ying-Chun Hu, Wen-Jun Huang, Kevin Kimble, Ying-Liang Lai, and Hong-Mao Li who each presented papers discussing chapters of the book. A more developed draft was discussed in John Morrison's graduate seminar at Columbia as well as in Nico Orlandi's philosophy of perception seminar at UCSC. The book benefited greatly from the constructive criticism of the participants in both seminars. In the Spring of 2016, I presented a heavily revised version of the manuscript to a graduate seminar at Rutgers. I am indebted especially to Austin Baker, Laura Callahan, Danny Forman, Ayoob Shahmoradi, and Eli Shupe for their insightful and probing comments. It is a privilege to be in a position to learn from such brilliant graduate students. In July 2016, the Centre for Integrative Neuroscience at the University of Tübingen hosted a workshop on a draft of the book with talks by Adrian Alsmith, Moritz Mueller, and Robin Dennis. I thank the three speakers for their critical comments as well as all the other participants for their questions and suggestions. In July 2017, the University of Potsdam held a workshop entitled *Perceptual Content: Workshop with Susanna Schellenberg* on a near-final draft of the manuscript. In the course of that memorable day, Andrew Chignell, Silvia De Toffoli, Stefanie Grüne, Johannes Haag, Till Hoeppner, Till Hopfe, Lionel Shapiro, and Bernhard Thöle gave me invaluable chapter by chapter feedback on the whole manuscript. Finally, in February 2018, I had the privilege of participating in a two-day workshop on the manuscript at the University of Zürich with talks by Nadja El Kassar, Pit Genot, Harman Ghijsen, Roberta Locatelli, Christoph Pfisterer, Stefan Riegelnik, Johannes Roessler, Eva Schmidt, and Keith Wilson. I am indebted to all the speakers and participants for their comments.

I did some of the work on this book as a visiting professor at the University of Tübingen funded by a Friedrich Wilhelm Bessel Research Award of the Alexander von Humboldt Foundation, and I am grateful for the support of the Humboldt Foundation as well as for the hospitality of the Philosophy Department and the Centre for Integrative Neuroscience as a whole, but especially to Chiara Brozzo and Hong Yu Wong for many fruitful conversations. Special thanks are due to Thomas Sattig for nominating me for the award. I benefited greatly from our many conversations about constitution and metaphysical necessity.

John Morrison, Ram Neta, and Nico Orlandi have read and given me comments on all or part of the complete manuscript. I am deeply grateful. Others have given me feedback on early versions of individual chapters. They include Kent Bach, David Chalmers, Jonathan Cohen, Stewart Cohen, Earl Conee, Tim Crane, Marian David, Fred Dretske, Bill Fish, Branden Fitelson, Todd Ganson, James Genone, Mikkel Gerken, Kathrin Glüer, Alvin Goldman, Dan Greco, John Greco, Ting Ho, Frank Jackson, Jeff King, Ole Koksvik, Nick Kroll, Shen-Yi Liao, Matt McGrath, John Maier, Neil Mehta, Angela Mendelovici, Carla Merino-Rajme, Alex Morgan, Casey O'Callaghan, Adam Pautz, David Rosenthal, Jonathan Schaffer, Charles Siewert, Nico Silins, Declan Smithies, Ernie Sosa, Joshua Spencer, Daniel Stoljar, Kurt Sylvan, Brad Thompson, and Chris Tucker. In addition to those mentioned above, I have benefited greatly from discussions with Ned Block, Bill Brewer, John Campbell, Frankie Egan, Megan Feeney, Santiago Echeverri, EJ Green, Gabe Greenberg, Clayton Littlejohn, Mike Martin, Chris Peacocke, François Recanati, Michael Rescorla, and Miguel Ángel Sebastián.

The ideas in this book have been presented and tested as the *Thacher Lecture 2017* at George Washington University, as the *Clark Lecture 2015* at Indiana University, and as keynote addresses at the *International Wittgenstein Conference 2017* in Kirchberg, the *3rd Philosophy Graduate Conference*, UNAM, Mexico City, the *Rochester Graduate Epistemology Conference 2016*, the *PeRFECt2* workshop at the University of Pennsylvania, the *Philosophy of Perception Workshop* on this book at TMU, Taipei, Taiwan, the *Portuguese Society for Analytic Philosophy, National Meeting*, the Azores, the *2015 University of Texas at Austin Graduate Philosophy Conference*, the *PETAF final conference*, Barcelona, the *Princeton-Rutgers Graduate Conference*, as well as at the following institutions, workshops, conferences, seminars, and reading groups (listed in reverse chronological order): *The Principles of Epistemology* conference at the Collège de France, Paris, the *Workshop on Perception* at the University of Tübingen, the *APA Pacific Division Meeting 2017*, the *Perceptual Awareness* workshop at the Institut Jean Nicod, the Consciousness/Self-Consciousness group at the Institut Jean Nicod, an invited symposium at the *Canadian Philosophical Association 2017* (with comments by Jim John), Stanford University, UCSC, Rice University, the *Bochum-Rutgers Workshop* in New York City, the CUNY Cognitive Science Group, University of Tübingen, the *Conference in Honor of the 30th Year of Goldman's Epistemology and Cognition* at the College of William and Mary, an invited symposium at the *ESPP 2016*, the *Epistemology of Perception* workshop at the University of Southampton, the *Facets of Perception* at the University of Tübingen, the *Unstructured Conference* at Rutgers University, the *Episteme Conference* in Mpumalanga, the *5th Lund-Rutgers Conference* at the

University of Lund, University of Pittsburgh, National Chung Cheng University, Taiwan, the *Metaphysics of Mind Conference*, Fordham University, Universitat de Barcelona, *Orange Beach Epistemology Workshop*, *The Epistemology of Perception* workshop at SMU, Universidad Autónoma Metropolitana, Mexico City, the *CSMN Workshop on the First Person Perspective* at the Norwegian Institute in Athens, USC, Johns Hopkins University, the *Representationalism vs. Relationalism* workshop at the University of Antwerp, *NeuPhi Online Talk* (with comments by Matt McGrath), UC-Irvine, the *Oberlin Colloquium on Philosophy of Mind*, with comments by Alex Byrne, the *Sanders Conference on Philosophy of Perception*, Princeton, CUNY, Notre Dame, Duke, the *Columbia-Barnard Perception Workshop*, the *Minds and Metaphysics* workshop at Ghent University, the *Rationality and Reference Conference* (with comments by Nick Kroll), Frank Jackson's graduate seminar at Princeton, Anil Gupta's graduate seminar at the University of Pittsburgh, UC-Berkeley, the NYU consciousness reading group, University of Miami, an invited symposium at the *APA Eastern Division Meeting 2012* (with comments by Adam Pautz), the New York area corridor reading group, the *Perception and Knowledge* workshop at the University of Graz, the *Metaphysics and the Philosophy of Mind* workshop at the University of Oslo, the *Oberlin Colloquium on Philosophy of Mind* (with comments by Alex Byrne), University of Massachusetts, Amherst, Temple University, the *Carolina Metaphysics Workshop* (with comments by Benj Hellie), *The Epistemology of Philosophy* conference at the University of Cologne, the *Perception, Action, and Time* workshop in Barcelona, Cambridge University, University of York, the *Epistemology* workshop at Aarhus University, University of Glasgow, Warwick University, the Rutgers epistemology group, Washington University, St. Louis, University of Missouri, St. Louis, Saint Louis University, University of Miami, the *Propositions and Same-Saying II* workshop at the University of Sydney, Université de Fribourg, CEU Budapest, the Arché Research Centre, University of St Andrews, the *Perception and Knowledge* workshop at the University of Stockholm, the *Australasian Association of Philosophy 2008*, the *Themes from Crispin Wright* conference at the Philosophy Program RSSS, ANU, the *Australasian Association of Philosophy 2009*, University of Turin, Philosophy Program RSSS, ANU, University of Waikato, University of Auckland, Victoria University of Wellington, Leeds University, University of Sydney, Yale, Rutgers University, UC Riverside, Farid Masrour's NYU graduate seminar, University of Canterbury, University of Otago, the *Hallucination* workshop on Crete, *Toward a Science of Consciousness 2008*, the *APA Pacific Division Meeting 2008* (with comments by John Campbell and Terry Horgan), the *Russell Conference in Philosophy*, Monash, University of Melbourne, the *Bled Epistemology Conference* 2007, and the *Australasian Association of Philosophy 2007*. I have benefited from discussions, probing questions, and helpful suggestions at each of these occasions.

Peter Momtchiloff has been a supportive and generous editor. I am deeply grateful for his help and encouragement throughout the project. He gathered substantial comments from three referees who I thank for their thorough and critical comments.

Thanks are due also to Edwin Pritchard for copy-editing the manuscript. Many thanks to Laura Callahan, Megan Feeney, Jenny Judge, Robert Long, Eli Shupe, and Martin Stone who helped with editing at various stages, to Alison Springle for her help with the references, and to Carolina Flores for preparing the index. Finally, many thanks to Georgi Gardiner, who read and commented on the entire penultimate draft of the manuscript.

This book integrates material on perception that I have been working on for over ten years. From the very start, I envisaged this work as a unified account of the epistemological, phenomenological, and cognitive role of perception. Over the years, the ways in which I conceived of the unifying element shifted from focus on representational content to focus on perceptual capacities (the employment of which constitutes representational content). This refocusing required rewriting and reworking the material that draws on previously published work from the ground up.

Chapter 1 is based on parts of "Perceptual Particularity," *Philosophy and Phenomenological Research* (2016), rewritten extensively. There is significant new material in Sections 1, 2, and 4.

Chapter 2 consists entirely of new material.

Chapter 3 is based on parts of "Perceptual Particularity" rewritten extensively.

Chapter 4 draws on material from "The Particularity and Phenomenology of Perceptual Experience," *Philosophical Studies* (2010) as well as "Externalism and the Gappy Content of Hallucination," in *Hallucination*, MIT Press (2013), rewritten from the ground up.

Chapter 5 is based on "In Defense of Perceptual Content" *Philosophical Perspectives* (2017). It exploits some ideas from "Perceptual Content Defended," *Noûs* (2011) as well as "The Relational and Representational Character of Perceptual Experience," in *Does Perception have Content?*, Oxford University Press (2014). However, the key arguments are different and the material is rewritten from the ground up.

Chapter 6 is based on material from "Perceptual Consciousness as a Mental Activity," *Noûs* (2017) as well as "Ontological Minimalism about Phenomenology," *Philosophy and Phenomenological Research* (2011).

Chapter 7 is a revised version of "Experience and Evidence," *Mind* (2011), with some critical changes to the key argument.

Chapter 8 is based on "Phenomenal Evidence and Factive Evidence" and "Phenomenal Evidence and Factive Evidence Defended: Replies to McGrath, Neta, and Pautz," a symposium with comments by Matt McGrath, Ram Neta, and Adam Pautz, *Philosophical Studies* (2016).

Chapter 9 is based on parts of "Perceptual Capacities, Knowledge, and Gettier Cases," in *Explaining Knowledge: New Essays on the Gettier Problem* (2017) and "The Origins of Perceptual Knowledge," *Episteme* (2017), rewritten extensively.

Chapter 10 draws on parts of "Perceptual Capacities, Knowledge, and Gettier Cases."

I thank the editors concerned for permission to use this material.

Large parts of this book were written at the Writers Room in Manhattan. I am grateful to the many wonderful people there for their encouragement and friendship, as well as for discussions about grammar, prose, and managing the agony of writing. Ram Neta and Nico Orlandi kept me going at critical junctions in the final stretch of finishing this book. I thank them for their loyal friendship. Above all, I am grateful to Ezra for constant inspiration with his insatiable intellectual curiosity and creative engagement with the world.

Contents

Part III. Consciousness

Introduction

GALILEO Vision is perfect. People have very good eyes.
APICIUS Whose weak eyes, then, need the help of your lenses?
GALILEO They are the eyes of the philosophers.

Fontenelle, *Dialogues des morts*, 1683

Perception is our key to the world. It plays at least three different roles in our lives. It justifies beliefs and provides us with knowledge of our environment. It brings about conscious mental states. It converts informational input, such as light and sound waves, into representations of invariant features in our environment. Corresponding to these three roles, there are at least three fundamental questions that have motivated the study of perception:

Epistemology Question: How does perception justify beliefs and yield knowledge of our environment?

Mind Question: How does perception bring about conscious mental states?

Information Question: How does a perceptual system accomplish the feat of converting varying informational input into mental representations of invariant features in our environment?

To be sure, many other questions have motivated the study of perception. To list just a few: What is the nature of the perceptual relation? What is the object of perception? How does perception guide action? What is the relation between perception and thought? But the way these questions are answered hinges on what stance is taken on the three fundamental questions.[1]

The last decade has seen an explosion of work on the mind and information questions in both philosophy of mind and cognitive science. While there has been fruitful interaction between work in these two fields, little has been done to integrate this work with issues in epistemology. Theories motivated by addressing the mind and information questions have been developed largely independently of concerns about

---

[1] No doubt, dependencies run in the other direction as well: what stance one takes on, say, the question of what the object of perception is, will affect one's answer to the three fundamental questions. But arguably there is an asymmetry in the order of explanation between the three fundamental questions and the other questions.

how perception furnishes knowledge of our environment and how it justifies our beliefs. Similarly, theories motivated by addressing the epistemology question have been developed largely independently of concerns about how perception brings about conscious mental states. To be sure, most accounts of perceptual justification rely heavily on the idea that perception justifies beliefs in virtue of its phenomenal character. However, such accounts typically take it as given that perception provides evidence and immediately proceed to addressing the question of what the relationship is between such evidence and relevant beliefs.

This split between philosophy of mind and cognitive science on the one side and epistemology on the other has hindered our understanding of perception. Questions in philosophy of mind are intimately connected with questions in epistemology, in particular with regard to perception: the role of perception in yielding conscious mental states is not independent of its role in justifying our beliefs and yielding knowledge. If this is right, then perception should be studied in an integrated manner.

This book develops a unified account of the phenomenological and epistemological role of perception that is informed by empirical research. As such, it develops an account of perception that provides an answer to the first two questions, while being sensitive to scientific accounts that address the third question. By analyzing mental states in light of scientific evidence while being sensitive to their epistemic, cognitive, and phenomenological role, this book aims to advance a rigorous way of doing philosophy of mind. It aims to be conceptually disciplined and empirically constrained. It is intended as a useful resource both for those familiar with philosophical and scientific debates about perception; as well as those unfamiliar with these debates.

The key idea is that perception is constituted by employing perceptual capacities—for example the capacity to discriminate and single out instances of red from instances of blue. Perceptual content, consciousness, and evidence are each analyzed in terms of this basic property of perception. Employing perceptual capacities constitutes phenomenal character as well as perceptual content. The primacy of employing perceptual capacities in perception over their derivative employment in hallucination and illusion grounds the epistemic force of perceptual experience. In this way, the book provides a unified account of perceptual content, perceptual consciousness, and perceptual evidence. What unifies the account is perceptual capacities. Due to the grounding role of perceptual capacities, we can call the view developed in this book capacitism.

Such a unified account of perception opens up a new understanding of the nature of perceptual content, perceptual particularity, the phenomenological basis of evidence, the epistemic force of evidence, the origins of perceptual knowledge, the relationship between content and consciousness, as well as the relationship between consciousness and reference. Moreover, it clears the way for solving a host of unresolved problems, such as the relation between attention and perceptual knowledge, the linguistic analysis of perceptual reports, the relation between acquaintance and awareness, the rational role of perceptual experience, and the perceptual basis for demonstrative reference.

One larger aim of this book is to bring back mental capacities as a way of analyzing the mind. Despite their prominence in the history of philosophy, capacities have been neglected in recent philosophical work. By contrast, appeal to mental capacities is standard in cognitive psychology and the brain sciences. This book develops the notion of capacities in light of empirical work in cognitive psychology, neuroscience, and developmental psychology. While it is based in contemporary empirical research, it also harks back to a long tradition of analyzing the mind in terms of capacities. It turns out that we can use contemporary insights and tools to modernize that tradition.

Analyzing the mind in terms of capacities has many advantages. One central advantage is that it allows for a counterfactual analysis of mental states on three interrelated levels. On one level, we focus on the function of mental capacities. On a second level, we focus on the mental capacities employed irrespective of the context in which they are employed. Here the focus is on what perception and corresponding cases of hallucination and illusion have in common. On a third level, we focus on the mental capacities employed, taking into account the context in which they are employed. Here the focus is on the difference between cases in which a capacity fulfills its function (perception) and cases in which it fails to fulfill its function (hallucination and illusion). These terms will be explained in more detail in Chapter 2.

Let me locate capacitism within the wider philosophical landscape. First, capacitism grounds mental states, consciousness, evidence, and content in the physical, nonmental world. In doing so, these features of the mind are rendered no less amenable to scientific investigation than any other features of the world. The naturalistic and physicalist view of perception presented shows how perception is our key to the world while situating perception within that world.

Second, capacitism is an externalist account of perceptual content, consciousness, and evidence. It is an externalist account since the perceptual capacities that constitute these features of the mind function to discriminate and single out particulars in our environment. Due to their function to single out particulars, perceptual capacities connect us to our environment. While capacitism is an externalist view, it is one that does justice to the internalist elements of perceptual experience. In contrast to, say, orthodox versions of reliabilism, it makes room for the cognitive and epistemic role that conscious mental states play in our lives. Moreover, the capacities employed in perception can be employed derivatively in hallucination and illusion. While they do not fulfill their function when employed in hallucination and illusion, the capacities nonetheless function to discriminate and single out particulars, thereby providing a relation to how things would be were they to fulfill their function. By doing justice to the internalist elements of perceptual experience, capacitism is a modestly externalist view.

Third, capacitism is a common factor view of perception. The same perceptual capacities can be employed in perception, hallucination, and illusion. The perceptual capacities employed constitute a metaphysically substantial common element. This common element shared by perceptions, hallucinations, and illusions presents itself on three levels: representational content (Chapter 4 and Chapter 5), perceptual consciousness (Chapter 6) and phenomenal evidence (Chapter 7 and Chapter 8). Thus, capacitism is at its core non-disjunctivist.

Fourth, despite being non-disjunctivist, capacitism is nevertheless an asymmetric account of perception, hallucination, and illusion. It holds that perception is metaphysically and explanatorily more basic than hallucination and illusion. After all, the function of perceptual capacities is indexed to perception. Perceptual capacities function to discriminate and single out particulars. They have this function, even when employed derivatively in hallucination or illusion.

Thus, capacitism walks a path between two traditional views: the common factor view and austere relationalism. The common factor view posits that a perception, hallucination, and illusion with the same phenomenal character share a common element that grounds that shared phenomenal character. Typically, the additional condition that makes for successful perception is considered to be a causal relation between the experiencing subject and the perceived object. This approach is analogous to the epistemological view that knowledge can be factorized into belief and some additional element, say, justification. By contrast, austere relationalism characterizes hallucination as falling short of perception, arguing that perception and hallucination do not share a common element (cf. Campbell 2002, Martin 2002a, Brewer 2006). This approach is analogous to the view that mere belief is to be analyzed as subjectively indiscriminable but falling short of knowledge.

Against austere relationalism, I argue that perceptions, hallucinations, and illusions with the same phenomenal character share a metaphysically substantial common factor which grounds that phenomenal character. This much I share with other common factor views. But in the spirit of austere relationalism, I argue that hallucinations and illusions can be understood only in terms of a deficiency of perceptions: perceptual capacities fulfill their function when employed in perception but fail to fulfill their function when employed in hallucination or illusion. Thus, there is an asymmetric dependence of the employment of perceptual capacities in hallucination and illusion on their employment in perception.

This book makes certain assumptions. It approaches questions about the nature of perception within the framework of anti-reductionist realism. The world is a certain way independently of how we perceive it to be. In most cases, there could have been other ways in which we could have perceived that same environment. The difference in these ways in which our environment can be perceived is due to differences in the perceptual capacities employed. Any given particular can be successfully singled out with a range of different perceptual capacities. I can successfully single out the color of a pomegranate with my capacity to discriminate red from other colors or with my capacity to single out cochineal from other colors. I could not successfully single out the color of the pomegranate with my capacity to discriminate and single out blue from other colors. The world sets the limits as to when a perceptual capacity is employed such that it succeeds in singling out a particular.

This book has four parts: foundations, content, consciousness, and evidence. Each part develops a component of capacitism. I introduce six arguments in the course of developing these components: the particularity argument (Part I), the perceptual content argument, the relational content argument (Part II), the argument for mental activism (Part III), the phenomenal evidence argument, and the factive evidence argument (Part IV).

1. Foundations

Part I develops the foundations on which the rest of the book builds. Chapter 1 addresses the particular elements of perception; Chapter 2 its general elements.

The phenomenon of perceptual particularity has received remarkably little attention in recent philosophical work. It is high time that this changed. After all, the central role of perception in our epistemic and cognitive lives is to provide us with knowledge of particulars in our environment, justify our beliefs about particulars, ground demonstrative reference, and yield singular thoughts. Chapter 1 tackles the problem of perceptual particularity, teasing apart its different aspects. In light of this discussion, it defends the particularity thesis, that is, roughly, the thesis that a subject's perceptual state is constituted by the particulars perceived. It does so by arguing that perception is constitutively a matter of employing perceptual capacities that function to discriminate and single out particulars. Thereby, the chapter provides an account of the particular elements of perception.

Chapter 2 develops an account of the general element of perception. The general element is constituted by the perceptual capacities employed. Drawing on work in cognitive psychology, neuroscience, and developmental psychology, the chapter provides a comprehensive theory of perceptual capacities. This theory includes an account of the function of perceptual capacities, their individuation and possession conditions, the physical and informational base of perceptual capacities, as well as their repeatability, fallibility, and the asymmetry of their employment in perception on the one hand and hallucination and illusion on the other.

The rest of the book exploits this view of the general and particular elements of perception to develop a unified account of content (Part II), consciousness (Part III), and evidence (Part IV).

2. Content

Chapter 3 argues that perceptual particularity is best accounted for in terms of perceptual content rather than in terms of epistemic, psychologistic, or ontological dependency properties. Chapter 4 develops my account of singular perceptual content. I call this view Fregean particularism. Fregean particularism advances a new understanding of singular modes of presentation: the representational content of a perception, hallucination, or illusion is constituted by the perceptual capacities employed and the particulars (if any) thereby singled out. These modes of presentation can be individuated at the level of content types and token contents. Perceptions, hallucinations, and illusions with the same phenomenal character are constituted by employing the same perceptual capacities; they thereby share a content type. But the token content of perception, hallucination, and illusion differs at least in part. If one perceives a particular, one employs a perceptual capacity that successfully singles out that particular. The token content of the relevant perceptual states is thereby constituted by the particular singled out and is thus singular content. If one fails to single out a particular (perhaps because one is suffering an illusion or hallucination), the token content is gappy.

Fregean particularism offers a non-disjunctivist account of perceptual content that synthesizes relationalist and representationalist insights. Relationalists argue that perceptual experience is constitutively a matter of a perceiver being related to her environment. Representationalists argue that perceptual experience is constitutively a matter of a perceiver representing her environment. However, the standard views in the debate are either austerely relationalist or austerely representationalist. According to austere relationalists, perception is constitutively relational but not constitutively representational (Campbell 2002, Martin 2002a, Travis 2004, Brewer 2006). According to austere representationalists, perception is constitutively representational but not constitutively relational (Dretske 1995, Tye 1995, Lycan 1996). Fregean particularism avoids the pitfalls of both austere views by arguing that perception is both constitutively relational and constitutively representational. The history of philosophy is a history of false dichotomies. The dichotomy between relationalists and representationalists is one such false dichotomy.

Chapter 5 takes a step back and traces the way in which excessive demands on the notion of perceptual content invite an austere relationalist account of perception. It argues that any account that acknowledges the role of discriminatory, selective capacities in perception must acknowledge that perceptual states have representational content. The chapter shows that on a relational understanding of perceptual content, the fundamental insights of austere relationalism do not compete with representationalism. Most objections to the thesis that perceptual experience has representational content apply only to austere representationalist accounts—that is, accounts on which perceptual relations to the environment play no explanatory role.

3. Consciousness

Chapter 6 exploits the thesis that perception is constitutively a matter of employing perceptual capacities to address the problem of consciousness. Orthodox views analyze consciousness in terms of sensory awareness of some entities. Such views differ widely on how they understand the nature of those entities. According to one cluster of views, they are understood to be strange particulars, such as sense-data, qualia, or intentional objects. According to a different cluster of views, they are understood to be abstract entities, such as properties. According to yet another cluster of views, namely austere relationalist views, they are mind-independent particulars in our environment, such as objects, property-instances, and events. What these views have in common is that they all analyze consciousness in terms of sensory awareness of some entities.

There are problems with all three versions of the orthodox view. In a nutshell, the problem with sense-data and qualia theories is the following: if the goal is to explain consciousness, it is unclear what the explanatory gain is of appealing to awareness of obscure entities, such as sense-data and qualia. On the face of it no explanatory progress has been made. The problem with explaining consciousness in terms of sensory awareness of abstract entities is that abstract entities are neither spatio-temporally located nor causally efficacious. It is unclear what it would be to be sensorily aware of such entities. Leaving aside complicating details, the problem with austere relationalist views—on which consciousness is analyzed in terms of awareness of mind-independent particulars—is that it leaves unexplained how we could be conscious when we are hallucinating rather than perceiving.

Chapter 6 breaks with this tradition. It argues that perceptual consciousness is constituted by a mental activity, namely the mental activity of employing perceptual capacities. I call this view mental activism. Mental activism avoids the problems of the orthodox view of analyzing consciousness in terms of sensory awareness of some entity. Insofar as employing perceptual capacities constitutes representational content, mental activism is a form of representationalism. Standard representationalist views purport to explain consciousness (phenomenal character) in terms of representational content. Some representationalists have it that phenomenal character is identical to representational content (Tye 1995). Such an identity claim arguably amounts to a category mistake. More cautious views have it that phenomenal character supervenes on or is grounded in representational content. Such views, however, say almost nothing unless an explanation is given of what it is about representational content such that it grounds or constitutes the supervenience base of consciousness. Mental activism argues that employing perceptual capacities constitutes both consciousness and representational content in such a way that consciousness supervenes on representational content. Thus, the view explains how and why consciousness supervenes on representational content.

4. Evidence

Locke famously wrote: "whence has [the mind] all the materials of reason and knowledge? To this I answer, in one word, from EXPERIENCE" (1690, II.i.2). Perception guides our actions, decisions are routinely made on the basis of perception, and most scientific knowledge derives at least in part from perception. Part IV provides an account of perceptual evidence that is sensitive to the nature of appearances. It sheds light on a host of issues at the mind-epistemology interface: the phenomenological basis of evidence, the rational source of perceptual evidence, and the ground of perceptual knowledge.

Building on the distinction between the content type of a perceptual experience (which perceptions, hallucinations, and illusions can share), and the token content of perceptual experience (which represents the perceived particular when things go well), Chapter 7 introduces a distinction between two levels of evidence. The content type furnishes a weak type of evidence, namely phenomenal evidence: evidence that corresponds to how our environment sensorily seems to us. In the case of an accurate perception, the token content furnishes a strong type of evidence, namely factive evidence: evidence that is determined by the environment to which we are perceptually related such that the evidence is guaranteed to be an accurate guide to the environment.

Illusions and hallucinations can mislead us: they may prompt us to act in ways that do not mesh with the world around us and they may lead us to form false beliefs about that world. Capacitism provides an account of evidence that shows in virtue of what illusions and hallucinations mislead us and prompt us to act: in hallucination and illusion we have phenomenal evidence. Moreover, it gives an account of why we are in a better epistemic position when we perceive than when we hallucinate: when we perceive, we have not only phenomenal evidence but also factive evidence. So in the good case we have more evidence than in the bad case.

I argue that the rational source of both phenomenal and factive evidence lies in employing perceptual capacities that function to discriminate and single out particulars. I thereby show that the epistemic force of perceptual states stems from the explanatory and metaphysical primacy of employing perceptual capacities in perception over their employment in corresponding hallucinations and illusions. Perceptual states have epistemic force due to being systematically linked to mind-independent, environmental particulars via the perceptual capacities that constitute those perceptual states. Hence the ground of the epistemic force of perceptual states lies in properties of the perceptual capacities that constitute the relevant perceptual states and thus in metaphysical facts about perceptual experience.

Chapter 8 discusses the repercussions of capacitism for the justification of beliefs, the credences we should assign to perceptual beliefs, and the luminosity of mental states. In light of this discussion, the chapter explores the consequences of capacitism for various familiar problem cases: speckled hens, identical twins, brains in vats, new evil demon scenarios, matrices, and Swampman.

From one's perspective one does not know whether one is perceiving, hallucinating, or suffering an illusion and one does not know whether one knows or fails to know. Not only does one not know whether one does not know, one does not know whether one knows. Chapter 9 exploits the consequences of capacitism for a view of perceptual knowledge. It argues that while factive evidence is sufficient for knowledge, phenomenal evidence is not. Thus, the chapter develops a sufficient evidence requirement for knowledge. In perceptual Gettier cases, it is standardly thought that the subject has sufficient evidence for knowledge, but fails to know for some other reason. Once we recognize the distinction between phenomenal and factive evidence, we can say that in perceptual Gettier cases, the subject has mere phenomenal evidence. Since she does not have factive evidence, however, she fails to have knowledge. In this way, perceptual Gettier cases are analyzed without appeal to any factor beyond evidence. Capacitism rejects the belief condition on knowledge and gives substance to the idea that knowledge is a mental state.

Chapter 10 shows how capacitism differs from competing views of evidence and knowledge: knowledge-first epistemology, reliabilism, and virtue epistemology. By grounding the epistemic force of perceptual experience in facts about its metaphysical structure, capacitism is not only an externalist view, but moreover a naturalistic view of the epistemology of perceptual experience. In contrast to standard externalist and naturalistic views, capacitism does not invoke reliability to explain the epistemic force of mental states. Moreover, in recognizing a metaphysically substantial common element between perception and hallucination, it avoids any commitment to disjunctivism. While capacitism makes room for phenomenal evidence, it does not amount to an internalist attempt at isolating a non-factive mental component of factive evidence. After all, phenomenal evidence is constituted by employing perceptual capacities—the very same capacities that also constitute factive evidence. Insofar as both kinds of evidence stem from properties of the perceptual capacities employed, capacitism provides a unified account of the rational source of perceptual evidence. Capacitism is a distinctive externalist view of evidence and knowledge that does not invoke reliability, remains steadfastly naturalistic, and in recognizing a metaphysically substantive common element between perception and hallucination avoids any commitment to disjunctivism.

While this book constitutes a unified whole, each chapter is written such that it can be read as an independent unit. To help those who read only one or two chapters, I refer to sections in previous chapters where background might help a deeper understanding. For those pressed for time, who nonetheless want to read the key parts, I recommend reading Chapter 1 (for the view on perceptual particularity), Chapter 2 (for the nature of perceptual capacities), Chapter 4 (for the key ideas on perceptual content), and then depending on proclivities either Chapter 6 (consciousness) or Chapter 7 (evidence).

PART I

Foundations

Chapter 1

Perceptual Particularity

When we attempt to reduce complex operations to simpler and simpler ones, we find in the end that discrimination or differential response is the fundamental operation. Discrimination is prerequisite even to the operation of denoting or 'pointing to'.

(Stevens 1939)

When we perceive our environment, we are perceptually related to particulars in that environment. What kind of mental state are we in when we are perceptually related to a particular? Is the mental state constituted by the particular? Assuming that the perceptual state is characterized by its content, is the content a singular proposition? To motivate these questions, consider Kim, who has three distinct, consecutive experiences. First, she sees a cup. Let's call it cup$_1$. Then, unbeknownst to her, the cup is switched with a numerically distinct but qualitatively identical cup. So in the second experience, she sees a different cup. Let's call it cup$_2$. In the third experience, she hallucinates a cup and so is not perceptually related to any cup. All three experiences are subjectively indistinguishable—from Kim's perspective, it seems as if she saw just one cup.

How do the three experiences differ? It is uncontroversial that they differ in that Kim is causally related to different environments. In the first experience, she is causally related to cup$_1$. In the second, she is causally related to cup$_2$. In the third, she is not causally related to any cup. In addition to this difference in causal relation, the question arises whether there are further differences between the three experiences. Is there a difference in the epistemic relation between Kim and her environment? Is there a difference in the ontological nature of the three experiential states? Is there a difference in their phenomenal character? Finally, do the three mental states differ in content?

Kim's case brings into focus two central questions that structure the debate on perceptual particularity. One question is whether perceptual states are constituted by particular elements, by general elements, or by both particular and general elements.[1]

---

[1] Campbell (2002), Travis (2004), and Brewer (2006) among others have it that perceptual states are constituted only by particulars. Jackson (1977), Lewis (1980), Harman (1990), Millar (1991), Davies (1992), Siewert (1998), Byrne (2001), and Hill (2009) among others have it that perceptual states are constituted only by general elements. Evans (1982), Peacocke (1983), Searle (1983), Burge (1991, 2010), Recanati (1993, 2010), Soteriou (2000), Martin (2002b), Johnston (2004), Chalmers (2006a), Schellenberg

If we assume that perceptual states are constituted by particulars, a second question is what property of the perceptual state grounds perceptual particularity: is perceptual particularity a matter of the epistemic relation between the perceiver and her environment, ontological features of the perceptual state, its phenomenal character, its content, or a combination of the above?[2] I will argue that perceptual states are constituted by both particular and general elements, and that perceptual content grounds perceptual particularity.

In Section 1, I present the particularity thesis, which to a first approximation is the thesis that perceptual states are constituted by the particulars perceived. Section 2 clarifies what is at issue in the debate on perceptual particularity. In Section 3, I discuss what could adjudicate the debate. I present several arguments in support of the particularity thesis and will show how the generalist could avoid their conclusion. Section 4 puts forward the particularity argument, the conclusion of which is the particularity thesis. By arguing that perceptual states are constituted at least in part by particular elements, it addresses the first question structuring the debate on perceptual particularity.

While this chapter remains neutral on whether perceptual states are constituted only by particular elements or by both particular and general elements, I take a stand on this question in Chapter 3. There I argue that perceptual states are constituted both by particular and general elements. I also address the second of the two central questions structuring the debate about perceptual particularity: I distinguish between four versions of the particularity thesis (epistemic, ontological, psychologistic, and representational) and argue for the representational version. Thus, Chapter 3 argues that perceptual particularity is grounded in perceptual content. The particularity thesis—which this chapter establishes—is, however, neutral between these four interpretations.

1. The Particularity Thesis

Particularity Thesis: A subject's perceptual state M brought about by being perceptually related to the particular α is constituted by α.

The particularity thesis entails that if Kim first sees cup_1 and then sees cup_2, she is in two distinct token perceptual states—even if she does not notice the switch. More

---

(2006, 2010), Bach (2007), Byrne and Logue (2008), García-Carpintero (2010), Crane (2011), Speaks (2011, 2014), and Genone (2014) among others have it that perceptual states are constituted by both particular and general elements. Many are neutral on the matter, for example, Siegel (2011).

  [2] Campbell (2002), Martin (2002b), Johnston (2004), Brewer (2006), and Genone (2014) account for perceptual particularity in terms of phenomenal character. Recanati (2010) accounts for it in terms of the epistemic relation between the perceiving subject and her environment. Evans (1982), Peacocke (1983), Searle (1983), Burge (1991), Soteriou (2000), Chalmers (2006b), Schellenberg (2006, 2010, 2011a), Byrne and Logue (2008), García-Carpintero (2010), Crane (2011), and Speaks (2011, 2014) account for perceptual particularity in terms of perceptual content.

generally, the thesis entails that if M is a perceptual state brought about by being perceptually related to the particular α, and M^* is a state brought about by being perceptually related to a numerically distinct particular β (and not perceiving α), then M and M^* are distinct perceptual states—even if α and β are qualitatively identical. The particularity thesis is stronger than the thesis that M and M^* differ, it makes a claim about what constitutes this difference.

It will be helpful to specify each element of the particularity thesis. A perceptual state is the mental state a subject is in when she perceives particulars in her environment. So a perceptual state is to be contrasted from the state one is in when one suffers an illusion or a hallucination. In paradigmatic cases of illusion, it seems to one that there is a property-instance, where there is no such property-instance. In paradigmatic cases of hallucination, it seems to one that there is an object, where there is no such object.[3] Perceptual states have phenomenal character. At this stage of the discussion, we can and should stay neutral on whether phenomenal character is the only crucial property of a perceptual state or whether a perceptual state is further characterized by representational or epistemic properties. Later, I will relinquish neutrality on all accounts. But I will remain neutral for now since the argument of this chapter can be accepted regardless of what stance one takes on this issue.

The relevant particulars perceived can be objects, events, or property-instances in our environment. It is uncontroversial that objects and events are particulars. Arguably, however, we are not just perceptually related to objects and events, but also to property-instances—for example, instances of shape, size, pitch, texture, and color properties, to name just a few. To support this idea, note that perceptual relations are a kind of causal relation. So when we perceive, say, the shape of the cup in front of us, that shape must be causally efficacious—otherwise we could not perceive it. Thus, given plausible assumptions about causation, the shape of the cup must be a concrete spatio-temporal particular rather than a universal. After all, universals are neither spatio-temporally located nor causally efficacious. I will assume an Aristotelian view on which properties are understood in terms of their instances. Hence, I will assume that we perceive property-instances. These property-instances could be, but need not be, understood as tropes. Regardless of whether or not property-instances are understood to be tropes, they are particulars and not universals.[4]

Here and throughout "A is constituted by B" is understood in the sense that A is at least partially constituted by B, leaving open that there may be other things that jointly with B constitute A. Moreover here and throughout "A is constituted by B" does not imply that A is materially constituted by B. So "A is constituted by B" does not imply that B is a material component of A. There are a number of ways to understand constitution given these constraints. For the sake of specificity, I will work with the following

---

[3] See Macpherson and Batty 2016 for a discussion of many variations of illusions and hallucinations.

[4] For a discussion of the nature of tropes, see Nanay 2012. For a defense of the thesis that property-instances are particulars to which we are perceptually related in much the same way that we can be perceptually related to objects and events, see Schellenberg 2011b.

notion of constitution: *A* is constituted by *B*, if and only if *A* is grounded in *B*, where grounding is understood as a relation that can hold between entities such as mental states and material, mind-independent particulars (and not just between propositions).[5] So when I say that *A* is constituted by *B*, I mean that *A* is at least partially grounded in *B* without *B* necessarily being a material component of *A*.[6] I will present an argument for the particularity thesis based on this notion of constitution, but my argument easily generalizes to alternative ways of understanding constitution given the above constraints.[7]

It follows from the particularity thesis so understood that any perception involves being perceptually related to at least one particular. After all, in any case of perception, a subject perceives at least one particular: an object, an event, or a property-instance. So every perception is constituted by a particular. One might deny that we perceive property-instances. In this case, the particularity thesis entails only that perception is constituted by particulars if one is perceiving an object or an event. While I hold that we perceive property-instances, the argument I will put forward stands even if the particulars to which we are perceptually related are limited to objects and events.

Let's call the view that endorses the particularity thesis *particularism*. Particularism is to be contrasted with *generalism*. According to generalism, a perceptual state brought about by being perceptually related to the particular *α* is constituted only by general elements, and—contra particularism—not even in part by *α*.[8] On the orthodox version of generalism, the general element consists of an existentially quantified content.[9] The main advantage of generalism is that it gives a neat explanation of what is in common between subjectively indistinguishable perceptions, hallucinations, and illusions by grounding phenomenal character in general content. However, while a generalist view has its advantages, it comes at a cost. As I will argue, it fails to explain a key element of perception, namely that perceivers discriminate and single out particulars.[10] I will develop an account that preserves the advantages of generalism while nonetheless accounting for perceptual particularity.

---

[5] For a discussion of the notion of constitution in terms of grounding, see Fine 2001, Schaffer 2009, and Rosen 2010. For a discussion of the notion of material constitution, see Paul 2010. Thanks to Thomas Sattig for many helpful discussions on the notion of constitution.

[6] As in the case of constitution, "*A* grounds *B*" does not entail that *A* is a component of *B*. For example, it is generally accepted that truthmakers ground the truth of the propositions they make true, and it is generally accepted that truthmakers are not components of the propositions they make true. It should be noted that on some Russellian views of propositions, truthmakers are components of the propositions that they make true.

[7] Alternative ways of understanding constitution given the above constraints include: *A* is constituted by *B*, if and only if the identity of *A* is metaphysically determined by *B*; *A* is constituted by *B* if and only if *A* is what it is in virtue of *B*; *A* is constituted by *B* if and only if *B* is an essential property of *A*; *A* is constituted by *B*, if and only if the existence or nature of *A* is grounded in the existence or nature of *B*.

[8] For generalist views, see Jackson 1977, Lewis 1980, Harman 1990, Millar 1991, Davies 1992, Siewert 1998, Byrne 2001, and Hill 2009.

[9] Another option is for the generalist to argue that perceptual content is constituted by properties only, where that content is not interpreted as an existentially quantified content.

[10] For a more detailed discussion of generalism, see Chapter 4, Section 1.2 "Austere representationalism."

2. Phenomenological Particularity and Relational Particularity

When a subject perceives her environment, she is aware of a particular. Now, our experience can be as of a particular, even if we are not in fact perceptually related to a particular. After all, when we suffer a non-veridical hallucination as of, say, a yellow rubber duck, it sensorily seems to us that there is a yellow rubber duck where in fact there is no such duck. In this sense, perceptual experiences are (as) of particulars. We can call this aspect of phenomenal character *phenomenological particularity*.

> *Phenomenological Particularity:*   A mental state manifests phenomenological particularity if and only if it phenomenally seems to the subject that there is a particular present.

A mental state manifests phenomenological particularity if and only if the particularity is in the scope of how things seem to the subject: phenomenological particularity does not require that there be a particular that seems to the subject to be present, only that it seems to the subject that there is a particular present. Every perceptual experience (as) of a particular manifests phenomenological particularity. Indeed, it is unclear what it would be to have a perceptual experience that seems to be of a material, mind-independent particular without it sensorily seeming to the subject that such a particular is present. If a subject has an experience that is intentionally directed at a particular and subjectively indistinguishable from perceiving a particular, it will seem to her as if a particular is present—regardless of whether she is in fact perceiving, hallucinating, or suffering an illusion. In short, phenomenological particularity is a feature of any perceptual experience—be it a perception, a hallucination, or an illusion. A generalist view can account for phenomenological particularity.[11]

We can distinguish the uncontroversial idea that perceptual experience manifests phenomenological particularity from the controversial idea that perception is characterized by *relational particularity*. A mental state is characterized by relational particularity if and only if that mental state is constituted by the particular perceived. More precisely:

> *Relational Particularity:*   A subject's perceptual state M brought about by being perceptually related to the particular α is characterized by relational particularity if and only if M is constituted by α.

It is relational particularity that generalists and particularists disagree about, not phenomenological particularity: the particularity thesis entails, and the generalist denies, that perceptual states are characterized by relational particularity. Thus, I will

---

[11] The notion of phenomenological particularity picks out what is sometimes called intentional directedness (e.g. Horgan and Tienson 2002), or direct presentational phenomenal character (e.g. Chalmers 2006a).

use "perceptual particularity" to mean relational particularity, not phenomenological particularity. Since I am concerned with relational particularity, even someone who denies that perceptual experience necessarily manifests phenomenological particularity can accept the argument of this chapter.[12]

Relational particularity and phenomenological particularity are often implicitly equated.[13] This is problematic. After all, a subject can be intentionally directed at what seems to her to be a material, mind-independent particular even if there is no such particular present. So a perceptual state could manifest phenomenological particularity without being characterized by relational particularity. Moreover, as I will argue, perceptions of numerically distinct yet qualitatively identical particulars yield perceptual states that are constituted by different particulars, yet they do not differ with regard to their phenomenal character. As I will show, it is only by recognizing the distinction between phenomenological and relational particularity that we can successfully account for the difference in the perceptual states brought about by perceiving qualitatively identical yet numerically distinct particulars.

3. Adjudicating the Debate on Perceptual Particularity

What could settle the question of whether perceptual states are constituted by particulars? There are at least three ways we could attempt to adjudicate the matter. First, we might consider the role that perception plays in our cognitive and epistemic lives and decide whether perception could play that role if perceptual states were constituted only by general elements. Second, we might introspect on our perceptual experiences in the hopes of gaining insight into their nature. Third, we might analyze the conditions under which a perceptual experience is accurate. After critically discussing each of these traditional approaches, I will argue for a new approach based on constitutive properties of perception: the argument I will put forward rests on the thesis that perception is constitutively a matter of discriminating and singling out particulars in our environment.

3.1. The role of perception in our cognitive and epistemic lives

Perception plays a number of roles at the intersection of mind and language. It grounds demonstrative reference, brings about *de re* mental states such as singular thoughts,

---

[12] See Montague 2011, Mehta 2014, Gomes and French 2016, and Mehta and Ganson 2016 for a discussion of phenomenological particularity.

[13] There is moreover a powerful tradition of sidelining relational particularity in favor of phenomenological particularity. For example, Crane—focusing on singular thought—puts all the weight on the cognitive or phenomenological role of a thought, that is, on what I call phenomenological particularity: "what matters is not that the [singular] thought happens to refer to just one thing, but that it has a specific *cognitive role*. Singularity is a matter of the cognitive—that is, the psychological or phenomenological—role of the thought" (Crane 2011: 25). Crane's focus is not on whether a thought is characterized by relational particularity, but rather on the nature of its singular character and thus on its phenomenological particularity.

and fixes the reference of singular terms. One might argue further that in virtue of playing these roles, perception grounds language in the world. For each one of these roles one could argue that perceptual states must be constituted by mind-independent particulars in the perceiver's environment for perception to play that role. One could argue, for example, that if perceptual content contains a demonstrative element, then the truth-evaluable content that characterizes a perceptual state must be constituted by the perceived particulars. Similarly, one might argue that perception could not fix the reference of singular terms, if perceptual states were not constituted by the referents of the singular terms. Or one might argue that perception could not ground language in the world, if perceptual states were not constituted by particulars in the environment.

We can formulate an argument in support of the particularity thesis premised on each of these roles that perception plays in our cognitive lives. Here is one such argument:

The Argument from Singular Thought

1. If a subject S perceives a particular α, then S's perceptual state M brought about by being perceptually related to α can give rise to a singular thought ST about α.

2. If S's perceptual state M brought about by being perceptually related to α can give rise to ST about α, then ST has singular content in virtue of M being constituted by α.

3. If ST has singular content in virtue of M being constituted by α, then S's perceptual state M brought about by being perceptually related to α is constituted by α.

From 1–3: If S perceives α, S's perceptual state M brought about by being perceptually related to α is constituted by α.

The crucial premise of this argument is Premise 2. Any support for Premise 2 will rely on an inference to the best explanation, namely the idea that any singular thought about the particular α based on perceiving α is best explained if the perceptual state is constituted by α. Analogous arguments can be formulated premised on the other roles of perception at the intersection of mind and language. Like the argument from singular thought, each of these arguments will include a key premise that a perceptual state could play the relevant role in our cognitive lives only if it were constituted by the perceived particulars. Shortly, I will discuss how the generalist could respond to arguments of this kind. Before I do so, however, I will present a second set of considerations to which one could appeal in arguing for the particularity thesis—considerations that focus on the role of perception in our epistemic lives.

Perception justifies singular thoughts and beliefs about particulars. Say I see a red apple hanging from the branch of a tree. On the basis of seeing the red apple, I form the belief, "That is a red apple." This belief is about a particular, namely, the red apple I am seeing. It is a kind of singular thought based on perception. My singular thought,

"That is a red apple," is justified, and it is plausible that it is justified by my perception. Arguably, my perception could not justify my singular thought if it were not constituted by the particular perceived. If the perceptual state manifests relational particularity in virtue of having singular content, then the idea is that singular content of perception provides evidential support for the singular content of the belief. More generally, the idea is that perception can provide evidence for thoughts and beliefs about particulars because perceptual states are constituted by the perceived particulars.[14]

Perception plays other roles at the intersection of mind and epistemology. We have knowledge of particulars in our environment. One way we gain such knowledge is via perception. If perception yields knowledge of environmental particulars, then arguably perceptual states must differ depending on which particular is perceived.[15] Consider the following example: I see a black pen on my desk. In virtue of seeing the pen, I have perceptual knowledge that this black pen that I see is on the desk. It is plausible that a condition for perception to yield such knowledge is that my perceptual state be constituted by the perceived black pen—for example, because I represent the black pen. After all, if I were to represent merely that there is some black pen on my desk, then my perceptual state would not yield knowledge that this pen, rather than some other pen, is on my desk. Now if the content of my perceptual state is constituted by the perceived black pen, then the content will be singular. And if the content of my perceptual state is singular, then my perceptual state is constituted by a particular. So the particularity thesis would be corroborated. We can formulate the point more generally such that it is not premised on the idea that perceptual content accounts for perceptual particularity: a condition for perception to yield knowledge of particulars is that perceptual states are constituted by the perceived particulars. If we formulate it this way, we remain neutral among the different possible interpretations of the particularity thesis. More formally:

The Argument from Perceptual Knowledge of Particulars

1. If a subject S perceives a particular α, then S can gain knowledge of α in virtue of perceiving α.

2. If S can gain knowledge of α in virtue of perceiving α, then S's perceptual state M brought about by being perceptually related to α is constituted by α.

---

[14] A further, albeit more contentious, role of perception at the intersection of mind and epistemology is the following: perception puts us in a better epistemic position than hallucination, because perception provides us with more and different evidence than hallucination. That is the case even if the perception and hallucination are subjectively indistinguishable. I will develop this view in Part IV of this book. Here it will suffice to give an example: if I perceive, say, a black pen on my desk, I am in a better epistemic position regarding my belief "That's a black pen" than if I merely hallucinate a black pen on my desk. I have evidence due to being perceptually related to a black pen. I do not just have evidence due to its seeming to me that there is a black pen present. For arguments in support of this idea, see Williamson 2000, Pritchard 2012, and Schellenberg 2013a, 2014a, 2016a, 2016b.

[15] This idea relies on the plausible assumption that for x to be knowledge, x must be a mental state. For a defense of the idea that knowing is a mental state, see Williamson 2000. See also Chapter 9.

From 1 & 2: If a subject S perceives α, then S's perceptual state M brought about by being perceptually related to α is constituted by α.

Analogous arguments can be formulated premised on the role of perception in justifying singular thoughts and in providing us with evidence for beliefs about particulars. Like the argument from singular thought, each of these arguments relies on an inference to the best explanation: perception can only play the role that it does, if perceptual states are constituted by particulars.

How would the generalist respond to arguments of this kind? In each case, the generalist could respond that

(a)   perceptual states are constituted only by general elements

and that

(b)   what explains the relevant role of perception is the general content of perception in conjunction with the causal relation to the perceived particular.

The generalist may use this strategy to explain how perception grounds demonstrative reference, forms the basis for *de re* mental states, fixes the reference of singular terms, yields knowledge of particulars, justifies singular thoughts, and provides evidence for beliefs about particulars. For instance, in the case of the argument from singular thought, the generalist could reject Premise 2 in favor of Premise 2*:

2*.   If a subject's perceptual state M brought about by being perceptually related to the particular α can give rise to a singular thought ST about α, then ST has singular content in virtue of the general content of M and the causal relation between the perceiver and α.

There are several ways the particularist could respond to this generalist strategy. One is to argue that such a strategy is incongruous: it allows that a causal relation can yield the singular content of a belief, while denying that the very same causal relation will yield the singular content of a perception. It is odd to posit that perceptual content is general, only to maintain that the content of beliefs based on perception can be singular via the very causal relations to particulars operating in perception itself. After all, if the causal relations to perceived particulars can make the content of perceptual beliefs singular, why would they not make the content of perception itself singular?

Another way the particularist could respond to this generalist strategy is to argue that the causal relation between the perceiver and the particulars perceived is not the kind of thing that could give rise, for example, to perceptual knowledge of particulars. A causal relation is not sufficient to secure knowledge, the particularist could say: the perceptual state needs to be constituted by the particular for perception to yield knowledge of particulars. Similarly, the particularist could argue that a causal relation between the perceiver and the particular perceived is not the kind of thing that could ground demonstrative reference or fix the reference of singular terms.

While the particularist could pursue these lines of argument against the generalist, I will not do so here. Instead, I will present a new argument that explains why perceptual states are constituted by particulars without relying on the fact that perception plays certain roles in our cognitive and epistemic lives. This will allow me to go a level deeper and explain *why* perception plays those roles. First, however, I will critically discuss two further traditional ways of adjudicating the debate about perceptual particularity.

3.2. Introspection

One might argue that the particularity thesis is supported by the phenomenal character of perception and so appeal to introspection to adjudicate the debate. On such a strategy, the aim is to establish the particularity thesis by taking phenomenological particularity to be a guide to relational particularity. Consider again Kim, who sees a cup. She is perceptually related to many particulars: the cup, its location, color, shape, and so forth. It seems to her that there are several particulars present. If it seems to her that there are particulars present, then her mental state is characterized by phenomenological particularity. A particularist who takes the introspective approach will then need to show how this phenomenological evidence supports the particularity thesis.[16] More formally, the argument could go as follows:

The Argument from Phenomenal Character
1. If a subject S perceives a particular α, then it seems to S that α is present.
2. If it seems to S that α is present, then S's perceptual state M brought about by being perceptually related to α is constituted by α.

From 1 & 2: If S perceives α, then S's perceptual state M brought about by being perceptually related to α is constituted by α.

The key premise of this argument is Premise 2. Any generalist is likely to reject it, but one does not need to be a generalist to do so. A good reason to reject the premise is the fact that an experience manifesting phenomenological particularity is no indication that the relevant perceptual state is constituted by the particulars (if any) perceived. After all, there are many examples of experiences that are seemingly of particulars for which we have no reason to posit that the relevant mental states are constituted by any perceived particulars. Hallucinations that are subjectively indistinguishable from perceptions manifest phenomenological particularity, but are not constituted by particulars—at least not by the object that seems to the subject to be present. Similarly, afterimages or experiences of phosphenes can manifest phenomenological particularity: it seems to one as if there is a particular patch of color in front of one's eyes. Such experiential states are not constituted by external, mind-independent particulars.

---

[16] For an argument that takes such an approach, see Martin 1998.

Thus, the fact perceptual states manifest phenomenological particularity does not support the thesis that perceptual states are characterized by relational particularity.[17]

3.3. Accuracy conditions of perception

A third way one might adjudicate the debate on perceptual particularity is to argue from the accuracy conditions of perception:

The Argument from Accuracy Conditions

1. If a subject S perceives a particular α, then S's perceptual state M has accuracy conditions that are determined by α.

2. If M has accuracy conditions that are determined by α, then S's perceptual state M brought about by being perceptually related to α is constituted by α.

From 1 & 2: If S perceives α, then S's perceptual state M brought about by being perceptually related to α is constituted by α.

All the arguments considered so far have been neutral on whether perceptual states have content. In discussing the argument from accuracy conditions, I will assume that perceptual states have content.[18]

The argument from accuracy conditions is supported by the following considerations. The accuracy conditions of a perceptual state specify the way the world would have to be for the content of the perceptual state to be accurate. The condition that needs to be met for a perceptual state to be accurate is not just that there is some particular in the world that satisfies the content. It is necessary to specify which particular in a subject's environment is represented to determine whether the subject's environment really is as it is represented. If perceptual content lays down a condition under which it is accurate in a way that is sensitive to which particular (if any) is perceived, then the particular to which the subject is perceptually related makes a difference to the content of her perceptual state. If that is the case, then the content of her perceptual state is constituted by that particular and is thus singular content. If that is right, then the accuracy conditions of a perceptual state track relational particularity.[19]

How would the generalist respond to this argument? Consider again Kim who sees a white cup. One way for the generalist to respond to this argument is to insist that all we

---

[17] For a more general critical discussion of the limits of introspection, see Pereboom 1994 and Schwitzgebel 2008. For a discussion of the relationship between phenomenal character and perceptual particularity, see Mehta 2014.

[18] One could argue that perceptual states have accuracy conditions without having representational content (see Martin 2010: 223). My discussion of the argument from accuracy conditions would need to be reformulated only slightly to acknowledge such a view.

[19] Soteriou argues along these lines: "We need to determine which particular objects in the subject's environment are being perceived if we are to determine whether the subject's environment really is as it seems to her to be. We need to determine which particular objects in the subject's environment are represented by her experience if we are to determine whether the subject's environment really is as it is represented to be. So we need to determine which particulars are being perceived if we are to determine the veridicality of the subject's experience" (2000: 180f.). See also Burge 1991 and Schellenberg 2014b.

need for Kim's perceptual content to be accurate is that there be some white cup present at the location where she sees one to be: it is irrevelant which particular white cup is present.

The particularist can undermine this generalist response by appealing to familiar examples going back to Grice (1961). Suppose I look at a slanted mirror and have a visual experience that is caused by a white cup on my left reflected in the mirror (Soteriou 2000). Not knowing that I am looking into a mirror, it seems to me that the cup is straight ahead. As it happens, there is a white cup behind the mirror just where it seems to me that there is a cup. Intuitively, the content of my perceptual state is inaccurate. After all, my perceptual state is caused by the cup on my left, not by the cup at the location behind the mirror. However, on the generalist conception, the content of my perceptual state would be accurate: there is a white cup at the location where there seems to me to be one. And according to the generalist, that is sufficient for the content to be accurate. The problem with the generalist approach is that it is counterintuitive that the content of my perceptual state is accurate, given that the cup that caused my perceptual state is not the one that (according to the generalist) renders my perceptual content accurate.

This suggests, contra the generalist, that perceptual content is singular rather than general. A view on which perceptual content is singular will hold that in this slanted mirror case, my perceptual state does not have singular content that is constituted by the cup located behind the mirror. After all, I am not perceptually related to that cup.

While the particularist could respond to the generalist challenge by appealing to such Gricean cases, there remains room for the generalist to simply reject the intuition that the content of my perceptual state is inaccurate in such cases. The generalist could argue that it simply does not matter whether the cup that caused the experience is in fact the same cup as the one that satisfies the general content of the experience. So, the search for an argument in support of the particularity thesis that will move the generalist is not yet over.

4. The Particularity Argument

I have considered several arguments that one could formulate in support of the particularity thesis: arguments that appeal to the role of perception in our cognitive and epistemic lives, arguments that appeal to what we can know about perception through introspection, and ones that appeal to the accuracy conditions of perception. In each case, I have shown how the generalist could contest their conclusions. I will now present a new argument in support of the particularity thesis—an argument that is based on constitutive properties of perception. Without further ado:

The Particularity Argument

I.   If a subject S perceives particular α, then S discriminates and singles out α (as a consequence of being perceptually related to α).

II. If S discriminates and singles out α (as a consequence of being perceptually related to α), then S's perceptual state M brought about by being perceptually related to α is constituted by discriminating and singling out α.

III. If S's perceptual state M brought about by being perceptually related to α is constituted by discriminating and singling out α, then S's perceptual state M brought about by being perceptually related to α is constituted by α.

From I–III: If S perceives α, then S's perceptual state M brought about by being perceptually related to α is constituted by α.

In support of Premise I we can say that it is unclear what it would be to perceive a particular without at the very least discriminating and singling it out from its surround. Consider a perceiver who sees a white cup on a desk. He employs his capacity to discriminate white from other colors and to single out white in his environment. Similarly, he employs his capacity to differentiate and single out cup-shapes from, say, computer-shapes and lamp-shapes. Such discriminatory activity allows for scene segmentation, border and edge detection, and region extraction. If there is no discriminatory activity, it is unclear how he could be perceptually aware of the cup. Now he might get the location of the cup wrong, he might get its color wrong, he might get its shape wrong— but perceiving the cup will involve discriminating it in some way from its surround. I argue that this thesis is modality general: it holds not just for vision but also for audition, olfaction, touch, and any other perceptual modalities.[20] To a first approximation, singling out a particular is a proto-conceptual analogue of referring to a particular. As I will argue in Chapter 2, while referring can be argued to require conceptual capacities, singling out particulars requires no such capacities. If these considerations are right, then discriminating and singling out a particular from its surround is a necessary condition for perceiving the particular. The necessity in question is metaphysical necessity (not logical or natural necessity). It follows that it is necessarily the case that if one is perceiving a particular, one is discriminating and singling out that particular.

Premise II is supported by the following general principle: if a subject is in a mental state in virtue of engaging in a mental activity, then that mental state is constituted at least in part by that mental activity. If the subject is, for example, in a mental state in virtue of employing concepts, then that mental state is constituted by employing those concepts. Closer to home: if a subject is in a perceptual state in virtue of discriminating and singling out a particular, then her perceptual state will be constituted by that discriminatory, selective activity.

---

[20] For discussion of olfaction, see Batty 2010; for tactile experiences, see Fulkerson 2011; for taste, see Smith 2007; for auditory experiences, see Nudds 2001, O'Callaghan 2010, Phillips 2013, Wu and Cho 2013. See Macpherson 2011 for different ways of individuating the senses. See DeRoy et al. 2014 for a discussion of a multisensory conception of perception, and DeRoy 2014 and de Vignemont 2014 on multimodal unity and binding.

A more careful way of supporting Premise II is by appealing to the relation between necessity and constitution.[21] As I argued, discriminating and singling out a particular from its surround is metaphysically necessary for perceiving the particular. As with any metaphysical necessity claim, we can ask what the source of this necessity is. The source of this necessity is that perceptual states are constituted by discriminating and singling out particulars. In other words, the fact that perceptual states are constituted by discriminating and singling out particulars is why discriminating and singling out particulars is necessary for perceiving particulars. Bringing this all together it follows that if we perceive a particular in virtue of discriminating and singling out that particular, then the perceptual state brought about by this activity is constituted by discriminating and singling out that particular. In short, perceiving is by its nature a matter of discriminating and singling out particulars.

One might worry that all sorts of things discriminate—including thermometers and sunflowers—without thereby perceiving. Sunflowers track the movement of the sun by turning their heads towards it and thermometers track the temperature. In response, neither Premise I nor Premise II posits that discriminating is sufficient for perceiving. Premise I holds that discriminating is necessary for perceiving. Premise II holds that discriminating is constitutive of mental states. So both premises are compatible with things discriminating without thereby perceiving or constituting mental states. The sunflower and the thermometer discriminate without thereby perceiving.

Premise III marks the transition from the thesis that perceptual states are constituted by discriminating and singling out particulars to the thesis that those perceptual states are constituted by the particulars thereby singled out. To give support to this premise, we need to take a closer look at what it means to discriminate and single out particulars. We discriminate and single out particulars by employing perceptual capacities. I will develop the notion of perceptual capacities in detail in Chapter 2. For now, all we need is the idea that a perceptual capacity functions to discriminate and single out particulars of a specific kind in our environment. Take, for example, Sam who possesses the perceptual capacity that functions to discriminate and single out instances of red. When Sam perceives an instance of red, she will employ that capacity and will thereby discriminate and single out that instance of red.

In light of this, we can specify the support for Premise III as follows: perceptual states are constituted by employing perceptual capacities that function to discriminate and single out particulars, and in the case of an accurate perception, they in fact discriminate and single out a particular of the right kind. Now if singling out a particular has any significance, then the subject's perceptual state is constituted by the particular when she perceives that particular. To think otherwise would be to sever the link between the function of the capacity and its output. After all, mental states are outputs

---

[21] On the relation between necessity and constitution, see Fine 2001 and Correia 2010. Many thanks to Thomas Sattig for helpful conversations and email exchanges about constitution and metaphysical necessity.

of employing capacities with a certain function, and these outputs are individuated by the particulars on which the capacities operate. A perceptual state of perceiving α is constituted by α in virtue of the perceptual state being constituted by employing a perceptual capacity that functions to single out particulars of the type under which α falls.

Now let's consider a perceiver who is perceptually related to two qualitatively identical rubber ducks. She cannot tell the rubber ducks apart, except by their locations. However, that does not show that she lacks the capacity to discriminate each duck from its surround. In perceiving the first rubber duck, she singles it out. Even if she cannot distinguish it from the other rubber duck except by its location, she is at any given moment discriminating and singling out the rubber duck she sees from its surround.

How would the generalist respond to the particularity argument? The generalist could aim to reject Premise I by arguing that surely one can see a wall that is uniformly colored and that fills out one's entire field of vision. In such a case, the generalist would argue, one does not employ any discriminatory, selective capacities since there is nothing present to discriminate. In response, when we stare at an undifferentiated and uniform field of color the *ganzfeld* effect sets in: after a few minutes, one simply sees black and experiences an apparent sense of blindness due to the lack of structure in one's environment.[22] But how do we explain what is going on before the ganzfeld effect sets in? The particularist can argue that the subject employs perceptual capacities insofar as she is discriminating the part of the uniformly colored wall to her right from the part of the wall to her left. While the different parts of the wall have the same color, they occupy different locations within the subject's egocentric frame of reference. So she is employing perceptual capacities to discriminate the parts of the uniformly colored wall within her egocentric frame of reference.

A second way the generalist could respond to the particularity argument is to reject Premise II. There are at least two approaches she might take. She could argue that we do not discriminate between property-instances, but rather between properties. Properties are not particulars, but rather universals. The generalist could then contend that since we discriminate between properties, there is no need to say that perceptual states are constituted by particulars. In response, the particularist can point out that the problem with this generalist strategy is that properties are abstract entities. They are neither spatio-temporally located nor causally efficacious. It is not clear what it would mean to perceptually discriminate between entities that are neither spatio-temporally located nor causally efficacious. What we discriminate between are particulars, be they objects, events, or property-instances. Moreover, the particularist can respond to this generalist challenge by arguing that even if it were the case that we discriminate between general properties and not property-instances, we would still discriminate objects and events and so discriminate particulars. All we need for

---

[22] For the first psychophysiological study on *ganzfelds*, see Metzger 1930. For a more recent seminal study, see Wackermann et al. 2008.

the particularity argument to go through is that there be at least one particular discriminated.

An alternative way for the generalist to reject Premise II would be to argue that perceptually discriminating α is matter of (i) the perceptual system producing a representation with a purely existential content, (ii) α satisfying that content, and (iii) α causing the perceptual processing that results in the representation. In response, the particularist can retort that this notion of discrimination is *ad hoc* and has no bearing on perceptual discrimination. After all, at the very minimum perceptual discrimination is a matter of tracking the difference between particulars, but the generalist understanding of discrimination given by (i)–(iii) does not even capture this minimal condition.

Finally, the generalist could respond to the particularity argument by rejecting Premise III. On this strategy, the generalist would concede that we discriminate and single out particulars, but would argue that the perceptual state is nevertheless not constituted by those particulars. There are at least two versions of this strategy. One is for the generalist to argue that while we discriminate property-instances and they can cause our perceptions, it is properties that we perceive and that constitute our perceptual states: we are aware of properties, instances of which cause our perceptual state in the good case. In response, the particularist can argue that it is unmotivated to accept that we discriminate property-instances and so particulars, only to then deny that those particulars are what we perceive.

A second version of this generalist strategy is to argue that while perceptual states are constituted by the perceptual capacities employed, they are not constituted by the particulars those capacities single out. To motivate this strategy, consider a factory in which leather boots are produced in an automated assembly line. The assembly line has the capacity to produce boots. While each pair of boots produced is a particular pair of boots, we need not refer to any particular pair to explain how the machine produces boots. What is relevant is just that every time a pair of boots is produced, the automated assembly line manifests a capacity to produce boots. If this is right, so the generalist objection would go, then the same holds for the perceptual case: while the input differs, the perceptual system operates the same way; it is not relevant whether we see this particular round shape or that particular round shape.[23]

In response, the particularist can acknowledge that the particular pair of boots produced at any given moment is irrelevant to explaining how the automated assembly line produces boots. However, explaining how the assembly line produces boots is not the issue here. The issue is the relation between the particular materials on which the assembly line operates and the products it thereby produces. The automated assembly line always operates on particular pieces of leather, thereby producing a particular pair of boots that is constituted by that very leather. Similarly, the perceptual system

---

[23] This objection is due to Neil Mehta.

employs perceptual capacities that operate on particulars in the environment, thereby yielding perceptual states that are constituted by those very particulars. A critical dis-analogy between the way in which boots are constituted and perceptual states are constituted is in the notion of constitution in play. The boots are materially constituted by the pieces of leather on which the assembly line operates. By contrast, perceptual states are constituted—but not materially constituted—by the particulars on which the perceptual capacities operate.

The important point here is that the employment of perceptual capacities cannot be dissociated from what the capacities function to do—and in fact do in the case of perception. Discriminating α and discriminating β, where α and β are distinct particulars, is doing different things. Insofar as those two activities differ, the perceptual states generated by employing the capacities in distinct environments will differ. We can think of this in terms of what it means for a capacity to have a function and how mental states brought about by employing such capacities should be individuated. The capacity has the function to discriminate and single out particulars. The output of a capacity with a certain function is the mental state yielded by employing that capacity. The capacity fulfills its function if it singles out a relevant particular. The output yielded by employing the capacity successfully is constituted by the particular that the capacity singles out.

5. Coda

Perception grounds demonstrative reference, yields *de re* mental states such as singular thoughts, it fixes the reference of singular terms, provides us with knowledge of particulars, and it justifies singular thoughts about particulars. I have provided an argument for the thesis that perceptual states are constituted by particulars that does not itself depend on perception playing these epistemological and cognitive roles. Thus, I have given an explanation of how it is that perception can play these roles in our epistemic and cognitive lives.

In doing so, I have argued for the thesis that perception is constitutively a matter of employing perceptual capacities that function to discriminate and single out particulars. We can call this the *capacity thesis*, and a view that accepts this thesis *capacitism*. The rest of this book develops this view.

Now, the particularity argument takes a stance on the first of the two questions structuring the debate on perceptual particularity, namely, the question of whether perceptual states are constituted by particular elements, by general elements, or by both particular and general elements. It establishes that perception is constituted by particulars, but it remains neutral on whether it is constituted also by general elements. Moreover, it is neutral on the second question structuring the debate on perceptual particularity, namely, the question of whether perceptual particularity is best accounted for in an epistemic, ontological, psychologistic, or representational way. I will argue that the particularity thesis is best understood in a representational way and will thereby argue that perceptual particularity is a matter of the singular content of perception. Thus, I will argue that perceptual states are constituted by both particular and general elements. To develop this argument, we will need a more developed understanding of the nature of perceptual capacities.

Chapter 2

Perceptual Capacities

In Chapter 1, I argued that perception is constitutively a matter of discriminating and singling out particulars by employing perceptual capacities. To be a perceiver is to possess certain capacities, to perceive is to employ them, and employing them constitutes perceptual states.

What are perceptual capacities? A perceptual capacity is a kind of discriminatory, selective capacity that we employ in perception, hallucination, or illusion. It is a low-level mental capacity that functions to differentiate, single out, and in some cases classify mind-independent particulars of a specific type—for example to discriminate and single out instances of red from instances of blue. While discriminating particulars can include classification, it does not require it. To say that perceptual capacities are low-level is not to say that they are subpersonal, but rather that they are cognitively less high-level than concepts (at least on most philosophical accounts of concepts). Perceptual capacities come in many varieties: there are perceptual capacities to discriminate luminance, motion, quantities, size, pitch, tone, and distances to name just a few. Some capacities are more basic than others. Some stand in complex hierarchical structures. Some are always employed jointly with other capacities.

Drawing on work in cognitive psychology, neuroscience, and developmental psychology, this chapter provides an analysis of perceptual capacities. It includes the following key elements:

Function of a Perceptual Capacity:	The function of a perceptual capacity C_α is to discriminate and single out mind-independent particulars $\alpha_1, \alpha_2, \alpha_3, \ldots \alpha_n$, that is, particulars of a specific type.
Individuation Condition:	A perceptual capacity C_α is individuated by the mind-independent particulars $\alpha_1, \alpha_2, \alpha_3, \ldots \alpha_n$ that the perceptual capacity functions to single out.
Possession Condition:	A subject S possesses a perceptual capacity C_α if and only if the following counterfactual is true of S: S would be in a position to discriminate

and single out a particular α_1, where α_1 is any particular of the type that C_α functions to discriminate and single out, if S were perceptually related to α_1, (i) assuming S is perceptually capable (awake, alert etc.), (ii) assuming no finking, masking, or other exotic case obtains, and (iii) where S being perceptually related to α_1 means that (a) the situational features are such that α_1 is perceivable by S (good lighting conditions etc.), (b) S has the relevant sensory apparatus that allows her to gain information about α_1, and (c) S is spatially and temporally related to α_1 such that S is in a position to gain information about α_1 via her sensory apparatus.

Fallibility Condition: If a subject S employs a capacity C_α, C_α can either fulfill its function or fail to fulfill its function, such that there is no difference at the level of employing C_α but only a difference at the level of fulfilling its function. The function of C_α is fulfilled if by employing C_α a relevant particular is singled out. The function of C_α fails to be fulfilled if by employing C_α no relevant particular is singled out.

Asymmetry Condition: The employment of a perceptual capacity C_α in cases in which C_α fulfills its function is metaphysically more basic than the employment of C_α in cases in which C_α fails to fulfill its function.

Repeatability Condition: A necessary condition for C_α to be a perceptual capacity is that C_α is repeatable.

Physical Base Condition: If a subject S is employing a perceptual capacity C_α, then there is a physical base of employing C_α that is constituted by physical processes, events, and structures (such as the neural activity) of S.

Informational Base Condition: If a subject S is employing a perceptual capacity C_α, then there is an informational base of employing C_α that is constituted by the subpersonal psychological mechanism (information processing, computations, and other subpersonal functional states, events, and processes) of S.

I will provide an asymmetric counterfactual analysis of perceptual capacities that is built around these eight conditions. But first it will be helpful to give a brief history of the notion of capacity in cognitive science and philosophy, and to lay out the benefits of analyzing the mind in terms of mental capacities.

1. Why Analyze the Mind in Terms of Mental Capacities?

The notion of a capacity is deeply entrenched in psychology and the brain sciences. Driven by the idea that a cognitive system has the capacity it does in virtue of its internal components and their organization, it is standard to appeal to capacities in cognitive psychology.[1] Critical in the advent of the notion of capacity in cognitive psychology was Chomsky's distinction between competence and performance, where a competence is a cognitive capacity, and a performance is generated by employing a competence. In the case of language, a competence is a tacit grasp of the structural properties of a language and the performance is the production of utterances (Chomsky 1995).

In contrast to the centrality of capacities in psychology and the brain sciences, questions about mental capacities have been neglected in recent philosophical work.[2] This is surprising given their importance in the history of philosophy, in the work of Aristotle and Kant in particular. Until the beginning of the twentieth century, capacities and related concepts such as abilities, skills, powers, and categories featured prominently in philosophical and scientific work on perception. Indeed, it was standard to analyze the mind in terms of capacities. With the linguistic turn the norms changed and it became standard to analyze the mind in terms of representational content instead. No doubt the linguistic turn brought with it much clarity and precision. However, in sidelining capacities a great deal was lost. The good news is that we are not forced to choose between analyzing the mind in terms of capacities and analyzing it in terms of representational content. Indeed, I will argue that employing mental capacities constitutes the representational content of mental states.

The main benefit of invoking capacities in an account of the mind is that it allows for an elegant counterfactual analysis of mental states: it allows us to analyze mental states on three distinct yet interrelated levels.

1) A first level of analysis pertains to the function of mental capacities.
2) A second level of analysis pertains to the mental capacities employed, irrespective of the context in which they are employed.
3) A third level of analysis pertains to the mental capacities employed, taking into account the context in which they are employed.

On the first level, we focus on the function of perceptual capacities, which is to discriminate and single out particulars of a specific type. A perceptual capacity has this function even if it is employed while failing to fulfill its function, as is the case in hallucination and illusion. Even in such a case, the capacity functions to discriminate and single out particulars of a specific type. Moreover, a perceptual capacity has this function even if it is more often than not employed while failing to fulfill its function.

---

[1] See Cummins 1985 for a good overview.
[2] There are notable exceptions. See, for example, Cartwright 1994 and Sosa 2010.

On the second level of analysis, we focus on what is in common between mental states in which the same perceptual capacities are employed. On this level, it is irrelevant whether or not a perceptual capacity is employed such that it fulfills its function. As I will argue in Chapter 6, in perceptions, hallucinations, and illusions with the same phenomenal character, the same perceptual capacities are employed. So on this second level of analysis, perceptions, hallucinations, and illusions with the same phenomenal character are on a par.

On the third level of analysis, we focus on the fact that perceptual capacities are employed in a specific environment, whereby a particular is either successfully singled out or the experiencing subject fails to single out a particular. In contrast to the second level, it matters, on this third level, whether or not a capacity is employed such that its function is fulfilled. So on this level, perceptions differ from hallucinations and illusions. As I will argue in Chapter 4, this is the level of analysis on which we determine the token content of the relevant experiential state.

2. The Function of Perceptual Capacities

Perceptual capacities function to discriminate and single out particulars. More precisely:

Function of a Perceptual Capacity: The function of a perceptual capacity C_α is to discriminate and single out mind-independent particulars $\alpha_1, \alpha_2, \alpha_3, \ldots \alpha_n$, that is, particulars of a specific type.

As discussed in Chapter 1, a particular, as understood here, is a mind-independent object, event, or property-instance. I use the notion of "singling out" rather than "referring" so as to remain neutral on whether perceptual capacities are conceptual or nonconceptual. While referring has been argued to require conceptual capacities, singling out particulars requires no such capacities. Singling out a particular can be understood as a proto-conceptual analogue of referring to a particular. Non-rational animals and infants as young as four months old can perceptually single out particulars in their environment, yet on at least some notions of "reference" they do not have the capacity to refer. Moreover, on many views of reference, referring to a particular presupposes that the relevant subject is in a mental state with content.[3] While I will, in Part II, argue that perception is representational, for now I remain neutral on whether perceptual experience has content. Thus, I use the term "singling out" so as not to presuppose that perceptual experience has content.

---

[3] For discussion, see Hawthorne and Manley 2012.

The notion of function in play is a notion of natural function. It is natural in that it is independent of interpretation. So what function a capacity has is not relative to an interpreter.[4] There are many different kinds of perceptual capacities. There are perceptual capacities that function to discriminate and single out objects of a specific type. Others function to discriminate and single out property-instances of a specific type. Still others function to discriminate and single out events of a specific type.

Natural functions can be given an etiological analysis; we can, however, work with the notion of a natural function while rejecting such an analysis. As I will argue, that is what we should do. According to etiological theories, something has a certain function because of what it is selected and adapted for (Ayala 1970, Wright 1973, Millikan 1989, Neander 1991).[5] Consider the heart's function to pump blood. The etiological theory explains this function by pointing to the fact that hearts were selected for pumping blood. While this is no doubt how it causally came about that hearts have the function to pump blood, *the fact* that hearts have this function is neutral on *how* they came to have it. Even if hearts came to have their function by some other means, they could still have the function to pump blood. More generally, we should distinguish what function something has from how it came to have that function. What is crucial for an analysis of capacities is what function they have, not how they came to have it.

In contrast to etiological theories, the view developed here is neutral on how mental capacities came to have their function. No doubt, we have the perceptual capacities that we do due to our phylogenetic and ontogenetic background. The point is that we can analyze the function of those capacities without appealing to how we came to have them. Indeed, there is no sense in which the phylogenetic or ontogenetic history of a subject is relevant for determining the function of her capacities. A subject who discriminates and singles out particulars in her environment via an implant can have perceptual capacities with the very same function as a subject who has those capacities due to her phylogenetic and ontogenetic background. While most mental capacities happen to have their function due to natural selection or some other natural process, nothing in the account developed here hinges on the matter.

For this reason, the account of mental states developed here does not face well-known problems of etiological theories of mental content. It does not, for example, face the problem of how to account for complex capacities, the possession of which cannot be explained in terms of natural selection, adaptation, or meme selection. Moreover, by contrast to etiological accounts, it does not face Davidson's Swampman objection (Davidson 1987: 443–4). Swampman is a creature that by astounding coincidence came into existence through a collision of particles caused by a lightning bolt. At the

---

[4] For this reason, the account of capacities developed here does not face Dennett's (1991) indeterminacy worries.

[5] For a critical discussion of etiological accounts of function, see Nanay 2010. As Nanay argues, such accounts are circular.

very same moment, Donald Davidson is struck by a lightning bolt and tragically dies. Swampman is a physical duplicate of Davidson, but his history is radically different. He did not partake in any evolutionary history, and there are no phylogenetic, ontogenetic, or other etiological ways to explain his mental states. For this reason, etiological accounts of function are forced to say that Swampman's component parts do not have any functions. But according to capacitism, the view developed in the course of this book, a function is in no way dependent on the history of the subject employing the relevant capacity. Therefore, capacitism posits that Swampman possesses all the capacities that Davidson possessed shortly before being struck by lightning. As I will argue in Part IV, neither the content nor the epistemic force of a mental state depends on the history or reliability of employing the capacities that constitutes that mental state. Since capacitism holds that the function of perceptual capacities is independent of the history of the subject employing those capacities, the view posits that Swampman not only has mental states with content, but also mental states with epistemic force.

A perceptual capacity has a certain function irrespective of whether it fulfills its function in any particular context of employment. To explain why, it is helpful to distinguish capacities from their employment. While a capacity is a kind of mental tool, the employment of a capacity is a mental activity. Consider Sam from Chapter 1 who possesses the perceptual capacity that functions to discriminate and single out red particulars. Just as Sam's heart has the function to pump blood, but may fail to pump blood, so Sam may employ her capacity while failing to single out any red particular. In such a case, the capacity failed to fulfill its function because the target of employing the capacity is not present: no red particular was discriminated and singled out.

A few clarifications are in order before we move on to developing the individuation conditions of perceptual capacities. First, for f to be a natural function does not imply that f is a biological function. While biological functions are natural functions, not all natural functions are biological functions. After all, a computer can have a natural function, but it does not have a biological function.

Second, it is crucial that the function of a perceptual capacity is not just a matter of discriminating particulars, but also of singling them out. Due to this, perceiving an instance of red is distinct from perceiving an instance of blue. Both cases may involve discriminating red from blue, but in the former case an instance of red is singled out, while in the latter case an instance of blue is singled out. So the capacities employed are distinct, and the perceptual states constituted by employing those capacities differ.

Third, while capacitism is compatible with functionalism, it does not commit one to functionalism. Functionalism individuates mental states not with regard to their internal constitution or their relation to the environment, but rather on the basis of their function in the cognitive system of which they are a part (e.g. Lewis 1966, Block 1978). Capacitism individuates mental states on the basis of mental capacities and mind-independent particulars: mental states are constituted by the mental capacities employed and the particulars (if any) thereby singled out. The function of those capacities is not understood in terms of the role those capacities play in the cognitive system of which they are a part. Thus, capacitism does not entail functionalism. There may, however, be good reasons to integrate capacitism in a functionalist view of the mind.

2.1. Material discrimination

When we perceptually discriminate α from β we discriminate an actual, mind-independent particular α to which we are perceptually related from a distinct actual, mind-independent particular β to which we are similarly perceptually related. Let's call this kind of discrimination *material discrimination*. When I speak of discrimination without further qualification, I mean always material discrimination. Discriminating between two particulars in this sense does not require attending to both particulars. It requires only registering their differences. Consider Dylan who is walking through thick foliage. It is unclear how she could be perceptually aware of, say, a leaf without registering how it differs in at least one respect from its surround. More generally, it is unclear how one could be perceptually aware of a particular without registering how it differs in at least one respect from its surround. The basic level of employing perceptual capacities is to discriminate one particular from another, where this discrimination is understood as registering their differences.[6]

Material discrimination is distinct from any notion of discrimination understood in terms of carving out possibility space. On such notions, to discriminate α is to discriminate α from other possible ways α could be. In particular, material discrimination is to be distinguished from the notion of discrimination in relevant alternative views of knowledge (Austin 1946, Dretske 1969, 1981, Goldman 1976), contextualism and pragmatic encroachment accounts (Hawthorne 2003, Stanley 2005, DeRose 2009), as well as contrastivism (Schaffer 2005). Subtleties aside, such views have it that to know that an object o has property F (in some circumstance), one must be able to rule out some relevant alternatives, that is, certain relevant situations in which o has, say, property G rather than F. On this notion of discrimination, to discriminate a property F that an object o instantiates is to discriminate F from relevant alternative ways o could be. As Pritchard puts it:

In the perceptual case at least, to be able to rule out an alternative is to be able to make the relevant discriminations between the target object and the object at issue in the alternative—e.g., to be able to discriminate between goldfinches and woodpeckers.   (Pritchard 2010: 246)

On such relevant alternative views of knowledge, discrimination is necessary for knowledge: to know one must discriminate the way things are from relevant other ways they might be. The notion of discrimination is a matter of modal appreciation.[7]

---

[6] For discussions of the role of pre-attentive discrimination in perception, see Julesz 1981, Watson and Robson 1981, Sagi and Julesz 1985, Malik and Perona 1990, Krummenacher and Grubert 2010, and To, Gilchrist, at al. 2011.

[7] Thanks to Laura Callahan for helpful discussions on this issue.

Material discrimination is distinct from discriminating relevant alternatives in two ways. First, material discrimination is a matter of noticing differences between actual, mind-independent particulars to which one is perceptually related rather than appreciating relevant alternatives. Second, material discrimination need not be cognitive (and typically is not), while any kind of modal appreciation and modal theorizing falls squarely in the cognitive realm. It is standard to distinguish perception and cognition. Perception is a kind of mental faculty that we share with non-rational animals. While human perception might be rife with top-down effects, there is no reason to think that modal appreciation is constitutive of perception.[8]

Material discrimination is distinct not only from appreciating relevant alternatives, but also from detecting differences between mental states via introspection. It has been argued that two phenomenal states M_1 and M_2 differ if and only if their subject can introspectively tell them apart (Shoemaker 1994). I am not denying that we *can* discriminate between phenomenal states in this way (though I will argue in Chapter 6 that the phenomenal character of two perceptual states can differ even if their subject cannot introspectively tell them apart). We can call this *introspective discrimination*. The important point here is that in perceiving our environment, we discriminate between external, mind-independent particulars, rather than mental states or aspects of mental states. According to capacitism, discriminating such particulars constitutes perceptual states and indeed phenomenal character, and so is more basic than introspective discrimination.

3. The Individuation Condition

Perceptual capacities are individuated by the external, mind-independent particulars that they function to single out.

> *Individuation Condition:*   A perceptual capacity C_α is individuated by the mind-independent particulars α_1, α_2, α_3, ... α_n that the perceptual capacity functions to single out.

Given that perceptual capacities are individuated externally, the perceptual capacity that functions to single out instances of red differs from the perceptual capacity that functions to single out instances of scarlet or vermilion. There will be a perceptual capacity to discriminate and single out instances of red, a distinct perceptual capacity to discriminate and single out instances of scarlet, and yet another perceptual capacity to discriminate and single out instances of vermilion. So perceptual capacities can be more or less fine-grained and we can single out the very same particular with capacities that are more or less fine-grained. Suppose you see a field of flowers that are shades of

---

[8] Accepting this is compatible with holding that perceptual knowledge results from the exercise of cognitive capacities operating on inputs received from perception. However, in Part III, I will develop a view of perceptual knowledge that does not put any such intellectualist conditions on perceptual knowledge.

red and yellow. You can employ your capacity to discriminate between red and yellow and thus be aware of a field of red and yellow flowers. Alternatively, you can employ your capacity to discriminate between crimson, scarlet, and vermilion, and between lemon, mustard, and ochre and thus be aware of the colors in front of you in a more fine-grained way.

The external, mind-independent property-instances that we can perceive do not just include instances of intrinsic properties, such as intrinsic shapes, colors, sounds, smells, textures, and the like.[9] We always perceive from a perspective. As a consequence, we perceive under situational features, that is, features such as the lighting conditions, color context, the acoustic conditions, and our location in relation to the particulars perceived. Thus, when we perceive a circular coin from different angles, there is a respect in which the coin looks circular throughout, but also a respect in which the coin's appearance changes. Likewise, when we perceive two trees of the same size located at different distances from us, there is a respect in which they look the same size, but also a respect in which they appear different (Peacocke 1983). Perception has both an *invariant* aspect—an aspect that remains stable across changes in perspective—and a *variant* aspect—an aspect that changes depending on one's perspective. How should we account for the variant aspect of perception?

One option is to understand the variant aspect in terms of situation-dependent properties.[10] A situation-dependent property is an external, mind-independent property that is determined by an intrinsic property and relevant situational features (e.g. the perceiver's location relative to the perceived intrinsic property, the lighting conditions, acoustic conditions etc.). Situation-dependent properties are exclusively sensitive to and ontologically dependent on intrinsic properties and situational features. Any perceiver occupying the same location would, *ceteris paribus*, be presented with the same situation-dependent property. As with intrinsic properties, perceivers differ, however, with regard to which situation-dependent properties are perceptually available to them and they differ in how they represent and are aware of situation-dependent properties. If this is right, then the external, mind-independent property-instances that we can perceive include situation-dependent properties, in addition to intrinsic properties.

The boundaries of the set of particulars that a capacity functions to single out is set by the world. It is not set by what a perceiver takes her perceptual capacity to function to single out. So the boundaries of my capacity to discriminate and single out squares is set by squares not by what I take to be squares. If in perception I take something to be a square that is not in fact a square, I employ my perceptual capacity to discriminate

---

[9] I am here following Byrne and Hilbert (2003) in treating color properties, and similar such properties, as external, mind-independent intrinsic properties. My argument, however, easily generalizes to alternative views of color, as long as there are external, mind-independent properties, such as reflectance properties or wavelength emittence properties, that form the basis for perception of colors.

[10] For a development of the notion of situation-dependent properties, see Schellenberg 2008. For critical discussions, see Cohen 2010 and Jagnow 2012.

and single out squares baselessly, while failing to single out a square. Thus I presuppose a strong form of realism.

As we have seen, perceptual capacities are with regard to their individuation conditions analyzed in terms of mere relations to the world and so without any appeal to mental entities, be they, states, capacities, or events. In this respect, capacitism builds on causal views of mental states (Kripke 1972, Putnam 1975, Burge 1979, Devitt 1981). However, as I will argue shortly, with regard to their possession conditions the situation is more complex: the possession of at least some perceptual capacities requires possessing other perceptual capacities.

4. The Possession Condition

Perceptual capacities cannot be analyzed independently of analyzing their possession conditions. To possess a perceptual capacity is to be in a position to discriminate and single out the external, mind-independent particulars that the capacity functions to single out when perceptually related to such particulars and some further conditions hold. So if we possess such a capacity, then—assuming no exotic case obtains—the following counterfactual holds: if we were perceptually related to a particular that the capacity functions to single out, then we would be in a position to discriminate and single out that particular. More precisely:

> *Possession Condition:* A subject S possesses a perceptual capacity C_α if and only if the following counterfactual is true of S: S would be in a position to discriminate and single out a particular α_1, where α_1 is any particular of the type that C_α functions to discriminate and single out, if S were perceptually related to α_1, (i) assuming S is perceptually capable (awake, alert, etc.), (ii) assuming no finking, masking, or other exotic case obtains, and (iii) where S being perceptually related to α_1 means that (a) the situational features are such that α_1 is perceivable by S (good lighting conditions etc.), (b) S has the relevant sensory apparatus that allows her to gain information about α_1, and (c) S is spatially and temporally related to α_1 such that S is in a position to gain information about α_1 via her sensory apparatus.

The condition requires only that a subject be in a position to discriminate and single out a particular of the type that C_α functions to single out when perceptually related to one, and not that she in fact do so. The reason for this is that even if the subject is perceptually related to a relevant particular, she might for a variety of reasons fail to single out the particular, perhaps because she does not notice the particular due to her attention being directed elsewhere.

It will be helpful to specify each qualification of what it is to be perceptually related to a particular. The qualification that the subject is perceptually capable rules out cases in which the subject is not at that particular moment able to employ her perceptual capacity (perhaps because she is intoxicated or sleepy), even though she is generally capable of doing so. The qualification that no finking, masking, or other exotic cases obtain rules out cases in which the subject mysteriously loses her capacity from one moment to the next. The inference from a claim about perceptual capacities to a counterfactual fails in such cases.[11] However, all the standard ways of fixing the disposition-to-counterfactual inference can be exploited for the capacity-to-counterfactual inference (see Lewis 1997). Finding a formulation of the capacity-to-counterfactual inference that is indefeasible in light of all possible finking, masking, and similarly exotic cases would be a project of its own. Therefore, I will here work on the independently plausible assumption that no such exotic cases obtain.

The first specification of what it means to be perceptually related rules out cases in which the subject is causally related to a relevant particular α_1, but it is, for example, too dark or too noisy for her to perceive the particular. The second specification rules out cases in which the relevant subject does not have the sensory apparatus to perceive α_1, perhaps because her sensory organs are damaged. The third specification rules out cases in which the subject is causally related to a relevant particular α_1, but not in a way that allows her to gain information about α_1 via her sensory organs—perhaps because α_1 is so close to her eyes that she cannot properly make it out or so far away that she is unable to discriminate it from its surround.

Successfully employing a perceptual capacity to discriminate and single out particulars of a type requires being differentially sensitive to particulars of that type in one's environment. However, the counterfactual analysis of perceptual capacities entails that one could possess a perceptual capacity despite not being able at that very moment to respond differentially to the relevant particulars. If one is sufficiently intoxicated, one might not be able to respond differentially to much at all. In such states, one nonetheless possesses perceptual capacities. Moreover, if one does not have the relevant sensory apparatus or one's sensory apparatus is impaired, one cannot be perceptually related to particulars that the perceptual capacity functions to discriminate and single out. In those cases too, one nevertheless can possess perceptual capacities. One will just not be in a position to employ them while fulfilling their function without being appropriately connected to a sensory apparatus. In short, while *successfully employing* a perceptual capacity requires being differentially sensitive to particulars of the relevant type in one's environment, *possessing* a perceptual capacity is not subject to this requirement.

There are several close alternatives to the counterfactual analysis provided. A conditional could, for example, be formulated in terms of a "might" or a "could."

---

[11] For a discussion of masking, see Johnston 1992; for a discussion of finking, see Martin 1996.

If the conditional were formulated in terms of a "might" or a "could," the link between possessing a perceptual capacity and successfully employing it would be too weak to entail a constitutive relation between the perceptual capacities employed and the perceptual states thereby constituted.[12] Therefore, it is crucial that the conditional is formulated in terms of a "would."

Now, one might wonder what the connection is between possessing specific capacities and possessing closely related capacities. One might wonder, for example, whether there could be a perceiver who possesses only the capacity to discriminate red from other colors without possessing any perceptual capacities to discriminate and single out other colors. More radically, can there be a perceiver who possesses only one perceptual capacity? In response, there is empirical evidence that possession of at least some perceptual capacities comes in clusters. For example, if one is able to discriminate angles from straight lines, one will also be able to discriminate curves from straight lines. And, if one possesses the capacity to discriminate, for example, red from blue and single out red, one will also possess the capacity to discriminate blue from red and single out blue.[13]

4.1. Possessing a capacity vs employing a capacity

What is the relation between possessing a capacity and employing it? It has been argued that one cannot count as possessing a capacity if one has never employed it successfully (Aristotle, *De Generatione Animalium* 2.3, 736b21–6 & 4.1, 766a5–10).[14] It has been argued, moreover, that if one employs a capacity without it fulfilling its function, then one does not count as possessing the capacity at that moment (Millar 2008). Aristotle attributes a view that is even more restrictive to the Megarians:

> There are some—such as the Megarians—who say that something is capable only when it is acting, and when it is not acting it is not capable. For example, someone who is not building is not capable of building, but someone who is building is capable when he is building; and likewise too in other cases. It is not hard to see the absurd consequences of this.
>
> (*Metaphysics*, Book Θ, 1046b)

On the Megarian view, one can possess a capacity only when one is successfully employing it.

Against all these views, I am arguing that we can possess a capacity even if we never employ it. Possessing a capacity is thus metaphysically more fundamental than employing a capacity: a subject cannot employ a capacity that she does not possess, but she can possess a capacity without ever employing it.

---

[12] For the distinction between "might"-conditionals and "would"-conditionals, see Lewis 1973: 21–4. For a discussion of "could"-conditionals, including a discussion of whether they are in fact conditionals, see Austin 1970: 211–13. See also DeRose and Grandy 1999.

[13] For discussions of this set of issues, see in particular Li et al. 2004, 2009, Scott et al. 2007. See also Luna et al. 2005, de Lafuente and Romo 2005, Chowdhury and DeAngelis 2008, Law and Gold 2008, Kahnt et al. 2011.

[14] See Caston 2002 for a helpful discussion. Thanks to Victor Caston for helpful exchanges on Aristotle's view of capacities and powers.

Aristotle's distinction between first and second potentiality of capacities and first and second actuality of capacities is helpful here (*De Anima* II.5, 417a22–417a30). We can distinguish between an English speaker's innate capacity to speak a language (first potentiality), her capacity to speak English when she is sleeping (second potentiality), and her capacity to speak English when she is speaking English (second actuality). If one has first potentiality of a capacity one is the kind of being that could possess that capacity. If one has second potentiality of a capacity one possesses that capacity (Aristotle also calls this the first actuality of a capacity). If one manifests the second actuality of a capacity one employs the capacity successfully.

A necessary condition for possessing a capacity is to be the kind of being who could possess that capacity and to meet some further constraint, such as being in an environment in which one has the opportunity to come to possess the capacity. Aristotle expresses this idea when he maintains that first potentiality is prior to second potentiality (or first actuality). A necessary condition for employing a capacity is to possess that capacity and to meet some further constraint, such as being in a suitable environment. Aristotle expresses this idea when he maintains that first actuality is prior to second actuality.[15]

5. The Fallibility Condition

So far, we have analyzed perceptual capacities in light of their function to discriminate and single out particulars in perception. What happens when we fail to single out what we purport to single out, such as in cases of hallucination and illusion? I argue that perceptual capacities are fallible in that the very same perceptual capacity can be employed in perception, hallucination, and illusion.

Fallibility Condition: If a subject S employs a capacity C_α, C_α can either fulfill its function or fail to fulfill its function, such that there is no difference at the level of employing C_α but only a difference at the level of fulfilling its function. The function of C_α is fulfilled if by employing C_α a relevant particular is singled out. The function of C_α fails to be fulfilled if by employing C_α no relevant particular is singled out.

The relevant alternative to understanding capacities as fallible is to understand them as infallible. Millar among others understands perceptual capacities (including recognitional capacities) in this way:

If I had judged falsely that the plants in the plot were azaleas I would not have exercised the recognitional ability in question. The general point here is that the notion of the exercise of a recognitional ability is a *success* notion. (Millar 2008: 333.)

---

[15] For distinctions analogous to the distinction between employing a capacity and possessing a capacity, see Schellenberg 2007, Glick 2012, Vihvelin 2013, and Whittle 2010.

If capacities are understood as infallible, then one cannot employ a capacity if one does not succeed in fulfilling its function. I will not here argue against infallibilist views of capacities, but will focus rather on why we should understand perceptual capacities as fallible.

By way of analogy, consider that if we possess a concept, then we can employ it even if we fail to refer. After all, if we say "That's a horse," pointing to where in fact there is no horse, we are arguably using the very same concept HORSE that we would use if we were successfully pointing at a horse. The difference between the former and the latter case is simply that in the former, but not the latter, we fail to refer. The failure occurs at the level of reference. There is no failure at the level of employing the concept. If that is right, then there is no reason to think that the two cases differ with regard to employing the concept HORSE.

The very same thing can be said of perceptual capacities. If we possess a perceptual capacity, then we can employ it even if we are not accurately perceiving. One could be prompted to employ a perceptual capacity due to non-standard circumstances: unusual brain stimulations or misleading distal inputs, for example. Given that capacities are determined by functional relations between the perceiver and her environment and not by individual token responses, we can employ a capacity even if a relevant particular is not present. If this is right, then like concepts, perceptual capacities are fallible.

If we employ a concept, but fail to refer, the concept employed remains empty. Analogously, if we employ a perceptual capacity, but fail to single out a particular, the capacity is employed *baselessly*. It is employed baselessly in the sense that the usual target of discrimination and selection—an external, mind-independent particular— is absent.

Let's consider some examples. In the paradigmatic case of hallucination, it seems to us that there is an object where in fact there is no such object. Consider Kim when she hallucinates a white cup. She employs her capacity to discriminate and single out an object of a certain type. Moreover, she employs her capacity to discriminate and single out white from other colors along with capacities to single out various other property-instances: luminance, shapes, textures, and so on. Since she is hallucinating and so not perceptually related to a white cup, all these capacities are employed baselessly.

In the paradigmatic case of illusion, it seems to us that an object has a property that it does not in fact instantiate. A subject who is suffering an illusion is not perceptually related to at least one particular that she purports to single out. Say she sees an object that instantiates property π, but given misleading circumstances, it seems to her (falsely) to be instantiating property ρ. In such a case, she employs her capacity to discriminate and single out an instance of ρ. But given that there is no ρ-instance present, she employs that capacity while failing to single out any particular. In the typical case, she will be employing several other capacities successfully. But insofar as she is suffering an illusion, she employs at least one capacity baselessly.

Now, in perception the particulars between which we discriminate are mind-independent particulars in our environment. This invites the question: what do we discriminate between when we employ perceptual capacities baselessly? In response: when we employ a capacity baselessly, we are not discriminating any mind-independent particulars. Indeed, we are not discriminating any particulars. We are employing a mental tool without that mental tool fulfilling its function. The important point for present purposes is that the fact that the mental tool is not fulfilling its function does not imply that we are not employing the mental tool.

5.1. The dependence of perceptual capacities on mind-independent particulars

I have argued that while perceptual capacities are individuated by the particulars they function to single out, they can nonetheless be employed baselessly. This invites the question of whether perceptual capacities are dependent on the particulars they function to single out.[16] There are at least three different ways of understanding this question, each of which requires its own response.

One way of understanding it is as a question about possessing capacities. Could a subject possess a perceptual capacity, even though she has never been perceptually related to a particular of the kind that the capacity functions to single out? In response: yes. After all, the capacity could be innate. The perceiver may have been unlucky and never been perceptually related to a relevant particular. So despite possessing the capacity, the perceiver will never have had a chance to employ her capacity to successfully single out a relevant particular.

A second way of understanding the question is as a question about employing capacities. Could a perceptual capacity be employed even if the relevant particular is not present? In response: yes. As noted, a perceptual capacity could be employed in the absence of any relevant particular. This occurs in cases of hallucination and illusion.

A third way of understanding the question is as an existence question. Could a perceptual capacity exist that functions to single out a kind of particular that does not exist and has never existed? In response: no. As I will argue in Chapter 6, any perceptual capacities must be grounded in perception in the sense that any perceptual capacity must have been employed successfully by someone, somewhere. If that is right, then a perceptual capacity could not exist if no particular of the kind exists that the capacity functions to single out.[17]

In sum, while perceptual capacities are individuated by the particulars they function to single out, they are dependent on particulars only in the following sense: a perceptual capacity could not exist if no particular that it functions to discriminate and single out exists or ever has existed.

---

[16] Thanks to Matt McGrath for raising this question.
[17] See Chapter 6, Section 4: "Grounded and Ungrounded Perceptual Capacities."

6. The Asymmetry Condition

While perceptual capacities are fallible and employable in perception, illusion, and hallucination alike, there is an asymmetry between employing a capacity in perception and employing that same capacity in hallucination or illusion.

> *Asymmetry Condition:*   The employment of a perceptual capacity C_α in cases in which C_α fulfills its function is metaphysically more basic than the employment of C_α in cases in which C_α fails to fulfill its function.

The reason for this asymmetry is that it is the function of a perceptual capacity to discriminate and single out particulars. It is not its function to fail to single out particulars. This is the case even if a perceptual capacity is more often than not employed unsuccessfully. As a consequence, there is both an explanatory and a metaphysical primacy of the employment of a perceptual capacity in perception over its employment in hallucination or illusion.

There is an explanatory primacy of employing a perceptual capacity in perception over its employment in hallucination or illusion since one can give an analysis of the capacity employed in hallucination or illusion only by appealing to its role in perception. Consider again Kim when she suffers a hallucination as of a white cup on a desk. Even though she fails to single out anything white, she is in a phenomenal state that is as of an instance of white in virtue of employing the capacity to discriminate and single out white from other colors. She would single out an instance of white *were* she perceptually related to a white cup—assuming again that no finking, masking, or other exotic case obtains. After all, she is employing a perceptual capacity the very function of which is to differentiate white from other colors and to single out white in her environment. In this sense, we need to refer to what Kim would discriminate between and what she would single out in perception to explain the role of the capacities she employs in hallucination.

Licensing this explanatory primacy, there is a metaphysical primacy of employing a perceptual capacity in perception over its employment in hallucination or illusion. There is such a metaphysical primacy since a perceptual capacity functions to do what it does in perception, namely discriminate and single out particulars. It does not function to do what it does in hallucination or illusion, namely fail to discriminate and single out the particular that one purports to single out. On one understanding of metaphysical primacy, we can associate things with natures and see if the nature of one thing makes reference to another. If so, the latter will be said to be relatively primary and the former secondary. We can then construct chains so that if the nature of *A* makes reference to *B*, and the nature of *B* makes reference to *C*, then *C* will be primary, *B* secondary, and *A* tertiary. According to capacitism, in hallucination and illusion the subject employs her perceptual capacities while failing to fulfill their function, and these capacities are by their nature defined in terms of success in the perceptual case. Thus, the perceptual case is relatively primary and the hallucination and illusion cases are secondary. For the reasons discussed under the fallibility condition, the asymmetry condition does not imply that we must have successfully used a perceptual capacity in the past to employ that capacity in hallucination.[18]

Another way of expressing the idea motivating the asymmetry condition is as follows: the fact that we can employ capacities while failing to single out particulars depends on the fact that we can employ such capacities to single out particulars. This idea is analogous to the idea that misrepresentation depends on representation. Indeed, the two ideas go hand in hand, since—as I will argue in Chapter 3—employing perceptual capacities yields representational content.

The proposed asymmetric counterfactual analysis of perceptual capacities differs in significant ways from Fodor's asymmetrical causal dependence account of mental representation (Fodor 1987, 1990). According to Fodor, a mental state represents properties or objects only if it is reliably tokened by the presence of the relevant properties or objects. A mental symbol represents, say, pigs only if it is reliably tokened by pigs. So reliability is a necessary condition for Fodor's account: symbols of cognitive systems represent because of regularities between those cognitive systems and environments. Such regularities also explain what it is for such symbols to represent in the first place.

Like all tracking theories (Dretske 1981, Millikan 1984), Fodor's account faces indeterminacy problems. It fails to ground determinate content, which is required not just for avoiding Quinean indeterminacy problems (e.g. undetached pig parts, pig time-slices), but also to allow for the possibility of misrepresentation (and thus for avoiding the "disjunction" problem) and for ruling out proximal contents (e.g. piggy retinal patterns). Fodor (1990) addresses these indeterminacy problems by adding several conditions to his original account. He stipulates (i) that the mental symbol must be actually caused (not just that it would be caused) by the object or property (i.e. by pigs), and (ii) that the mental symbol has actually been caused by the wrong kinds of objects or properties (i.e. non-pigs), and thus that misrepresentation is not simply possible but that it has actually occurred. Adding these extra conditions, however, undermines the power of the account to explain mental content.

The key problem with accounts of mental content that depend on reliability conditions is the following: if a mental state M reliably represents P (e.g. pig), then M will also reliably represent the disjunction $P \lor Q$ (e.g. pig or a bull terrier; pig or undetached pig part). After all, P and $P \lor Q$ will be co-instantiated. The reliability relation does not cut finely enough to privilege P over the alternatives. In contrast to Fodor's asymmetrical causal dependence account, capacitism does not face these problems since it does not depend on the reliability of perceptual capacities.

---

[18] For a helpful discussion of asymmetry arguments, see Marušić 2016.

7. The Repeatability Condition

A perceptual capacity must be repeatable. More precisely:

> *Repeatability Condition:*   A necessary condition for C_α to be a perceptual capacity is that C_α is repeatable.

The repeatability condition implies that it must be possible to employ C_α in at least two distinct contexts for C_α to be a perceptual capacity. Now it might be that one possesses a perceptual capacity that one has—for whatever reason—employed only once, or indeed never. The requirement is not that one has in fact employed a perceptual capacity more than once, but that it is possible to employ that capacity in at least two distinct contexts. The contexts may differ in at least the following five ways.

One way is with regard to the particulars singled out. In one context, the perceptual capacity C_α can be employed to discriminate and single out the particular α_1; in another it can be employed to discriminate and single out the particular α_2, where α_1 and α_2 are numerically distinct particulars each of which C_α functions to discriminate and single out.

Second, the contexts could differ with regard to whether the perceptual capacity is employed while fulfilling its function, or employed while failing to fulfill its function. In one context, a perceptual capacity C_α can be employed while succeeding in singling out the particular α_1; in another it can be employed while failing to single out any particular.

Third, the contexts could differ with regard to the situational features that determine the conditions under which a particular is perceived—features such as lighting conditions, acoustic conditions, or the angle and distance from which the particular is perceived. The perceptual capacity C_α can be employed to discriminate and single out the particular α_1 under distinct situational features.[19]

Fourth, the contexts could differ temporally. The perceptual capacity C_α can be employed to discriminate and single out the particular α_1 at time t_1 and at time t_2.

Fifth, the contexts could differ spatially. The perceptual capacity C_α can be employed to discriminate and single out the particular α_1 at location L_1 and at location L_2.

In each of these five ways in which the contexts could differ, the same perceptual capacity C_α can be employed in two distinct contexts. As these examples of distinct contexts show, the bar for a perceptual capacity to be repeatable is low.

Now, it may be that at least some particulars are correlated with a unique perceptual capacity. This is plausible if one allows that perceptual capacities are quite high-level. Let's assume that Robin possesses a perceptual capacity to discriminate and single out his mother. This perceptual capacity will be individuated by exactly one particular in the world. Nonetheless, the perceptual capacity is repeatable. After all, Robin can employ his capacity to single out his mother today and also tomorrow.

---

[19] For a discussion of situational features, see Schellenberg 2008.

Capacitism is neutral on whether perceptual capacities function to single out only low-level properties such as colors, shapes, sounds, smells, and the like, or whether there are perceptual capacities that function to single out individual people, skyscrapers, pine trees as such. Nothing in the account presented in this book hinges on how the debate on whether perception represents only low-level properties or also high-level properties is resolved.

8. The Physical Base and Informational Base of Perceptual Capacities

We can analyze perceptual states at three distinct levels:

    I. the mental state level
    II. the information-processing, computational level
    III. the physical, neural level.

Employing perceptual capacities lies at the mental state level.[20] Computational states, events, and processes (as well as any other subpersonal functional states, events, and processes) that support mental states lie at the information-processing level. Neural networks and neural activity (as well as other biological or mechanical structures, states, events, and processes) in which the other two levels are realized lie at the physical level.

What are the computational and neural underpinnings of employing perceptual capacities? What is the relation between mental states brought about by employing perceptual capacities and the non-mental states, events, and processes in virtue of which they obtain? Any employment of a perceptual capacity has a physical base.

Physical Base Condition: If a subject S is employing a perceptual capacity C_α, then there is a physical base of employing C_α that is constituted by physical states, events, and processes (such as the neural activity) of S.

The physical base condition allows for multiple realizability. So the fact that employing perceptual capacities has a physical base does not imply an identity relation between employing a perceptual capacity and its physical base. Nor does it imply that there is an identity relation between the mental states constituted by employing perceptual capacities and the physical base of their employment.[21]

---

[20] I use "mental" to refer to personal-level states, events, and processes and "information processing" to refer to states, events, and processes that are at a subpersonal level. To avoid terminological confusions, it is important to note that some have used "mental" to refer to states, events, and processes at the subpersonal, computational level (see e.g. Fodor 1975).

[21] The locution "of the subject S who is employing C_α" in the physical base condition need not be understood as implying that the physical base is a biological component of S. The physical base could be an implant.

Any employment of a perceptual capacity has not only a physical base, but also an informational base.

> *Informational Base Condition:*   If a subject S is employing a perceptual capacity C_α, then there is an informational base of employing C_α that is constituted by the subpersonal psychological mechanism (information processing, computations, and other subpersonal functional states, events, and processes) of S.

There are complex relations between the information-processing level and the physical level. After all, neural networks encode information. One central question is what the relation is (if any) between information-processing modularity and neural modularity—assuming here standardly, though not uncontroversially, that there are information-processing modules (Barrett and Kurzban 2006, Evans and Frankish 2009). Information-processing modules are informationally encapsulated, functionally specialized computational mechanisms that are dedicated to perceptual or cognitive tasks: specific perceptual discrimination, biological classification, face recognition, to give just a few examples (Fodor 1983, Coltheart 1999, Barrett and Kurzban 2006, Carruthers 2006). Neural modularity is a claim about the relation between information-processing modules and physical neural networks, namely that there is a one-to-one mapping between information-processing modules and locations of neural activity.

It has been argued that information-processing modules have localized neural bases and that evidence of neural modularity, and more specifically of neuroanatomical localization, is required to support claims of information-processing modularity.[22] There is, however, compelling evidence that information-processing modularity does not entail physical neural modularity.[23] After all, information-processing modules are functionally characterized and could change over time—in response, for example, to damage (Segal 1996). So while at any given time there must be some neural structure (or analogous physical structure) that realizes each module's processing mechanism and establishes its informational connections with other subsystems, these structures could change. Furthermore, distinct information-processing modules might be grounded in the same neural structures. As with any complex biological or informational systems, there may be considerable sharing of physical parts between information-processing modules (Carruthers 2006). Moreover, given the flexibility of neural networks and physical structures more generally, any commitment to physical modularity should be rejected (Lloyd 2011). Thus, there is good evidence that information-processing modules need not have localized neural bases and that neuroanatomical localization is not required to support claims of information-processing modularity

---

[22] For discussion, see Fodor 1983 and Panksepp and Panksepp 2001. Note that they use the terminology of mental modules rather than information-processing modules. For a helpful discussion of modularity, see Toribio 2002.

[23] For general discussion, see Koch et al. 2016.

(Frankish 2011). And indeed we can accept the physical base condition on the employment of perceptual capacities without endorsing any one-to-one mapping between information-processing modules and locations of neural activity.

What about the relation between the mental state level and the information-processing level? The view that perceptual states are constituted by employing perceptual capacities fits neatly with computationalism, according to which personal-level mental states are grounded in computational states. Now, some reductive versions of computationalism have it that mental states are fully analyzable in computational terms. According to such views, personal-level mental states can be deduced from computational states, events, and processes: mental states simply are computational states at a certain stage of information processing.

We can accept that mental states are grounded in computational states, however, without endorsing such a reductive view. After all, states, events, and processes on the mental level can be grounded in states, events, and processes on the computational level even if no identity relations hold between the two levels. Accepting a grounding relation does not entail that personal-level mental states can be identified with or reduced to computational states, events, and processes. Moreover, states, events, and processes on the computational level can cause states, events, and processes on the mental level even if no identity relations hold between the two levels. In short, mental states, events, and processes can be grounded in, explained in terms of, or obtain in virtue of computational states, events, and processes, without any identity relations holding between the two levels.

This approach allows us to accept the existence of states, events, and processes on both levels and to understand vision science, and the cognitive sciences more generally, as investigating the metaphysical and explanatory dependencies between the two levels. On this approach, the focus is not on whether there are identity relations between states, events, and processes on the two levels, but rather on the causal and grounding relations between the two (Strevens 2004, Craver 2007, Godfrey-Smith 2008, Silva and Bickle 2009, Craver and Darden 2013). This allows us to acknowledge that an account of information processing is a necessary element of any complete account of perception, while also acknowledging that central questions, such as the nature and source of perceptual consciousness and the epistemic force of perceptual states, cannot be adequately addressed solely at the computational level.

As I have argued, employing perceptual capacities is grounded in subpersonal computational mechanisms and physical neural networks that encode information. Thus, capacitism entails that perceptual states can be scientifically explained in terms of informational and physical states, events, and processes, without thereby reducing perceptual states to those non-mental features. In this way, capacitism posits that perceptual states are genuinely mental, yet can nonetheless be the object of scientific inquiry.[24]

---

[24] For helpful discussions of computational accounts of perception, see Egan 1992 and Cohen 2010.

9. The Generality of Perceptual Capacities

A perceptual capacity is general in that it can be employed to single out any particular of the type that the capacity functions to discriminate and single out. In the typical case, no specific particular needs to be singled out in any specific employment of a perceptual capacity.[25] Any particular will do, as long as it falls under the type of particulars that the capacity functions to discriminate and single out. For example, the perceptual capacity C_{SQUARE} can be employed to discriminate and single out any perceivable square object. In this sense, it is semantically general in much the way as the concept SQUARE is semantically general. Semantic generality should be distinguished from syntactic generality. While perceptual capacities are semantically general, they are syntactically singular: they function to single out particulars in the environment—not general kinds or universals. In this respect, they are akin to singular terms, such as demonstratives and indexicals. Not only are perceptual capacities syntactically singular, the perceptual states they yield are syntactically singular as well.

9.1. Perceptual capacities and modes of presentation

By employing a perceptual capacity in perception, we single out a particular in a certain way. Let's say we are perceptually related to a triangle. We can single it out via its three-sidedness, or via its three-corneredness. When we single it out via its three-sidedness we employ a different capacity than when we single it out via its three-corneredness. Similarly, when we hear a cello in the midst of the cacophony of an orchestra, we can single it out in virtue of its rich timbre or its reverberating sound. When we see a scarlet gemstone, we can single it out in virtue of it being red or in virtue of it being scarlet.

Perceptual capacities can be understood as the mental counterpart of Fregean modes of presentation. They parallel modes of presentation in at least two respects. As a mode of presentation is a way of referring to an object, so employing a perceptual capacity is a way of singling out a particular. Just as there is a many-one relation between senses and references, there is a many-one relation between perceptual capacities and particulars: the same particular can be singled out with a range of different perceptual capacities. In Part II, I develop the relation between perceptual capacities and modes of presentations further. I argue there that employing perceptual capacities constitutes perceptual content, and that this content is structured by singular modes of presentation.[26]

9.2. Perceptual capacities, concepts, and nonconceptual content

A perceptual capacity can be understood either as a conceptual or a nonconceptual capacity. Which stance one takes will depend largely on how one understands the nature of concepts and their possession conditions. Depending on how concepts are understood it is more or less plausible to think of perceptual content as conceptually

---

[25] Exceptions are perceptual capacities that function to single out one unique particular, such as Robin's perceptual capacity to single out his mother.
[26] See Chapter 4, Section 3.1.

structured. For this reason, the debate over whether perceptual content is conceptual or nonconceptual is almost entirely terminological. One of the advantages of analyzing perceptual states (and, as I will argue, perceptual content) as constituted by employing perceptual capacities is that it allows us to sidestep the issue of whether perceptual content is conceptual or nonconceptual.[27]

Concepts have been understood in terms of mental representations, stereotypes, functional roles, and inferential roles, to name just a few standard views. Nonconceptual content has been understood in terms of image-like or map-like representations, as constituted by employing nonconceptual, perceptual capacities, or in terms of the idea that we represent naked properties and objects.

If concept possession requires the ability to draw inferences, then it is wildly implausible that the capacities employed in perception are conceptual capacities.[28] After all, perception is a low-level mental faculty that we share with animals that have no inferential capacities. This implies that, if concept possession requires the ability to draw inferences, then it cannot be the case that all perceptual capacities are conceptual capacities. If, on the other hand, it is held that all perceivers possess concepts—even perceivers that have no inferential abilities or any other such high-level cognitive abilities—then it is more plausible that perceptual capacities are conceptual capacities. On such a view of concepts, the requirements for concept possession are cognitively so minimal that it becomes unproblematic to say that a honeybee possesses concepts and hence unproblematic to say that perceptual capacities are conceptual.

While the debate on whether perceptual content is conceptual or nonconceptual is almost entirely terminological, there are elements of the debate that are not terminological. Focusing on those elements, I argue that perceptual content is nonconceptual. The key motivations are to accommodate the fact that at least some aspects of perceptual content can be image-like or map-like, and moreover to account for the richness and fineness of grain of perceptual experience.[29]

If perceptual content is constituted by employing such nonconceptual capacities, then perceptual content is nonconceptual. The thesis that perceptual content is constituted by employing perceptual nonconceptual capacities gives a substantive analysis of the nonconceptual content of perception.

The thesis that perceptual content is nonconceptual is supported by the fact that on standard views of concepts, perceptual experience is richer and more fine-grained than our concepts. For example, the shades of color a perceiver is able to discriminate in perception are typically significantly more fine-grained than her color concepts. If that is right (and on most notions of concepts it is), then richness and fineness of grain

---

[27] For discussion of nonconceptual content, see Peacocke 1998, Heck 2000, and Speaks 2005. For recent arguments for the idea that perceptual content is conceptually structured, see Glüer-Pagin 2009 and Bengson et al. 2011.

[28] For a view on which possessing concepts requires inferential capacities, see Brandom 1994.

[29] The key arguments in this book can, however, be accepted if perceptual capacities are understood as conceptual rather than as nonconceptual capacities.

of perceptual experience supports the thesis that perceptual content is nonconceptual.[30] Additional evidence is provided by the fact that non-rational animals perceive. If non-rational animals do not possess concepts, then perceptual capacities cannot necessarily be conceptual. As mentioned, however, whether this additional evidence has any force depends on the notion of concept with which one is operating.

The conceptualist might object that if singular thoughts or perceptual beliefs inherit their content from perception, then perceptual content must have the same structure as the content of belief. If that is right, then perceptual content must be conceptual rather than nonconceptual. In response, the nonconceptualist can say that such beliefs can be based on perception without their content being exactly like perceptual content. After all, the fact that perceptual beliefs are based on perception does not imply that perceptual content is conceptual. While it is plausible that at least some elements of perceptual content are similar to the content of a belief based on that perception, the similarity need not be a matter of both mental states having conceptual content.

The conceptualist might object further that only something that is conceptually structured can justify beliefs; so if perceptual experience justifies beliefs, then perceptual content must be conceptually structured. In response, the nonconceptualist can say that all we need for experience to play a justificatory role is that its content is propositionally structured. But content can be propositionally structured without being conceptually structured. Moreover, there are reasons to question whether something must be propositionally structured in order to provide evidence.

In sum, there is good reason to understand perceptual content and perceptual capacities as nonconceptual. The thesis that perceptual content is constituted by employing perceptual capacities allows for a substantive way of analyzing perceptual content as nonconceptual. However, the thesis is also compatible with understanding (at least some) perceptual capacities as conceptual capacities. Indeed, one of the benefits of analyzing perceptual content as constituted by perceptual capacities is that it allows one to sidestep the largely terminological debate over whether perceptual content is conceptual or nonconceptual.

10. Coda

I have developed an asymmetric counterfactual analysis of perceptual capacities. The asymmetry stems from the primacy of the employment of perceptual capacities when the capacities fulfill their function over their employment when they fail to fulfill their function. The analysis is counterfactual, since (subtleties aside) one qualifies as possessing a perceptual capacity only if one would be in a position to discriminate and single out a particular of the type that the capacity functions to single out, were one perceptually related to such a particular. Moreover, the analysis is externalist insofar as capacities are individuated by the external, mind-independent particulars that they function to discriminate and single out.

---

[30] It should be noted that on certain views of demonstrative concepts, one could argue that our concepts are as finely grained as our experiences.

PART II
Content

Chapter 3

Content Particularism

In Chapter 1, I defended the particularity thesis. To recall, the particularity thesis states that a subject's perceptual state M brought about by being perceptually related to the particular α is constituted by α.[1] The particularity thesis is neutral on how α enters into the constitution conditions for M. We can specify the constitution conditions for M in a number of ways by articulating versions of the particularity thesis. In this chapter, I will discuss four versions of the particularity thesis and will argue that the content version is the most fundamental. In light of this discussion, I will present the singular content argument, the conclusion of which is the singular content thesis.

1. Varieties of Particularity

How is perceptual particularity understood? We can take an epistemic approach and understand perceptual particularity in terms of a special epistemic relation to the particulars perceived. We can take an ontological approach and understand perceptual particularity in terms of the ontological dependence of the perceptual state on the particulars perceived. We can take a psychologistic approach and understand perceptual particularity in terms of the phenomenal character of perceptual states by arguing that phenomenal character is constituted by the particulars perceived. Finally, we can take a representational approach and understand perceptual particularity in terms of features of perceptual content. Corresponding to these four approaches, we can formulate the following four more specific particularity theses:

Epistemic Particularity Thesis: A perceptual state M brought about by being perceptually related to the particular α has the property that M is constituted by a special epistemic relation between the perceiver and α.

Ontological Dependence Thesis: A perceptual state M brought about by being perceptually related to the particular α has the property that M is constituted by α in virtue of being ontologically dependent on α for its existence.

---

[1] As in Chapter 1, when I speak of constitution, I mean always partial constitution. See Chapter 1 for a discussion of the notion of constitution.

Psychologistic Particularity Thesis:	A perceptual state M brought about by being perceptually related to the particular α has the property that M's phenomenal character is constituted by α.
Singular Content Thesis:	A perceptual state M brought about by being perceptually related to the particular α has the property that M's content is constituted by α.

While one can distinguish these four specifications of the particularity thesis, they are not mutually exclusive and indeed they can be combined in various ways. One could endorse both the epistemic and the psychologistic particularity theses, by arguing that perceptual states are constituted by a special epistemic relation to the perceived particulars in virtue of their particularized phenomenal character (cf. Campbell 2002, Martin 2002b, Johnston 2004, Brewer 2006). Alternatively, one could endorse all four theses by arguing that in virtue of being acquainted with a particular one is in a mental state with singular content, which grounds the particularized phenomenal character of perceptual states and is characterized by an existence-dependent condition.

While one could combine the versions of the particularity thesis in such ways, once all four are on the table, two questions arise: Which are true? Of the true ones, which is the most fundamental?[2] So as not to keep you in suspense: I will argue that the epistemic particularity thesis and the ontological dependence thesis are both true but that both depend on the truth of the singular content thesis. I will argue, moreover, that there are powerful reasons to reject the psychologistic particularity thesis (though if it were true its truth would also depend on the more fundamental truth of the singular content thesis). I will argue that the epistemic and ontological particularity theses both presuppose the singular content thesis, since they presuppose that perception is a matter of employing discriminatory capacities, which is already constitutive of representational content.

Let's start with the epistemic particularity thesis. According to this thesis, perceiving the particular α is constituted by a special epistemic relation to α. The special epistemic relation may be an acquaintance relation. Notoriously, there is barely any agreement on how to understand the acquaintance relation. Russell understood "acquaintance" as follows: "I say that I am *acquainted* with an object when I have a direct cognitive relation to that object, i.e. when I am directly aware of the object itself" (1911: 108).[3]

Is the epistemic particularity thesis true? The thesis is supported by the fact that there is an epistemic difference between perceiving α and perceiving β. There is such an epistemic difference since perceiving α puts one in a position to gain perceptual

---

[2] The relevant notion of fundamentality is that p is more fundamental than q, if p explains the truth of q. For present purposes this characterization will suffice. For a detailed discussion of the notion of fundamentality, see Fine 2001, Schaffer 2009, and Rosen 2010.

[3] Russell was famously restrictive about what kinds of things we could be acquainted with, arguing that those things include only universals, sense-data, and (perhaps) ourselves. There is no reason on the present account to limit the scope of what we could be acquainted with in such a way. For a discussion of acquaintance relations, see Jeshion 2010.

knowledge of α and perceiving β puts one in a position to gain perceptual knowledge of β. Given that we can gain knowledge of particulars through perception and given that there is such an epistemic difference between perceiving distinct particulars, it is plausible that the perceptual state brought about by being perceptually related to a particular involves standing in a special epistemic relation to that particular. For present purposes these reasons suffice for accepting the epistemic particularity thesis.

But is the epistemic particularity thesis the most fundamental in the sense that it explains the truth of the other theses? To answer this question, let's consider what the fundamentality of the epistemic particularity thesis would entail. For the epistemic particularity thesis to be fundamental, it would have to be possible for one to be brutely epistemically aware of the particular in a way that is not further explained in ontological, psychological, or representational terms. After all, if the thesis were the most fundamental, then it would have to be possible for one to be epistemically aware of a particular without thereby bringing to bear any personal-level representational capacities by means of which one is so epistemically aware.[4] But it is not clear what it would be to be brutely epistemically aware of a particular in perception. Indeed, as I will argue, any epistemic awareness of a perceived particular presupposes and is best explained via representational content. First, being epistemically aware of a perceived particular at minimum requires the employment of perceptual capacities whereby one discriminates and singles out that particular from its surround. Second, the employment of such perceptual capacities generates a perceptual state that is charac-terized by representational content for the following two reasons: the employment of perceptual capacities generates a perceptual state that is *repeatable* and has *accuracy conditions*. Being repeatable and having accuracy conditions are jointly key signa-tures of representational content. I will give support to each claim in turn.

The very same perceptual capacity C_α can be employed to single out particular α_1 or to single out particular α_2. As argued in Chapter 1, if one singles out α_1 rather than α_2, one is in a distinct perceptual state, namely, a perceptual state that is constituted by α_1 (and not by α_2). This is the case even if α_1 and α_2 are qualitatively identical. So the same perceptual capacity can be employed in distinct environments and yield distinct per-ceptual states. Moreover, the same perceptual capacity can be employed to single out α_1 at time t_1 and at time t_2 and thus yield the same perceptual state at t_1 and t_2.[5] If this is right, then there is a repeatable element that is constitutive of perceptual states, namely, the perceptual capacities employed and, moreover, employing perceptual capacities generates a perceptual state that has a repeatable element. Now, when one discriminates and singles out a particular from its surround, one may do so more or less accurately, and the perceptual state generated thereby will be more or less accurate.[6] After all, a

---

[4] This claim is compatible with the fact that subpersonal processing yields personal-level perceptual states.

[5] One could argue that different time-slices bring about a difference in perceptual states. If one holds this, then the relevant perceptual state would be different, but it would be different only in this respect.

[6] One might object here that not all discriminatory capacities yield things that have accuracy conditions. For example, thermometers discriminate temperatures, but we do not say that the state thereby produced has accuracy conditions. In response, it is apt to say that the temperature indicated by the thermometer

perceiver can single out an object and correctly single out only very few of its properties; or she can single out the same object and correctly single out many of its properties. The first perceptual state will be less accurate with regard to the environment than the second.[7] So employing perceptual capacities yields perceptual states that exhibit key signatures of representational content: it yields something that is at least in part repeatable and that can be accurate or inaccurate. With a few plausible further assumptions, these considerations establish that employing perceptual capacities yields perceptual states with content. In Chapter 5, I will defend this thesis in more detail.

One might argue that one gains perceptual knowledge of particulars simply in virtue of employing capacities by means of which one singles out the relevant particulars and thus argue that the epistemic relation is as fundamental as the singular representational content of the relevant perception. In response, the content particularist can say that it is in virtue of the subject being in a perceptual state with representational content—where that content is constituted by the perceptual capacities employed and the particulars thereby singled out—that the subject gains knowledge of the particular perceived. So while employing perceptual capacities in the good case constitutes representational content and yields knowledge of the particular perceived, it is only because one represents those particulars by employing perceptual capacities that employing perceptual capacities yields such knowledge.

I conclude that the epistemic particularity thesis is not the most fundamental of the four versions of the particularity thesis. It is dependent on the singular content thesis, insofar as it depends on claims about the employment of perceptual discriminatory capacities, the employment of which is already constitutive of representational content. I will use an analogous argument against the putative fundamentality of the psychologistic particularity thesis.

But first, let's assess the ontological dependence thesis. The ontological dependence thesis has it that a perceptual state M brought about by being perceptually related to the particular α has the property that M is constituted by α in virtue of being ontologically dependent on α for its existence. The thesis that an accurate perception of particular α has the property that the existence of that perception ontologically depends upon the existence of α entails that perceptual states are modally dependent on the particulars perceived. To show why the ontological dependence thesis holds, let's consider the following scenario: let M be a perceptual state brought about by being perceptually related to the particular α. Suppose that α does not exist. Can M still exist? It cannot, since, in the scenario where α does not exist, no perceptual state can be brought about by being perceptually related to α. After all, α is not there to be perceived.[8]

---

either matches the temperature in the environment or fails to match the temperature in the environment. In this sense, the state of the thermometer in which it indicates a particular temperature has accuracy conditions. Thanks to Neil Mehta for pressing me on this point.

[7] For a discussion of the relationship between singling out objects and singling out the properties this object instantiates, see Pylyshyn and Storm 1988, Pylyshyn 2007, and Fodor 2008.

[8] I am presupposing a timeless sense of 'exist' here. This avoids the counterexample that M is a perceptual state brought about by being perceptually related to a distant star, even though that star no longer

While true, the ontological dependence thesis is a poor candidate to be the most fundamental truth in this vicinity. Plausibly, if M is ontologically dependent on α this is because there is some feature of M that is constituted by α. Otherwise we are left with a brute and mysterious dependence claim. But what is the feature of M that is constituted by α? If it is a matter of either epistemic awareness or representational content, then the singular content thesis is the most fundamental, since (as just argued) epistemic awareness presupposes representational content. The remaining alternative on the table would be to explain ontological dependence via psychologistic particularity, but I will now argue that there are reasons to reject the psychologistic particularity thesis, and moreover that if it were true it too would presuppose the singular content thesis. This will lead me to the conclusion that the singular content thesis is the most fundamental version of the particularity thesis.

The psychologistic particularity thesis posits that perceptual states have the property that their phenomenal character is at least in part constituted by the particulars perceived. This thesis is endorsed by austere relationalists, who argue that perception is fundamentally a matter of standing in an awareness relation to external and mind-independent particulars and lacks any personal-level representational component (see Campbell 2002, 2010, Travis 2004, Soteriou 2005, Brewer 2006, 2011, Fish 2009, Genone 2014, French 2014).[9] According to austere relationalism, the phenomenal character of perceptual states is best understood in terms of perceptual relations to particulars in the environment.[10] One central motivation for this view is to understand phenomenal character not in terms of awareness relations to strange entities such as qualia, phenomenal properties, universals, or intentional objects, but rather in terms of the very things we are aware of when we perceive. On this approach, the distinction between phenomenological and relational particularity collapses—at least in the case of perception.[11]

There are reasons to reject the psychologistic particularity thesis. After all, it implies that when Kim sees cup_1 at t_1 and cup_2 at t_2, the phenomenal character of her perceptual state at t_1 and at t_2 will differ even though cup_1 and cup_2 are qualitatively identical. It is implausible that the phenomenal character of her perceptual states changes between seeing cup_1 and cup_2, keeping in mind that Kim is unaware that cup_1 was switched with cup_2. It is implausible since there is no difference in the environment other than the numerical identity of the perceived cups. It is unclear why the numerical identity of the

---

actually exists—it went supernova long ago, but the light from that explosion will not reach us for a while. In this case, the star exists in the relevant sense: it is to be found somewhere in the spatio-temporal manifold, even if lacks current existence.

[9] Martin's view is committed to some aspects of phenomenal character being understood in a nonrepresentational, relational way (see e.g. Martin 2002a). But beyond that commitment his view is not committed to austere relationalism.

[10] For a critical discussion of such austere relationalist views and a discussion of the various versions of the view, see Schellenberg 2011a. See also Chapter 5.

[11] Austere relationalists could still hold that hallucination involves phenomenological but not relational particularity. It would be an open question, however, what constitutes phenomenological particularity in the case of hallucination.

perceived cups should affect phenomenal character. Arguably phenomenal character is multiply realizable in that phenomenal states with the very same phenomenal character could be brought about by relations to numerically distinct but qualitatively identical objects. However, accepting that phenomenal character is multiply realizable in this way just is to deny the psychologistic particularity thesis.

Austere relationalists could avoid this counterintuitive consequence by arguing that phenomenal character is multiply realizable. The idea is that the very same phenomenal character could be realized by relations to numerically distinct but qualitatively identical objects. If phenomenal character is multiply realizable, then a subject could be in a perceptual state characterized by the very same phenomenal character regardless of whether she is perceptually related to cup_1 or cup_2. Indeed, Martin argues that perceptions of numerically distinct but qualitatively identical objects have the same phenomenal character. However, by introducing another aspect of the phenomenal state, which he calls "phenomenal nature," he argues that there is a phenomenal difference between the two perceptual states despite the sameness in phenomenal character:

> Once we reflect on the way in which an experience has a subject matter…then we need a way of making room for the essentially or inherently particular aspects of this as well as the general attributes of experience. We need to contrast the unrepeatable aspect of its phenomenology, what we might call its *phenomenal nature*, with that it has in common with qualitatively the same experiential events, what we might call its *phenomenal character*.   (2002b: 193f.)

The notion of a phenomenal nature captures an unrepeatable aspect of the phenomenal state that, according to Martin, cannot be specified without reference to the actual object of the experience.[12]

Positing such object-dependent and unrepeatable phenomenal natures entails that any two experiences of distinct objects necessarily differ phenomenally, even if the relevant objects are qualitatively identical. This consequence is counterintuitive as a thesis about perceptual consciousness. It is counterintuitive even if one acknowledges that two experiences can exhibit phenomenal differences while being subjectively indistinguishable. To show why, consider cases in which there is a threshold level difference in phenomenal character due to a threshold level difference in the perceived particulars, for example, color sorites cases in which one consecutively perceives three subtly distinct shades of a color, for example, red_{47}, red_{48}, and red_{49}.[13] We cannot perceptually tell the difference between red_{47} and red_{48}. We cannot perceptually tell the difference between red_{48} and red_{49}. Yet we can perceptually tell the difference between

---

[12] Assuming that there is such an unrepeatable aspect of phenomenal character, it is not obvious why it must be due to the particular *object* perceived, rather than the particular *event* in which the particular object is perceived. On a sufficiently holistic view of experience, every experience may be understood as necessarily phenomenally distinct insofar as it is a distinct and unique event of experiencing. On such a holistic view, one could say that the phenomenal character of any perceptual state is distinct regardless of what object, if any, the experiencing subject is related to.

[13] See Fara 2001 and Morrison 2013 for discussions of phenomenal indiscriminability and the intransitivity of matching sensible qualities.

red_{47} and red_{49}. As I will discuss in Chapter 8, in order to avoid violating Leibniz's law, it is plausible that there is a difference in the phenomenal character of the perceptual state brought about by being perceptually related to red_{47} and the phenomenal character of the perceptual state brought about by being perceptually related to red_{48} even if the perceiver does not notice the difference. But this case is different in kind from Kim's case. After all, in the color sorites case, there is a qualitative difference between the shades perceived. Since there is a qualitative difference between the perceived particulars, the differences are at least in principle subjectively accessible.[14] Were our perceptual apparatus more sensitive, we would detect the difference between red_{47} and red_{48}. The case of numerically distinct but qualitatively identical objects is different in kind, since in this case there is no qualitative difference between the perceived particulars. So no matter how good our perceptual apparatus is, we could not detect a difference between the particulars perceived. In short, an austere relationalist who argues that perceptual relations to qualitatively identical, but numerically distinct objects necessarily yields distinct phenomenal character must accept the counterintuitive consequence that phenomenal character is detached from what is potentially available to consciousness.

A proponent of the psychologistic particularity thesis might retort that a hallucination, although indistinguishable to the subject from a corresponding perception, will have a different phenomenal character than the corresponding perception. Thus, she will reject the link between accessibility and phenomenal character. In response, we can say that by rejecting the link between accessibility and phenomenal character the proponent of the psychologistic particularity thesis is changing the subject matter.

Now, consider an austere relationalist who accepts that phenomenal character is multiply realizable without endorsing Martin's thesis that the particular object perceived makes a difference to what Martin calls phenomenal nature. Such an austere relationalist has it that perceptions of numerically distinct but qualitatively identical objects have the very same phenomenal character. While someone who takes this approach avoids the counterintuitive phenomenological consequences discussed above, he would be committed to rejecting the psychologistic particularity thesis. This brings out a dilemma for the austere relationalist. If he holds that two perceptions of numerically distinct but qualitatively identical objects do not differ phenomenally, then he must reject the psychologistic particularity thesis. If he holds that these perceptions do differ phenomenally, he must accept the counterintuitive consequence that phenomenal character can be detached from what is potentially subjectively available to the perceiver.

As I have argued, we should reject the psychologistic particularity thesis. Even if it were true, the thesis could not be fundamental: if the thesis were true and fundamental, then it would, like the epistemic particularity thesis, presuppose that we are brutely aware of perceived particulars. In this case, we are not brutely epistemically aware but

[14] For a recent discussion of perceptual consciousness and access, see Gross and Flombaum 2017.

rather brutely phenomenally aware. The same considerations that were brought to bear in support of the singular content thesis being more fundamental than the epistemic particularity thesis can be brought to bear in support of the singular content thesis being more fundamental than the psychologistic particularity thesis. In a nutshell, the point is that it is not clear what it would mean to be brutely phenomenally aware of a particular. It is unclear what it would mean to perceive a particular without at the very least employing discriminatory, selective capacities. But employing discriminatory, selective capacities is to be in a perceptual state with content. The dependence of the psychologistic particularity thesis on the singular content thesis is an explanatory dependence: the singular content thesis explains why the psychologistic dependence thesis holds. Therefore, if the psychologistic particularity thesis were true, the singular content thesis would be more fundamental. However, as I have argued, there are powerful reasons to reject the psychologistic particularity thesis altogether.

Finally, let's consider the singular content thesis. It posits that perceptual particularity is a matter of perceptual content being singular content. As I am using the term, perceptual content is the content of a perceptual state, that is, the state we are in when we perceive. (I will argue also that hallucinations and illusions have content, but that the content of those experiential states is not singular.) The singular content thesis entails that if M is a perceptual state brought about by being perceptually related to the particular α, and M^* is a perceptual state brought about by being perceptually related to a numerically distinct particular β (and not perceiving α), then the content of M is not identical to the content of M^*. This is the case even if α and β are qualitatively identical. The antithesis of the singular content thesis is the general content thesis, according to which perceptual content is entirely general, for example, an existentially quantified content.

There are several ways of understanding singular content. The orthodox view has it that singular contents are Russellian propositions that are constituted at least in part by particulars. This constitution relation provides a metaphysical basis for the notion of a singular content.[15] A Fregean can equally lay claim to understanding singular content as having a metaphysical basis. In addition to the content being constituted by particulars, the Fregean holds further that the content is structured by modes of presentation under which those particulars are grasped. These modes of presentation will be understood as *de re* or singular modes of presentation, rather than as *de dicto* modes of presentation. A *de dicto* mode of presentation lays down a condition that something must satisfy to be the object determined by the content. So a *de dicto* mode of presentation constitutes a way of thinking about objects irrespective of whether there is an object present. By contrast, a *de re* mode of presentation is constituted at least in part by the particular singled out.[16] Thus, the content covaries with the environment. So the relation between content and the relevant particulars is not simply one of satisfaction.

---

[15] For an excellent, recent defense of Russellian singular propositions, see King 2015.

[16] There are many possible ways of understanding *de re* modes of presentation given this constraint. It has been argued that they are radically object-dependent such that a mental state does not have content

An advantage of the Fregean approach over the Russellian approach is that it allows for more fine-grained propositions, insofar as every particular perceived will be represented under a mode of presentation. Moreover, it acknowledges the fact that any mind-independent particular can be represented in different ways, namely, by being grasped under different modes of presentation. By operating with such fine-grained propositions, the Fregean view avoids counterexamples to Russellian representational views.[17] Suppose you are looking at a page of graph paper and so a page of symmetrically arranged tiles. You can see the tiles as being grouped. There are a number of ways the tiles can be grouped depending on which tiles are seen to be more prominent. Now, let's say that at time t_1 you see one set of tiles as prominent and at time t_2 you see another set of tiles as prominent *ceteris paribus*. In such a case, there is no difference in the environment: the tiles perceived are exactly the same at t_1 and t_2. The only difference is how the mind groups the tiles.[18] Since there is no change in the environment to which you are perceptually related, it is not clear how a Russellian would account for the change in representational content. A Fregean has no problem dealing with such a case. A Fregean will say that you represent the tiles under different modes of presentation at t_1 and t_2.

A more general advantage of the Fregean approach is that it accounts for the fact that thought is fundamentally perspectival. Applied to perception, it accounts for the fact that perception is fundamentally perspectival—perspectival not only in that we perceive from a location and so in an egocentric frame of reference, but also in that we always perceive particulars under specific conditions (location, lighting conditions, acoustic conditions) with a specific set of perceptual capacities. There is always a way in which we discriminate and single out particulars in our environment. Consider Sasha who hears jazz for the first time. When listening to John Surman's recording of 'Doxology' for the first time, she will not discern much. As she becomes an expert, she will discern significantly more when listening to the very same recording. One explanation is that she develops more fine-grained perceptual capacities that allow her, for example, to discriminate between the sound of the trumpet and the sound of the piano even when they are playing at the same time and that allow her to hear differences between chords. More radically, we can say that we cannot perceive a particular in our environment without perceiving it from our location with our specific perceptual capacities.[19] In this sense, we cannot perceive without being constrained by our perspective. The Fregean approach acknowledges this.

properly speaking if the subject is not related to the relevant mind-independent object. For such a view see Evans 1982 and McDowell 1984. Alternatively, one can argue that the mental state has a defective content if one fails to refer and so understand *de re* modes of presentation as constitutively related to particulars rather than ontologically dependent on the presence of the relevant particulars. For a development of such a view, see Schellenberg 2010.

[17] See, for example, Neander 1998 and Macpherson 2006.

[18] For a discussion of this case, see Nickel 2007.

[19] For an excellent discussion of how best to understand the mental capacities we bring to bear in perceptual experience, see Speaks 2005.

2. The Singular Content Argument

I have considered four specific versions of the particularity thesis and argued that the singular content thesis is the most fundamental. In light of this, we can now formulate the following version of the particularity argument:

The Singular Content Argument

I. If a subject S perceives a particular α, then S discriminates and singles out α.

II. If S discriminates and singles out α, then S's perceptual state M brought about by being perceptually related to α is constituted by discriminating and singling out α.

III. If M is constituted by discriminating and singling out α, then S represents α (under a mode of presentation) such that M has the property that its content is constituted by α.

From I–III. If S perceives α, then S's perceptual state M brought about by being perceptually related to α has the property that its content is constituted by α.

As the singular content thesis is a representational specification of the particularity thesis, the singular content argument is a representational specification of the particularity argument. Insofar as it is a specification of that argument, the considerations in support of the premises of the particularity argument hold equally well for the premises of the singular content argument. So if we accept the arguments in support of the premises of the particularity argument, then we should accept the premises of the singular content argument. I will call the view established by the singular content argument *content particularism*. In the rest of this chapter, I will specify the commitments of this view.

The singular content argument relinquishes neutrality on both central questions that structure the debate on perceptual particularity. Recall that one question was: are perceptual states constituted by particular elements, by general elements, or by both particular and general elements? The other was: if we assume that perceptual states are constituted at least in part by particulars, what property of the perceptual state grounds perceptual particularity? The singular content argument establishes that perceptual particularity is accounted for by perceptual content and that perceptual states are constituted jointly by the perceived particulars and the general elements by means of which those particulars are singled out. After all, if perceptual states are constituted by employing perceptual capacities and the same perceptual capacity can be employed in many different environments, then perceptual states will be constituted by general elements, namely, the perceptual capacities employed. More generally, if one accepts that the same content could be true in one environment, but false in another, then arguably the content of experience is constituted by at least some general elements.

In what sense are perceptual capacities general? As I argued in Chapter 2, perceptual capacities are repeatable and as a consequence semantically general: a perceptual capacity can be employed to single out any particular that falls under the type of particular that the capacity functions to discriminate and single out. While perceptual capacities are semantically general, the employment of a perceptual capacity yields a mental state that is syntactically singular insofar as perceptual capacities function to single out particulars (and not general kinds or universals).

As we have seen, perceptual capacities having such a function is compatible with the fact that a perceptual capacity can be employed while failing to single out a particular. In virtue of perceptual capacities being syntactically singular, every employment of such a capacity will yield a representation that is either singular (good case) or defective (bad case). According to content particularism, relational particularity and syntactic particularity are two sides of the same coin.

So while perceptual capacities are general, the representations yielded by employing general perceptual capacities are not only syntactically singular, in the good case, they are moreover semantically singular. Insofar as the capacities are repeatable and yield perceptual states that are either accurate or inaccurate with regard to their environment, they yield states with content. Those contents are singular since the capacities single out particulars. If this is right, then singular content is constituted both by the particulars singled out and by the general perceptual capacities by means of which those particulars are singled out.

2.1. Discriminative accounts vs attributive accounts of perception

It is important to distinguish the *discrimination thesis* that perception is constitutively a matter of employing perceptual capacities by means of which we discriminate and single out particulars from the *attribution thesis* that perception is constitutively a matter of attributing properties to objects.[20] In arguing for the discrimination thesis I am not endorsing the attribution thesis. On the view developed here, property-instances, objects, and events are all particulars out in the world and if we notice them, we represent them by discriminating them and singling them out from their surround. There is no need to say that in doing so we attribute properties to objects to events.

Denying the attribution thesis is compatible with allowing that there are cases that cannot be analyzed without positing that the perceiving subject is attributing properties. After all, in denying the attribution thesis I am denying only that perception is constitutively a matter of attributing properties to her environment. According to capacitism, any attribution of properties will be grounded in discrimination.

Burge has forcefully defended the view that perception is constitutively a matter of attributing features (and so properties) to objects, thereby guiding singular reference (see Burge 2010). According to Burge, singular context-bound perceptual representations must be guided by general attributive representational content: perceptual content

---

[20] For a view on which the structure of perception is attributional, see Burge 2010. For a critical but sympathetic discussion of Burge's view, see Block 2014.

stems from attributing general features to objects. So Burge has it, for example, that seeing is always seeing as. There are reasons to be suspicious of Burge's central thesis. Barcan Marcus (1961), Donnellan (1966), and Kripke (1972) have each shown that one can refer to an object in one's environment even if the properties one attributes to it are not instantiated by that object.[21] The point generalizes to perception: we can successfully single out an object in perception even if we are mistaken about its location, color, texture, and a whole range of other properties.[22] Now the problem with Burge's account is not that it cannot handle the situation in which false attribution guides perceptual reference: if, for example, I know you think something is a martini—even though I know it is not—the description 'martini' can guide me to the thing you are talking about. The same holds for perception. False attributions can guide perceptual representation. While cases of false attribution are compatible with Burge's view, their existence, however, suggests that what ultimately guides perceptual representation is not attribution of general features, but rather something more fundamental, for example discriminating and singling out particulars.

Content particularism neither implies nor presupposes that perception has an attributional structure. So the Barcan Marcus, Donnellan, and Kripke cases are no problem for content particularism. On the view developed, singling out a particular is not in any way dependent on the attribution of general features. So the view denies the core Burgean thesis that there is a constitutive connection between perceptual reference and attribution of general features. In contrast to Burge, I am arguing that the property-instances that we perceive are particulars; the general elements in perceptual experience are the perceptual capacities employed—not attributive representational contents as Burge has it. So while Burge argues that perception is constitutively a matter of attributing properties to objects and events in our environment, I am arguing that perception is constitutively a matter of employing perceptual capacities by means of which we discriminate and single out particulars, such as property-instances, objects, and events.[23] As mentioned, this is compatible with some cases of perception involving attribution.

There are several further advantages of content particularism over Burge's attributive view of perception. An attributive view is committed to the idea that in any case of perception an object is perceived to which a property can be attributed. This is a problem, since there are many cases of perception in which we do not see any objects, but only events or property-instances. Content particularism does not depend on the idea that we are perceptually related to objects. It depends only on the idea that we are perceptually related to particulars. Those particulars could be property-instances and

---

[21] Barcan Marcus, Donnellan, and Kripke each articulate their points in terms of description, but the point easily generalizes to predicating or attributing properties of objects.

[22] The generalist would have to rely on a vague notion of partial satisfaction to deal with the fact that we can single out an object despite getting many of its properties wrong.

[23] For a discussion of how visual reference is made by deploying perceptual attentional capacities, see Green 2017.

so need not be objects. Thus, content particularism can account for cases in which we perceive only property-instances. Olfactory, gustatory, and tactile experiences may not have an attributional structure, or at least not typically have such a structure.[24] Since content particularism neither implies nor presupposes that perception has an attributional structure, it applies not just to visual and auditory experiences, but also olfactory, gustatory, and tactile experiences among other sensory modes.

Yet a further advantage is that the discrimination thesis avoids over-intellectualization objections to the attribution thesis. The thesis that experiences have attributional structure over-intellectualizes perception in that it posits that perception necessarily involves seeing something as something. The thesis that perception necessarily involves seeing something as something posits that perception has a sentential or proto-sentential form. But there are many cases of perception that do not have any such sentential or proto-sentential form. If I see a green leaf, I am not necessarily aware of the leaf as green. I may just be aware of green at a particular location. When I see a landscape the content of my perception may be map-like, pictorial, or iconic without involving any kind of proto-sentential form. Map-like, pictorial, or iconic content need not have any kind of attributional structure and does not have any kind of sentential or proto-sentential form.

2.2. *Content particularism and weak representationalism*

As I have argued, consecutive experiences of numerically distinct yet qualitatively identical objects should *ceteris paribus* have the same phenomenal character. After all, there is no qualitative difference in our environment. If this is right, then any view that accepts the singular content thesis and accepts a representationalist view of phenomenal character will want to accept that the content of two perceptual states can differ regarding the particulars represented without differing in phenomenal character. So content particularism is committed to weak representationalism, that is, a view on which the phenomenal character of experience is grounded in its representational content, while rejecting any kind of identity relation between content and phenomenal character.[25] According to weak representationalism, there can be differences in content that are not reflected in phenomenal character. The relevant alternative is strong representationalism, that is, a view on which what it is for a state to have a certain phenomenal character is identical to what it is for that state to have a certain representational content.[26] By contrast, weak representationalism makes

---

[24] For discussion, see Smith 2007, Batty 2010, 2011, and Fulkerson 2011. For discussions of whether auditory experiences have attributional structure, see Nudds 2001, O'Callaghan 2010, Ivanov 2011, Phillips 2013, and Matthen 2015.

[25] There are many reasons to deny an identity relation between perceptual content and phenomenal character. The main reason is that any such identity claim would amount to a category mistake.

[26] For a helpful classification of different versions of representationalism, see Chalmers 2004.

room for the distinction between phenomenological and relational particularity, while nonetheless grounding both in the representational content of experience.

In Chapter 4, I will develop an account of both the content of perception and the content of illusion and hallucination. As I will argue, the content of a perception, an illusion, and a hallucination with the same phenomenal character is constituted by employing the very same perceptual capacities. Employing such perceptual capacities yields a content type—more specifically, a potentially particularized content schema. In this sense, experiential states with the same phenomenal character share a meta-physically substantial common element. So the view developed here is non-disjunctivist. In the case of a successful perception, the subject singles out the particulars she purports to single out, and as a consequence, her mental state is characterized by a singular token content. In the case of an illusion or hallucination, the token content is gappy since the subject fails to single out at least one of the mind-independent particulars she purports to single out.[27]

The singular content thesis is neutral on whether objects and events are discriminated from their surround via discriminating property-instances (or clusters thereof) or vice versa.[28] The thesis is compatible with a view according to which we single out colors and shapes in our environment by tracking objects without accessing the objects in consciousness as such. Likewise, it is compatible with a view according to which we single out objects in our environment via the properties they instantiate without accessing these property-instances in consciousness as such. Moreover, the thesis is neutral on whether property-instances or objects are accessed at all in experience. The singular content thesis is committed only to there always being at least one particular represented in perception.

Now, I am not denying that when we perceive a particular, the particular is *experienced* as a particular. In a phenomenological sense, one always experiences a particular as a particular. Indeed, even in hallucination—at least a hallucination that is subjectively indistinguishable from a perception—one will experience one's environment as containing particulars. That is what the notion of phenomenological particularity captures. While content particularism allows that the numerical distinctness of particulars need not be revealed in phenomenal character, it is not, however, a problem for the view if a particular is experienced as a particular. There are different constraints operating on a theory of perceptual content: it should account for the accuracy conditions of perceptual experience and ground phenomenal character. Content particularism can account for there being differences in accuracy conditions when seeing α rather than seeing the numerically distinct but qualitatively identical β, while allowing that the phenomenal character of the two perceptual states is exactly the same.

---

[27] For a first stab at this view, see Schellenberg 2010, 2011a, and 2013b.

[28] See Burnston and Cohen 2012 for a discussion of whether we see objects in virtue of seeing properties or whether we see properties in virtue of seeing objects.

3. Coda

I distinguished several ways of interpreting the particularity thesis and argued that the content interpretation is the most fundamental. In doing so, I argued that perceptual states are constituted by the particulars perceived in that the perceptual state is characterized by singular content.

Chapter 4

Fregean Particularism

It is Monday morning and I am riding the train through the post-industrial wasteland of northern New Jersey. I gaze out of the window and, suddenly, I see a deer. Let's call it Frederik. The next morning, I am again on the train, riding through northern New Jersey. And, again, I see a deer. Let's call it Ferdinand. It is the same time of day. Everything looks exactly the same on Tuesday as it did on Monday—including the deer. However, unbeknownst to me, the deer I see on Tuesday is not the same as the one I saw on Monday. So I am seeing different particulars.

As the particularity argument established, my perceptual state on Monday is constituted by Frederik, while my perceptual state on Tuesday is constituted by Ferdinand. As the singular content argument established, the content of my perceptual state on Monday is constituted by Frederik, while the content of my perceptual state on Tuesday is constituted by Ferdinand. As before, "constituted" is understood in the sense of "at least partially constituted."

There are many open questions. What is the nature of singular perceptual content? When we suffer a non-veridical hallucination as of an object, then it seems to us that there is a particular object present, where in fact there is no such object. If veridical perceptual states have singular content, what is the content of a hallucination? Since in hallucination, we are not perceptually related to the particulars we seem to see, a hallucination cannot have singular content. What content, then, does a hallucination have? Finally, what accounts for the phenomenal character of hallucination, whereby it seems to us that a particular is present when no such particular is actually before us?

These questions can be put into focus by articulating two desiderata for any account of perception. One desideratum is to explain perceptual particularity, that is, to explain in virtue of what a perceptual state is constituted by the perceived particular. Let's call this the *particularity desideratum*. The other desideratum is to explain what accounts for the possibility that perceptions of qualitatively identical yet numerically distinct particulars could have the same phenomenal character. Let's call this the *phenomenal sameness desideratum*. More generally, the phenomenal sameness desideratum is to explain what accounts for the possibility that perceptions, hallucinations, and illusions of distinct environments could have the same phenomenal character.[1]

---

[1] One might argue that the only case in which two consecutive perceptions genuinely have the same phenomenal character are ones in which one consecutively perceives qualitatively identical, yet numerically distinct, particulars. If one holds this, one would hold that the phenomenal sameness desideratum does not

In Section 1, I will discuss these two desiderata in turn. In Section 2, I will consider several ways one might attempt to satisfy both desiderata and will show why they do not succeed. In Section 3, I will develop a particular way of understanding singular content that satisfies both desiderata. I will call this view *Fregean particularism*. Fregean particularism is the view of content that falls out of capacitism, that is, the view that perception is constitutively a matter of employing perceptual capacities. In Section 4, I will compare Fregean particularism to competitor views. In developing this account of singular content, I will consider many views along the way. I will argue against them only to the extent that it helps motivate Fregean particularism and situate it within a broader philosophical context.

1. Two Desiderata for an Account of Perception

We can understand the claim that two experiential states have the same phenomenal character as follows:

Phenomenal Sameness: If two experiential states e_1 and e_2 of the experiencing subject S have the same phenomenal character, then S would be unable to discern any difference between e_1 and e_2, even if her perceptual and introspective abilities were ideal.

An experiential state, as understood here, is the state one is in when one is either perceiving, hallucinating, or suffering an illusion. It is important to distinguish the case in which two experiences have the same phenomenal character from the case in which they are merely subjectively indistinguishable. We can all agree that we might have two consecutive experiences e_3 and e_4 that are so similar that they are subjectively indistinguishable. We may be unable to tell them apart because we fail to properly attend to the details presented to us. Or we might attend to all the details presented to us, but nonetheless be unable to tell the two experiences apart because we lack the requisite perceptual capacities. Neither is a case in which e_3 and e_4 have the same phenomenal character. After all, in the first kind of case, we could notice the difference between e_3 and e_4 if we paid better attention; in the second kind of case, we could notice the difference between e_3 and e_4 if our perceptual capacities were better.

The classic case of two perceptions that have the same phenomenal character is the case of consecutively perceiving qualitatively identical yet numerically distinct objects, *ceteris paribus*. More generally, if in two consecutive perceptions there is no qualitative difference in the environment (despite there being a difference in the numerical identity of the perceived objects) and if the subject is perceptually related to the environment in

---

apply to cases in which a hallucination seemingly has the same phenomenal character as a perception. I will here assume that a hallucination could have the same phenomenal character as a perception and so will take the phenomenal sameness desideratum to apply more generally. However, the argument of this chapter would need to be adjusted only slightly to apply to the more restrictive view on which a perception and a hallucination could never have the same phenomenal character.

the very same way, then, *ceteris paribus*, there is no difference in phenomenal character between the two perceptual states. In short, phenomenal character can be exactly the same even if the environment varies.

Moving on to the particularity desideratum: we can all agree that when a subject perceives a particular, she is causally related to the particular she perceives. It is uncontroversial and compatible with almost any view of perception that there is such a causal relation between a subject and a perceived particular—though views differ dramatically with regard to how much explanatory weight the causal relation can carry. Consider the case of two experiences, one of which is a perception of an object, the other of which is a hallucination with the same phenomenal character. It is uncontroversial and compatible with almost any view of perception that there is a difference in causal relation between the two experiences. When a subject perceives an object, she is causally related to the mind-independent object she is perceiving. When a subject suffers a hallucination with the same phenomenal character, she is not causally related to a mind-independent object that it seems to her she is perceiving. As argued in Chapter 1, acknowledging that there is a difference in causal relation between the two experiences is not sufficient to establish the particularity thesis, that is, the thesis that a subject's perceptual state M brought about by being perceptually related to the particular α is constituted by α. To satisfy the particularity desideratum, we need to explain in virtue of what a perceptual state is constituted by the perceived particular.

Recall that in Chapter 1, we distinguished between phenomenological and relational particularity. To recap: a mental state manifests phenomenological particularity if and only if it seems to the subject that a particular is present. A mental state is characterized by relational particularity if and only if the mental state is constituted by the particular perceived. The distinction between phenomenological and relational particularity allows us to reformulate the opening questions more specifically. Why think that when we perceive a particular our perceptual state is constituted by the particular perceived and thus is characterized by relational particularity in addition to phenomenological particularity? How should we account for the fact that when we suffer a hallucination, our mental state manifests phenomenological particularity, despite lacking relational particularity? In answering these questions, we can show how it is that in the case of an accurate perception, we are sensorily aware of particulars, and how it is that even when we are suffering a hallucination, our experience can be as of environmental particulars despite the fact that we are not perceptually related to at least one of the particulars to which it seems to us we are related.

1.1. Relationalism and representationalism

There are two radically different conceptions of perception. According to *relationalism*, a perceptual state is constitutively a matter of standing in an awareness or an acquaintance relation to the environment. According to *representationalism*, a perceptual state is constitutively a matter of representing the environment. So while representationalists analyze perceptual states in terms of their representational content, relationalists analyze perceptual states in terms of awareness or acquaintance relations to mind-independent particulars.

Relationalism and representationalism are widely considered to be in conflict.[2] But the debate between relationalists and representationalists sets up a false dichotomy. The source of this false dichotomy is that the standard views in the debate are either austerely relationalist or austerely representationalist. To a first approximation, *austere relationalism* has it that perception is constitutively relational and lacks any representational component. To a first approximation, *austere representationalism* has it that perception is constitutively representational and lacks any relational component that has repercussions for the experiential state.[3] Against both, I argue that perceptual relations to the environment and the content of experience are mutually dependent. I do so by exploiting insights from Chapters 1 through 3. I argue that by employing perceptual capacities we are related to our environment—at least in the case of perception. Thus, perception is constitutively relational. I argue moreover that the perceptual capacities employed constitute the representational content of our perceptual state. Thus, perception is constitutively representational. In this way, I will show that there is no tension between perception being constitutively both relational and representational. But first let's take a closer look at what it means for perception to be relational and what it means for perception to be representational.

Perceiving subjects have been argued to be perceptually related to many different kinds of entities. These entities fall into two groups: abstract or mind-dependent entities, such as qualia, sense-data, propositions, or intentional objects, on the one hand; and, on the other hand, concrete, mind-independent objects, property-instances, or events, such as a white coffee cup resting on a desk. In the current discussion, the thesis that perception is relational means always that perception is constitutively a matter of a subject being perceptually related to concrete, mind-independent objects, property-instances, events, or a combination thereof.

When I speak of perception as being representational without qualification, I mean no more than the idea that perception is a matter of a subject representing her environment such that her perceptual state is characterized by representational content. There

---

[2] For a recent articulation of this view, see Campbell 2002. Though see Schellenberg 2010 for a representationalist view that does not fit this dichotomy; see Beck (forthcoming) for a relationalist view that does not fit this dichotomy. See also Soteriou 2013 (Chapter 4), McDowell 2013, and Logue 2014.

[3] For austere representationalist views, see McGinn 1982, Davies 1992, Tye 1995, Lycan 1996, Byrne 2001, and Hill 2009 among many others. For austere relationalist views, see Campbell 2002, Travis 2004, Johnston 2004, 2014, Brewer 2006, Fish 2009, Logue 2012, Genone 2014, French 2014, 2016, Raleigh 2014, 2015, and Gomes and French 2016 among others. As I will discuss in more detail in Chapter 5, Martin (2002a, 2004) leaves open the possibility that experience could have content, but his positive view of perception is structurally similar to that of austere relationalists. Campbell (2002) calls his view the "relational view," Martin (2002a, 2004) calls his "naïve realism," while Brewer (2006) calls his the "object view." I will refer to the view with the label "austere relationalism," since the most distinctive features of the view are arguably the central role of relations between perceiving subjects and the world as well as its austerity. There is room in logical space to reject representationalism without endorsing a relationalist view. For such a view, see Gupta 2012.

are many different ways of understanding the nature of content given this constraint. I will discuss the different choice points in more detail in Chapter 5. For now, it will suffice to say that the content can be conceived of as a Russellian proposition, a Fregean sense, an indexical content, a map of the environment, an image-like representation, or in any number of other ways. Moreover, the content can be understood to be either conceptual or nonconceptual, propositional or nonpropositional, and as constituted by the particulars perceived or as independent of the particulars perceived. Finally, there are many different ways of understanding the relationship between phenomenal character and content. Indeed, accepting the thesis that perceptual experience is representational is compatible with thinking that the content and phenomenal character of mental states are entirely independent. So the thesis that perceptual experience is representational is agnostic on all possible ways of understanding the relationship between content and phenomenal character. I am using the term "representationalism" for any view that endorses the thesis that perceptual experience is constitutively a matter of representing. Representationalism, so understood, is neutral on the relationship between perceptual content and perceptual consciousness.

It will be helpful to contrast the distinction between relationalism and representationalism with an orthogonal distinction between two ways of individuating experiential states. On a *phenomenalist view*, experiential states are individuated solely by their phenomenal character. Versions of this view have been defended by Price (1932), Moore (1953), Tye (1995), Lycan (1996), Byrne (2001), and Block (2003) among others. On an *externalist view*, experiential states are individuated not only by their phenomenal character but also by the external, mind-independent particulars (if any) perceived. Needless to say views differ wildly on just how perceived particulars make a difference to perceptual states. Versions of externalism have been defended by Peacocke (1983, 2009), Searle (1983), McDowell (1984), Byrne (2001, 2009), Campbell (2002), Martin (2002b), Burge (2003, 2010, 2014), Johnston (2004), Soteriou (2005), Brewer (2006), Schellenberg (2006, 2010, 2011a), Hill (2009), Fish (2009), Logue (2014), and Genone (2014) among others.[4]

The motivations for thinking that perception is constitutively representational typically go hand in hand with the motivations for embracing the phenomenalist view. Similarly, the motivations for thinking that perception is constitutively relational typically go hand in hand with the motivations for embracing the externalist view. However, the fault line between relationalism and representationalism does not coincide with the fault line between phenomenalist and externalist views. Sense-data theory, as defended by Price (1932) and Moore (1953), is a phenomenalist view that rejects representationalism.[5] Moreover, one can argue for an externalist view that endorses

---

[4] On some versions of externalism, phenomenal character is itself constituted by external objects, events, and property-instances. Such naïve realist views defend externalist views of phenomenal character.

[5] One could argue that Price's notion of perceptual acceptance introduces a conceptual and thus representational element; however, arguably Price's notion of perceptual acceptance plays a role only at a higher level, namely the level of perceptual beliefs (Price 1932, Chapter VI).

representationalism (Peacocke 1983, 2009, Searle 1983, McDowell 1984, Byrne 2001, 2009, Burge 2003, 2010, 2014, Schellenberg 2006, 2010, 2011a, and Hill 2009).

In what follows, I will consider the austere versions of both representationalism and relationalism in more detail and will assess how they fare in satisfying the particularity and phenomenal sameness desiderata. As I will argue, austere representationalists can easily satisfy the phenomenal sameness desideratum, but not the particularity desideratum. By contrast, austere relationalists can easily satisfy the particularity desideratum, but not the phenomenal sameness desideratum. I will offer a synthesis of these approaches that satisfies both desiderata.

1.2. Austere representationalism

The key idea of austere representationalism is that to have a perception, illusion, or hallucination is to be in an experiential state with representational content that corresponds one-to-one with the phenomenal character of the experiencing subject: any changes in content go hand in hand with changes in phenomenal character and vice versa. Insofar as the representational content corresponds one-to-one with phenomenal character, it is phenomenal content.

If representational content is phenomenal content, then two experiential states with the same phenomenal character cannot differ in content—irrespective of what particular, if any, the subject is related to. So a perceptual state can have the same phenomenal content as a mental state brought about by suffering a hallucination or illusion. According to austere representationalism, if I see Frederik on Monday and Ferdinand on Tuesday, my perceptual states will have the very same content. More generally, there can be an exact duplicate of an experiential state and its content, brought about by being perceptually related to particular α, in an environment in which the experiencing subject is perceptually related to the numerically distinct particular β. Furthermore, there can be an exact duplicate of an experiential state and its content in an environment in which the experiencing subject is not perceptually related to any relevant mind-independent particular. So if experiential content is phenomenal content, then it is general content.[6] There are many different ways of understanding general contents. They can be thought of as *de dicto* modes of presentation, Russellian propositions, or existentially quantified content to name just a few options.[7]

Stated more precisely, austere representationalism is committed to the following three theses:

1. Experiential states have content.
2. A perception, an illusion, and a hallucination can have the same phenomenal character.

---

[6] For a discussion of phenomenal perceptual content, see Bayne 2010.
[7] For a discussion of the phenomenal content of perceptual experience, see Berger 2015.

3. The content of an experiential state corresponds one-to-one with its phenomenal character in that any changes in content go hand in hand with changes in phenomenal character and vice versa.[8]

It follows from these three theses that:

4. Perceptual content is not constituted by the mind-independent particulars perceived.

So austere representationalists are committed to denying that perceptual content is singular content, and thus cannot satisfy the particularity desideratum by appeal to the singular content of perception. I will embrace the first two theses of austere representationalism, but will reject the third. By rejecting the third thesis, the commitment to the fourth thesis can be avoided.

First, however, let's take a closer look at austere representationalism. One way of understanding experiential content under the constraint of the austere representationalist thesis is that it is existentially quantified content of the form that there is an object x that instantiates a property F:

$$(a_{p,i,h})   (\exists x)Fx$$

A perception, illusion, and a hallucination may each have content of this form. Most objects instantiate a multitude of properties. For example, most visually perceivable objects instantiate spatial, color, and location properties. Most auditorily perceivable objects instantiate pitch, loudness, duration, and timbre properties. I will work with the simplifying assumption that there can be an experience (as) of an object that instantiates only one property. My argument, however, easily generalizes to the more realistic case in which one experiences an object instantiating a multitude of properties.

The thesis that experiential content is existentially quantified content posits that an experiential state represents only that there is an object that instantiates the relevant properties in the external world. No element of the content depends on whether such an object is in fact present. So it is possible to be in a mental state with the relevant content regardless of what object is present or even whether there is an object present. The perceived object does not fall out of the picture altogether: although no reference to the particular object perceived is necessary to specify the content, the austere representationalist can say that a subject perceives an object o at a particular location only if o satisfies the existential content of the subject's experiential state. So the content is accurate only if there is an object at the relevant location that instantiates the properties specified by the content. The crucial point is that whether an object of the right kind is present bears only on the accuracy of the content. It has no repercussions for what is represented.

---

[8] McGinn (1982), Davies (1992), Tye (1995), Lycan (1996), Byrne (2001), and Pautz (2009) among others have defended views that are committed to these three theses.

The main advantage of austere representationalism is that it easily and elegantly explains how a perception, hallucination, and illusion could have the same phenomenal character. Indeed, accounting for this possibility is one of the main motivations for analyzing experiential content as phenomenal content. As Davies puts it: "the perceptual content of experience is a phenomenal notion: perceptual content is a matter of how the world *seems* to the experiencer...If perceptual content is, in this sense, 'phenomenological content'...then, where there is no phenomenological difference for a subject, then there is no difference in content" (1992: 26). By equating experiential content with phenomenal content, austere representationalists can easily satisfy the phenomenal sameness desideratum.

The main problem with austere representationalism is that it does not satisfy the particularity desideratum. The view cannot account for the difference between the perceptual content brought about by a subject perceiving cup_1 at time t_1 and her perceptual state brought about by being perceptually related to the qualitatively identical cup_2 at time t_2. Davies suggests, for example, that "if two objects are genuinely indistinguishable for a subject, then a perceptual experience of one has the same content as a perceptual experience of the other" (1992: 25f.).[9] According to austere representationalism, sameness of phenomenal character entails sameness of content. A view according to which two experiential states with the same phenomenal character cannot differ in content—irrespective of what particular, if any, the subject is related to—cannot satisfy the particularity desideratum in terms of perceptual content. Therefore, if perceptual content should reflect relational particularity, then perceptual content cannot be equated with phenomenal content.

Now an austere representationalist could say that the perceptual relation between the perceiving subject and the perceived object does play a role. After all, the austere representationalist could argue that the form of a veridical perception is a conjunction of two elements, namely, the content and the relation to the perceived particular:

$$(b_p) \quad HS<(\exists x)Fx> \text{ and } RS\alpha$$

Subject S stands in a representation relation H to the existentially quantified content that there is an object x that instantiates the property F and S stands in a perceptual relation R to particular α. By contrast, the form of a hallucination is:

$$(b_h) \quad HS<(\exists x)Fx>$$

---

[9] McGinn (1982) and Millar (1991) argue for a similar thesis. This view is subject to well-known counterexamples, which I will not rehearse here. They have been discussed in detail by Soteriou (2000) and Tye (2007) by expanding on Grice's (1961) discussion of so-called "veridical hallucinations." Searle (1983) aims to account for particularity within the framework of existentially quantified contents by building causal conditions into the existential contents. In short, the idea is that a descriptive condition picks out an object as the cause of the experience. By doing so, Searle builds causal relations to particular objects into perceptual content. Given Searle's view about the relationship between content and phenomenal character, this approach is at odds with the phenomenal character of experience.

We can call this view *conjunctivism*. Conjunctivism has it that two elements are in place in a successful perceptual experience. In the case of a hallucination, the subject stands in relation only to the proposition that there is an object that has a certain property. Conjunctivism is a representational view that individuates perceptual experiences not just by the relevant mental states, but also by the perceptual relation between the experiencing subject and the environment. The problem with conjunctivism is that the experiential state is in no way affected by the particular perceived (if any). Therefore, the particularity desideratum is not satisfied. Although conjunctivism builds perceptual relations between subjects and particulars into the form of perception, this relational element has no effect on any aspect of the perceptual state, for example, its content or phenomenal character. So conjunctivism is simply a version of austere representationalism that makes explicit that in the case of an accurate perception a perceptual relation holds between the subject and the perceived particulars.

With austere representationalists, I will argue that phenomenal character does not track relational particularity. Yet against austere representationalists, I will argue that perceptual content is singular content. First, however, let's assess how austere relationalism fares with regard to the particularity and phenomenal sameness desiderata.

1.3. Austere relationalism

Austere relationalists argue that no appeal to representational content is necessary in a philosophical account of perception and that perception constitutively involves at least three components: a subject, her environment, and a perceptual relation between the subject and particulars in her environment. This perceptual relation is understood as, for example, an acquaintance or a sensory awareness relation. So austere relationalists have it that perception is constitutively a matter of a subject S standing in an acquaintance or an awareness relation R to a mind-independent particular α:[10]

$$(c_p) \quad RS\alpha$$

In this way, austere relationalism conceives of the form of perception in a way that a hallucination could not possibly fit. As Brewer formulates the idea:

The course of perceptual experience...provide[s] the subject with the grounds for her actual beliefs about the world, and also for the various other beliefs which she might equally have acquired had she noticed different things, or had her attention instead been guided by some other project or purpose. It does so, though, not by serving up any fully formed content, somehow, both in advance of, but also in light of, these attentional considerations, but, rather, by presenting her directly with the actual constituents of the physical world themselves. (2006: 178)

---

[10] This summary does not do justice to the subtleties of austere relationalism. On one alternative formulation, austere relationalism holds that perception constitutively involves a subject's standing in an awareness relation to a property-instance, scene, or event. On another alternative formulation, perception is said to involve an event in which such a relation obtains. For a detailed discussion of the view and an analysis of the different versions of austere relationalism, see Chapter 5 and Schellenberg 2011a and 2014a.

Austere relationalism is a radical version of disjunctivism, that is, in short, the view according to which perceptions and hallucinations share no common element or do not belong to the same fundamental kind.[11] Traditionally disjunctivists argued that while hallucinations are not representational, perceptions do represent mind-independent particulars.[12] Austere relationalism is a radical version of disjunctivism insofar as it denies not only that hallucinations are representational, but that perceptions are as well.

Austere relationalism is structurally similar to sense-data theory and is motivated in part by its insights. So it will help to contrast the two views. Both views understand phenomenal character as constituted by the particulars perceived. However, while sense-data theorists argue that the particulars perceived are sense-data, austere relationalists argue that the particulars in question are material, mind-independent objects, property-instances, or events. This difference has many repercussions. One repercussion is that sense-data theorists take the structure of a perception to be the very same as that of a hallucination. In both cases a subject's experience consists in being acquainted with sense-data. Since hallucinations and perceptions have the very same structure, sense-data theorists can easily satisfy the phenomenal sameness desideratum. A second repercussion is that since sense-data theorists have it that a subject can be in the very same experiential state regardless of whether she is perceptually related to a mind-independent particular, the view is committed to denying that perceptual states are constituted by the particulars perceived. Therefore, sense-data theorists cannot satisfy the particularity desideratum.

In contrast to sense-data theorists, austere relationalists conceive of the fundamental structure of a perception in a way that precludes hallucinations from having that structure. After all, since a hallucinating subject is not perceptually related to the material, mind-independent particular she seems to be seeing, a hallucination cannot be modeled on the $RS\alpha$-form of perception. This way of thinking about perceptual experience has many virtues. The most salient for the present discussion is that austere relationalists can easily satisfy the particularity desideratum. Insofar as the subject is perceptually related to particular α, her perceptual state is constituted by α.

However, austere relationalism comes at a price. Austere relationalists account for relational particularity in terms of phenomenal character.[13] As a consequence, the phenomenal character brought about by being perceptually related to α necessarily differs from the phenomenal character brought about by being perceptually related to β. This is the case even if α and β are qualitatively identical. Moreover, the phenomenal character of a perception will necessarily differ from the phenomenal character of a hallucination. So austere relationalists cannot satisfy the phenomenal sameness desideratum.

---

[11] The metaphysical thesis that perception and hallucination share no common element was first articulated by McDowell (1982). Among others, Martin (2002a) formulates the key idea of disjunctivism as being that perceptions and hallucinations do not belong to the same fundamental kind.

[12] See, for instance, Hinton 1973, Snowdon 1981, and McDowell 1982.

[13] For discussion, see Chapter 3.

The natural solution to the problem is to argue that it is not the phenomenal character of a perceptual state, but rather its content, that grounds relational particularity. Since the austere relationalist holds that perceptual states do not have representational content, this solution is not open to her. In the rest of this chapter, I will present a way of satisfying the particularity desideratum while respecting the intuition that perceptions of numerically distinct, yet qualitatively identical particulars do not differ phenomenally. I will argue that although perceptions of numerically distinct particulars necessarily differ with regard to their content, this difference is not revealed in phenomenal character. But first I will make some clarificatory remarks about accuracy conditions.

2. Varieties of Singular Content

If the content of perception is singular content, then what is the content of a hallucination? A hard-line response to this question is to argue that hallucinations have no representational content. Such a view is motivated by a particular understanding of what it means to represent an object: singular content is radically object-dependent, such that an experiential state has representational content only if the experiencing subject is perceptually related to a particular in her environment. So only if a subject is related to an object, can she represent the object. Drawing on this understanding of the conditions for representing an object, the conclusion is drawn that a hallucinating subject is not in a mental state with content: it only seems to her that she is representing. So there is only the illusion of content.[14]

A view on which perceptual content is radically object-dependent amounts to a disjunctivist view of experiential content. Content disjunctivists accept the austere relationalist thesis that perception and hallucination share no common element or do not belong to the same fundamental kind. In contrast to austere relationalists, however, they hold that a perceiving subject represents the particulars to which she is perceptually related.

Content disjunctivists face the same problems as any other disjunctivists. One problem is that the cognitive significance and the action-guiding role of experiential content is downplayed. When a subject hallucinates, the way things seem to her plays a certain cognitive role. If it seems to her that she is perceptually related to a white cup, she may, for example, reach out and try to pick it up. If one denies that hallucinations have representational content, this cannot be explained. It is not clear how the mere illusion of content could motivate the subject to act. Consider Harman's example of Ponce de León who was searching Florida for the fountain of youth (Harman 1990). The fountain of youth does not exist, yet Ponce de León was looking for something particular. As Harman argues convincingly, he was not looking for a mental object.

---

[14] Versions of this view have been defended by Hinton (1973), Snowdon (1981), Evans (1982), and McDowell (1982, 1984).

He was looking for a mind-independent object that, as it so happened, unbeknownst to him, did not exist. A second problem—and the problem most salient for present purposes—is that, insofar as content disjunctivists hold that hallucinations do not represent, they leave unclear what explains the phenomenal character of hallucinations. So it is not clear how content disjunctivists satisfy the phenomenal sameness desideratum. While content disjunctivists acknowledge that a hallucination could seemingly have the same phenomenal character as a perception, they do little if anything to explain this phenomenon.

The problems of disjunctivism are avoided if perceptual content is not understood as radically object-dependent. That would allow that hallucinations can have at least some kind of content. One way to develop such a view is to argue that the content of a hallucination involves a gap that in the case of a perception is filled by a particular. Traditionally, gappy contents are thought of in terms of Russellian propositions.[15] On the gappy Russellian view, the content of hallucination expresses that the object that seems to be present seems to instantiate property F. The content of a hallucination will be an ordered pair of a gap and a property:

$$(d_h) \quad <\_\_, F>$$

In the case of an accurate perception of an object o, the gap is filled by that object:

$$(d_p) \quad <o, F>$$

There are several problems with the Russellian gappy content view. One problem is that the content of hallucination has too little structure to account for hallucinations as of multiple objects. If I hallucinate a green dragon playing a red piano, the content of my experience will contain multiple gaps and nothing that marks their difference other than these gaps being bound with distinct properties. Putting aside the problem of how a gap could be bound by properties, it is unclear how such a view could account for the difference in phenomenal character between hallucinating a green dragon playing a red piano and hallucinating a green elephant riding a red bicycle.

A second problem is that to account for a hallucination as of an object that seems to be instantiating a property that is in fact an uninstantiated property, such as supersaturated red or Hume's missing shade of blue, the Russellian must conceive of the content of hallucination as potentially constituted by uninstantiated properties. By doing so, she commits herself not just to a controversial metaphysics of properties but also to a controversial view of phenomenal character. The view is metaphysically controversial since accepting the existence of uninstantiated properties requires some kind of Platonic 'two realms'-view on which there is more to reality than the concrete physical world. The view is phenomenologically controversial since it is not clear

---

[15] See Braun 1993. Such a Russellian way of thinking about gappy contents has been defended also by Bach (2007) and Tye (2007). For a Fregean gappy content view, see Schellenberg 2006. This chapter develops ideas from that project.

what it would be to be sensorily aware of a property. After all, properties are not spatio-temporally located and not causally efficacious. The Russellian could respond to the phenomenological problem by distinguishing between being sensorily and cognitively aware of something. This would allow her to accept that we cannot be sensorily aware of properties, but argue that hallucinating subjects are cognitively aware of properties. However, now the problem arises as to how a perception and a hallucination could have the same phenomenal character. After all, being cognitively aware of something is phenomenally distinct from being sensorily aware of something.[16] If this is right, then it is unclear how the Russellian could satisfy the phenomenal sameness desideratum.[17]

These problems are avoided if perceptual content is understood as constituted by Fregean modes of presentation of mind-independent particulars, rather than bare properties and objects. In the rest of this chapter, I will develop and defend Fregean particularism, which will include a Fregean account of gappy contents. By doing so, I will present a way of satisfying both the particularity and the phenomenal sameness desiderata.

3. Fregean Particularism

The austere versions of relationalism and representationalism are not the only options. An alternative is to argue that perceptual experience is constitutively both relational and representational. On such a view, a perception, a hallucination, and an illusion with the same phenomenal character share a metaphysically substantial common element. However, there are also substantial differences with regard to their content: while the token content of perception is singular content, the form of illusion and hallucination is derivative of the form of perception. Perception plays multiple roles: it yields conscious mental states, it justifies beliefs, and it provides us with knowledge of our environment. To account for these multiple roles, perceptual content needs to serve multiple explanatory purposes. At the very least, perceptual content must have both a component that grounds perceptual consciousness and a component that, in the case of an accurate perception, grounds perceptual particularity. By grounding perceptual particularity the content can account for the epistemic role that perception plays in our lives.

I will develop Fregean particularism by exploiting the basic insights of capacitism. Recall that according to capacitism, perceiving a particular is constitutively a matter of employing perceptual capacities by means of which that particular is discriminated and singled out. If one possesses a perceptual capacity, one can employ it even if no particular of the kind that the capacity functions to single out is present. Therefore, the

---

[16] For a discussion of cognitive phenomenology, see Kriegel 2011, Montague 2011, and Wu 2014, Goff 2018.

[17] For a more detailed discussion of these two problems and for a discussion of alternative ways that the Russellian might respond to these two problems, see Chapter 6.

very same perceptual capacities that are employed in perception (good case) can also be employed in illusion and hallucination (bad cases). As I argued in Chapter 3, employing perceptual capacities constitutes content. After all, employing perceptual capacities is repeatable and yields phenomenal states that either accurately or inaccurately reflect the environment of the experiencing subject. The thesis that content is constituted by employing perceptual capacities that function to single out particulars implies that perceptual content is singular. After all, if the fact that perceptual capacities single out particulars in some situations but not others has any semantic significance, then the token content yielded by employing perceptual capacities in perception will be constituted by the particulars singled out.[18] Putting the same idea in different terms: for something to be the object of a singular content, the content must be constituted by that very object.

By contrast, an austere representationalist view (or any other view on which perceptual content is general) holds that the content is the very same regardless of what particular (if any) the experiencing subject is related to. A general content lays down a condition that something must satisfy to be the object determined by the content. The condition to be satisfied does not depend on the mind-independent particular that satisfies it. So the relation between content and object is simply the semantic relation of satisfaction.

3.1. Perceptual capacities and modes of presentation again

The idea that content is constituted by employing perceptual capacities by means of which we (purport to) single out particulars is analogous to the Fregean idea that modes of presentation are a way of grasping or referring to particulars. Indeed, it is analogous to the Fregean idea that modes of presentation both have a cognitive significance and are a means of referring to particulars. A mode of presentation is the specific way in which a subject refers to a particular. While Frege introduces the distinction between sense and reference with a perceptual case, he does not develop the notion for perceptual content. His focus was never on lowly mental faculties like perception. Nonetheless, we can apply his view of modes of presentation to the case of perception.[19] Applied to that case, the idea is that a mode of presentation is the specific way in which a subject singles out a perceived particular. We can think of perceptual capacities as the mental counterpart of modes of presentation. While a mode of presentation is a component of a thought or a proposition, a perceptual capacity is a mental tool. According to Frege, concepts are mappings from objects onto truth-values (Frege 1879). Similarly, perceptual capacities are mappings from particulars onto accuracy conditions.

---

[18] As previously, when I speak of constitution, I mean partial constitution. For a discussion of the notion of constitution in play, see Chapter 1.

[19] For an alternative way of understanding the relationship between Fregean modes of presentations and perception, see Millar 2016.

As we saw in Chapter 3, one key motivation for introducing modes of presentation is to capture a fineness of grain in content that reference to mind-independent particulars alone could not achieve. On a Russellian understanding, alternative possible modes of presentation can be expressed only insofar as one may have different cognitive attitudes to the same content. The way in which one perceives or thinks of the object is not expressed in the content proper.

Paralleling the distinction between singular and general content, there are two standard ways of thinking about Fregean modes of presentation. If one focuses on the role of modes of presentation as accounting for cognitive significance, then it is natural to think of them as *de dicto*. A *de dicto* mode of presentation is general in that it can be the very same regardless of what (if anything) the experiencing subject is perceptually related to. If, by contrast, one focuses on the role of modes of presentation as a way of referring to a particular, then it is natural to think of them as *de re*. A *de re* mode of presentation is singular in that what particular (if any) the subject is perceptually related to has repercussions for the token content.

A *de dicto* mode of presentation lays down a condition that something must satisfy to be the particular determined by the content. Chalmers, among others, understands Fregean senses in this way: "Fregean content is supposed to be a sort of phenomenal content, such that necessarily, an experience with the same phenomenology has the same Fregean content" (2006a: 99, see also Thompson 2009). A *de dicto* mode of presentation constitutes a way of representing mind-independent particulars irrespective of whether the relevant particulars are present. If the content of experiential states were constituted by *de dicto* modes of presentation, then the content of a perception, a hallucination, or an illusion with the same phenomenal character would be

$$(e_{p,h,i}) \quad <MOP_d^o, MOP_d^F>$$

where MOP_d^o is a *de dicto* mode of presentation of an object and MOP_d^F is a *de dicto* mode of presentation of a property. Such an account of perceptual content implies a two-stage view of determining reference: first, we represent a general content, and in a second step, we refer to mind-independent particulars based on this content.[20] Representing a *de dicto* mode of presentation is, on this view, independent of the second step, in which a particular may be determined. Such a two-stage view faces the problem of how the content grounds the ability to refer to external particulars. Insofar as a *de dicto* mode of presentation can be the very same regardless of what (if anything) the experiencing subject is perceptually related to, this way of thinking about content amounts to a version of austere representationalism and faces all the difficulties of that view. Any view on which perceptual content is constituted by *de dicto* modes

---

[20] For an argument against such a two-stage view of determining reference, see Johnston 2004: 150f. Johnston does not distinguish between *de dicto* and *de re* modes of presentation, and as a consequence sees the problem articulated in the main text as a problem for any Fregean view *tout court*. As I will show, it is only a problem for a view on which Fregean senses are *de dicto* rather than *de re*.

of presentation fails to satisfy the particularity desideratum for the same reasons that austere representationalism does.

This problem is avoided if perceptual content is analyzed as constituted by *de re* rather than *de dicto* modes of presentation. Understanding modes of presentation as *de re* is motivated by recognizing that modes of presentation play a dual role: they have a cognitive significance, and they single out or refer to mind-independent particulars. Understanding perceptual content as constituted by *de re* modes of presentation recognizes that representing a particular is not independent of singling out the particular that is the referent of the sense. By contrast to *de dicto* modes of presentation, *de re* modes of presentation are singular in the good case.

Now, on one way of understanding *de re* modes of presentation, a subject can have a contentful experience only if she is (perceptually) related to the very particular that she purports to single out. This view is a version of content disjunctivism, which we critically discussed in Section 2. What we need is an understanding of *de re* modes of presentation on which modes of presentation ground the relational particularity of accurate perceptions and the phenomenological particularity of perceptions, hallucinations, and illusions.[21]

3.2. Content types and token contents

I argued that regardless of whether we are perceiving, hallucinating, or suffering an illusion, we employ perceptual capacities by means of which we purport to single out mind-independent particulars. Since in the bad case, we fail to single out the particulars that we purport to single out, our perceptual capacities are employed baselessly. They are employed baselessly insofar as they do not fulfill their function to operate on environmental particulars. This failure is not at the level of employing the relevant capacity, but rather at the level of singling out a particular. Employing perceptual capacities accounts for the fact that we are intentionally directed at an apparent particular, a process that invests the hallucinatory and illusory state with structure. Moreover, the argument from Chapter 3—that employing perceptual capacities yields a perceptual state with representational content in virtue of the capacities being repeatable and constituting a phenomenal state that is either accurate or inaccurate—generalizes from perception to hallucination and illusion. So given that even in the bad case, the subject is employing perceptual capacities, there is good reason to think that her mental state has content.

We have distinguished between employing perceptual capacities *tout court* (regardless of what if anything is singled out) and employing perceptual capacities either while successfully singling out a particular or failing to do so. We can apply this distinction to content and thereby distinguish between *content types* that are constituted by the

---

[21] For a detailed discussion of Fregean modes of presentation and their individuation conditions, see Schellenberg 2012.

perceptual capacities employed and *token contents* that are constituted both by the perceptual capacities employed and the particulars (if any) thereby singled out.

Recall that in Chapter 2, we distinguished between three levels at which to analyze mental states. The first level of analysis pertains to the function of the mental capacity. The second level of analysis pertains to the mental capacity employed, irrespective of the context in which it is employed. The third level of analysis pertains to the mental capacity employed, taking into account the context in which it is employed. Applied to the notion of perceptual content, we can say that the second level of analysis pertains to the content type of a mental state, while the third level of analysis pertains to the token content of a mental state. The content type and the token content are both constituted by capacities that have a certain function. So the first level of analysis explains how the content type and the token content are connected beyond the one being a token of the other.

As I will argue in more detail in Chapter 6, employing perceptual capacities in a sensory mode constitutes perceptual consciousness, such that if two experiential states have the same phenomenal character, they will be constituted by employing the same perceptual capacities in the same sensory mode. Since employing perceptual capacities yields a content type, there is a one-to-one correspondence between perceptual consciousness and content type. By contrast, there is a one-to-many correspondence between perceptual consciousness and the token content of an experiential state.

A perception, a hallucination, and an illusion with the same phenomenal character will all be characterized by the same content type. After all, they all result from employing the same perceptual capacities. Thus, the phenomenal sameness desideratum is satisfied. However, their content token will differ at least in part. After all, in the case of perception, the perceiver successfully singles out the particulars she purports to single out, while, in the case of hallucination and illusion, the experiencing subject fails to single out at least one particular she purports to single out. Thus, the particularity desideratum is satisfied.

3.3. Token contents: singular modes of presentation and gappy modes of presentation

How should we understand the token content of a perceptual state? According to Fregean particularism, the token content of an accurate perception e_1 of a cup α_1 and the property-instance π_1 will be

$$(content_{e1}) \quad <MOP_{ra}(\alpha_1), MOP_{r\pi}(\pi_1)>$$

where $MOPr_{ra}(\alpha_1)$ is a singular mode of presentation of the cup α_1 that is the product of employing a perceptual capacity that functions to single out the kind of object under which α_1 falls. So "α_1" is functioning as the name of an object. "$MOPr_{ra}$" is a functional expression that expresses a function from objects to singular modes of presentation. $MOP_{r\pi}(\pi_1)$ is a singular mode of presentation of the property-instance π_1 that is the product of employing a perceptual capacity that functions to single out instances of the property under which π_1 falls. So while $MOP_{ra}(\alpha_1)$ is a *de re* mode of presentation of the object α_1, $MOP_{rn}(\pi_1)$ is a *de re* mode of presentation of the property-instance π_1. I am assuming that the *res* of a *de re* mode of presentation can be any mind-independent particular perceived, be it an object, a property-instance, or an event. To avoid any confusion, I will speak of singular modes of presentation rather than *de re* modes of presentation. For any given particular there will be many possible modes of presentation. For the content specified by $MOP_{ra}(\alpha_1)$ to be determinate, it is important that it is conceived of as one particular mode of presentation of the relevant object. Similarly, for the content specified by $MOP_{rn}(\pi_1)$ to be determinate, it is important that it is conceived of as one particular mode of presentation of the relevant property-instance.

A perception e_2 that has the same phenomenal character as e_1 and is of a qualitatively identical yet numerically distinct cup α_2 and property-instance π_2 will have the distinct content

$$(content_{e2}) \quad <MOP_{ra}(\alpha_2), MOP_{rn}(\pi_2)>$$

Given injectivity, $MOP_{ra}(\alpha_1) \neq MOP_{ra}(\alpha_2)$ and $MOP_{rn}(\pi_1) \neq MOP_{rn}(\pi_2)$. So token contents differ depending on the particular to which the subject is perceptually related. This is the case even if the particulars are qualitatively identical.

In the case of a hallucination that has the same phenomenal character as e_1, the same perceptual capacities are employed as in e_1. But the environmental requirements for successfully singling out the particulars are not met. So no particulars are singled out. As a consequence, the capacities are employed baselessly and so the ensuing token content is defective.

One way of understanding the idea that the content is defective is to say that it is gappy. There is nothing metaphysically spooky about gaps. The gap simply marks the failure to single out a particular. So the content of a hallucination in which we purport to single out an object that instantiates a property is

$$(content_h) \quad <MOP_{ra}(\_\_), MOP_{rn}(\_\_)>$$

where $MOP_{ra}(\_\_)$ specifies the kind of object that would have to be present for the experience to be accurate and $MOP_{rn}(\_\_)$ specifies the properties that this object would instantiate were the experience a perception rather than a hallucination. More specifically, $MOP_{ra}(\_\_)$ is a gappy mode of presentation that is the product of employing a perceptual capacity that functions to single out objects of the kind that the hallucinating subject purports to single out while failing to single out any such object. It accounts for the intentional directedness of the experience at a (seeming) particular object. $MOP_{rn}(\_\_)$ is a gappy mode of presentation that is the product of employing a perceptual capacity that functions to single out property-instances of the kind that the hallucinating subject purports to single out while failing to single out any such property-instance. It accounts for the intentional directedness of the experience at a property-instance. In short, $MOP_{ra}(\_\_)$ is a gappy, object-related mode of presentation and $MOP_{rn}(\_\_)$ is a gappy, property-related mode of presentation. So for a perceptual capacity to be employed baselessly amounts to the ensuing token content being gappy.[22]

An example will help clarify the idea. Consider Hallie who suffers a hallucination as of a white coffee cup. The content of her hallucination specifies both the kind of object that would have to be present for her experience to be accurate and the properties that this object would have to instantiate. The content is indeterminate insofar as it does not specify any particulars. The content would be accurate if the subject were related to a particular white cup. It is important that the content would be accurate regardless of whether the subject is perceptually related to this or that qualitatively identical white cup. This is just to say that the content of a hallucination does not reflect relational particularity.

Depending on how one understands the nature of properties that subjects experience, one might argue that the content of hallucination is gappy only in the object-place, but not in the property-place. On such a view, the content of hallucination would be: $(content_h)'$ $<MOP_{r\alpha}(\_\_), MOP_{r\pi}(\pi_1)>$. By contrast, I am arguing that a hallucinating subject who seems to be perceiving a property instantiated by an object is not related to a property-instance. After all, she is not related to any relevant object that could be instantiating the property. Due to this, the content of a hallucination is not just gappy in the object-place, but also in the property-place. Of course, it is possible that while hallucinating, one accurately perceives many mind-independent particulars. In this case, only some of the modes of presentation constituting the content will be gappy.[23]

I will discuss the nature of gappy contents in more detail shortly, but for now let's turn to illusions. In the case of an illusion that has the same phenomenal character as e_1, the same perceptual capacities are employed as in e_1, but, as in the case of hallucination, the environmental requirements for successfully singling out at least one of the particulars that the subject purports to single out are not met. Since the subject fails to single out a property-instance, the token content that ensues from employing the relevant perceptual capacity is gappy:

$$(content_i) \quad <MOP_{r\alpha}(\alpha_1), MOP_{r\pi}(\_\_)>$$

---

[22] Burge has been read as defending a gappy content view. However, as Burge writes of his view, "I have heard interpretations…according to which there is a 'hole' in the representational aspects of the proposition, where the hole corresponds to the object (which completes the proposition). I regard these interpretations as rather silly" (1977/2007: 75). Burge argues that there are demonstrative elements in the content of a mental state that are in place regardless of whether they refer to the object of experience. As he puts it, "I do not think that a physical *re* in the empirical world…is itself 'part of' the belief.… In my view, the Intentional side of a belief is its only side. In many cases, in my view, a belief that is in fact *de re* might not have been successfully referential (could have failed to be *de re*) and still would have remained the same belief. Moreover, the belief itself can always be individuated, or completely characterized, in terms of the Intentional content" (1991: 209). The way I am using the terms, what Burge refers to as *de re* would be more aptly labeled *de dicto*. More importantly, insofar as on Burge's view the intentional content of two experiences can be the very same regardless of the environment, the content does not reflect relational particularity.

[23] For an alternative account of modes of presentation, see Rescorla 2014.

So the token content of an illusion is gappy only in the property-place.

In sum, we can distinguish four different kinds of token contents of perceptual experience with same phenomenal character:

$$(content_{e1}) \quad <MOP_{ra}(\alpha_1), MOP_{rn}(\pi_1)>$$
$$(content_{e2}) \quad <MOP_{ra}(\alpha_2), MOP_{rn}(\pi_2)>$$
$$(content_h) \quad <MOP_{ra}(\underline{\quad}), MOP_{rn}(\underline{\quad})>$$
$$(content_i) \quad <MOP_{ra}(\alpha_1), MOP_{rn}(\underline{\quad})>$$

Each of these four experiences instantiates the following content type:

$$(content_{Type}) \quad <MOP_{ra}[\underline{\quad}], MOP_{rn}[\underline{\quad}]>$$

where $MOP_{ra}[\underline{\quad}]$ can be tokened by $MOP_{ra}(\alpha_1)$, $MOP_{ra}(\alpha_2)$, $MOP_{ra}(\alpha_3)$, $MOP_{ra}(\underline{\quad})$, or any other singular mode of presentation of a particular.

So Fregean particularism is characterized by the following three conditions:

1. The content of any two perceptions e_1 and e_1^* that have the same phenomenal character and in which the subject is perceptually related to the same particular α_1 in the same way will include the token singular mode of presentation $MOP_{ra}(\alpha_1)$, where $MOP_{ra}(\alpha_1)$ is constituted by employing the perceptual capacity C_α that functions to single out particulars of the type under which α_1 falls. More specifically, $MOP_{ra}(\alpha_1)$ is the output of employing perceptual capacity C_α that takes particulars of the kind under which α_1 falls as inputs. So $MOP_{ra}(\alpha_1)$ is constituted by the perceptual capacity employed and the particular α_1 thereby singled out.

2. A perception e_2 that has the same phenomenal character as e_1, but in which the subject is perceptually related to the numerically distinct particular α_2, will be constituted by employing the same perceptual capacity C_α. However, since the input in e_2 is a different particular than in e_1, the ensuing token content $MOP_{ra}(\alpha_2)$ is different. This is the case, even if α_1 and α_2 are qualitatively identical. So singular modes of presentation are injective: if $\alpha_1 \neq \alpha_2$, then $MOP_{ra}(\alpha_1) \neq MOP_{ra}(\alpha_2)$.

3. A hallucination or an illusion that has the same phenomenal character as e_1 is constituted by employing the same perceptual capacity C_α but, since there is no relevant particular present, the perceptual capacity is employed baselessly. As a consequence, the token content $MOP_{ra}(\underline{\quad})$ is gappy.[24]

3.4. Content types: potentially singular modes of presentation

So far I have specified the token contents. How should we understand the content types? According to Fregean particularism, a perception, a hallucination, and an illusion with the same phenomenal character share a metaphysically substantial common element: the

---

[24] For an earlier version of this view, see Schellenberg 2006.

perceptual capacities employed. Employing perceptual capacities yields a content type that experiential states with the same phenomenal character have in common. So, Fregean particularism avoids any disjunctivist commitments. There is a stock of distinct content types $MOP_{r\alpha}[\underline{}]$, $MOP_{r\beta}[\underline{}]$, $MOP_{r\chi}[\underline{}]$, $MOP_{r\delta}[\underline{}]$, ... which combine with particulars to form singular modes of presentation of objects, property-instances, and events.

Now, why are these content types not just general contents? In response, content types are potentially particularized contents. To motivate this, consider again Hallie who hallucinates a cup. On the basis of her hallucination, she thinks, "That is a white cup." Since there is no white cup present, she fails to refer and the content of her thought is not singular. However, it is not general either. After all, she purports to refer to a mind-independent particular. Failing to be a singular content does not imply that the content is general. There are other options. One alternative is to say that the content has the form of a singular content while failing to be a token singular content. It is a potentially singular content. As in the case of a failed singular thought, the content of hallucination is neither a general content nor a singular content. It is structured by two levels: the content type and the token content; more specifically, a potentially particularized content type and a gappy token content. In virtue of its singular form, the experience manifests phenomenological particularity. The potentially particularized content type can be analyzed as a schema that gives the conditions of satisfaction of any perceptual state with that content.

Although in the case of an accurate perception the token content is at least in part constituted by the particulars perceived, the very same content type can be tokened if no relevant particular is present. The token content of a hallucination is naturally not constituted by any mind-independent particulars perceived. While the content type is not dependent on particulars (if any) perceived it is nonetheless relational. It is relational since it is constituted by employing perceptual capacities that function to discriminate and single out particulars. As a consequence, relations to particulars are implicated in the very nature of content, even at the level of the content type.

One might object that the content of a hallucination and the content of a perception could never be tokens of the same type. After all, the former is gappy and the latter is not. In response, particulars can be tokens of the same type even if the particulars differ significantly. For them to be tokens of the same type they need only to exhibit the feature relevant to classification under that type. There are many ways to type contents. One is with regard to whether or not they are gappy. On this way, gappy contents and non-gappy contents would be tokens of different types. However, another way to type contents is with regard to the perceptual capacities employed that constitute the content. This is the kind of content types in play here.

3.5. *Accuracy conditions*

Accuracy conditions are often equated with content (see e.g. Dretske 1995, Tye 2009, Burge 2010). But this cannot be right. Accuracy conditions need to be distinguished both from content and from the truthmaker of that content. The accuracy conditions of perceptual content specify the way the environment of a perceiver would have to be for the content of her perceptual state to be accurate. More schematically, the idea is that:

(AC)   The content c of a perceptual state brought about by being perceptually related to environment E is accurate if and only if E is the way c represents E to be.

There are many other ways to articulate accuracy conditions, but I take this to be the most neutral one. To get clearer about what is at stake, let's consider an example. Say I see a white cup to my right. I can articulate the content of my perceptual state as follows:

(C$_1$)   That white cup is to my right.

This content determines accuracy conditions, which can be articulated in the following way:

(AC$_1$)   The content c_1 of a perceptual state brought about by being perceptually related to that white cup to my right is accurate if and only if that white cup is to my right.

I talk of accuracy conditions rather than truth conditions, since speaking of accuracy conditions allows one to acknowledge that the accuracy of perceptual content comes in degrees: perceptual content can be more or less accurate with regard to the environment of the perceiving subject.

Indeed, our environment is rarely and perhaps never exactly the way we represent it to be. We perceive plates to be round, although their shapes are much more complicated. We see surfaces to be colored, but it has been argued that surfaces do not have color properties (e.g. Hardin 1988, 2003, 2008, Boghossian and Velleman 1989, Maund 1995, 2006, 2011, and Averill 2005). We experience our environment to be populated by objects, but it has been argued that there really are no objects or at least not the kind of objects that we seem to see (e.g. Unger 1979, van Inwagen 1990). To accommodate these various respects in which the environment differs from how we perceive it to be, we must either relax our notion of an accuracy condition or resign ourselves to wide-spread (albeit explicable) perceptual error.[25]

We can all agree that if it perceptually seems to us that there is a red dragon playing the piano where in fact there is simply a white coffee cup, then we are not accurately perceiving the environment. Moreover, we can all agree that although we do not perceive the microphysical structure of the objects to which we are causally related, we can nonetheless accurately perceive our environment. As soon as we move beyond these parameters, the situation quickly gets complicated.

---

[25] See Mendelovici 2013 for a discussion of reliable misrepresentation. See Pasnau 2016 for an argument that we should not suppose that the phenomenal character of perceptual experience reveals anything about mind or world.

On many views of perceptual content, it seems to be assumed that the more detail is represented, the more accurate one's perception.[26] But more detail is not necessarily better. We can perceive our environment accurately even if we do not represent every detail in view. After all, if we see a white cup on a desk and represent the white cup on the desk, but fail to represent the speck of dust next to the white cup, we would hardly count as not accurately representing our environment. Moreover, were we to represent all details perceptually available to us, we would suffer from information overload. Indeed, it may be that perception does not aim at truth or accuracy, but rather aims at guiding action. If this is right, then rather than speaking of "accuracy conditions," we should perhaps be speaking of "action-guiding conditions" or "knowledge-guiding conditions." Even if we take this stance, however, we could say that the accuracy conditions of perception are indexed to the action-guiding role of perception or the knowledge-guiding role of perception.[27]

I have argued that if a subject is in a perceptual state with a particular content, then this content is either accurate or inaccurate. Accepting this is compatible with accepting that any given scene can be represented in many different ways. Even if there are many ways that the world can be represented, there is only one way the world is. To motivate this, consider Norway's jagged coastline: Norway's coastline has exactly one objective length, but we attribute very different numeric lengths to it depending on how detailed our method of measurements are. We will come up with a different number if we measure around each tiny crevice and indentation, than if take a less exacting approach. While the results of these measurements will be different, they can each be accurate representations of the coast of Norway relative to the method of measurement chosen. To take an example closer to home: a scene can be photographed once with a standard lens and once with a wide-angle lens. Although the representations of the scene will differ according to the lens that is used, both can be accurate.

One objection waiting in the wings is that ($content_h$) is not an adequate way of characterizing the content of a hallucination since it cannot account for the fact that the content of a hallucination is inaccurate: given the presence of a gap, the content cannot determine an accuracy condition. In response, it is necessary to distinguish two ways in which a content can be inaccurate. One way is for the content to make a claim about the environment that is not accurate. A second way is for it to fail to make an accurate claim about the environment. To illustrate this second sense of inaccuracy, suppose that I claim that Pegasus lives in my apartment. This claim is inaccurate. Given that "Pegasus" does not refer, the inaccuracy in question is that I have failed to make an accurate claim about who lives in my apartment. If inaccuracy is understood in

[26] This is suggested, for instance, by the analogy Burge (2010: 489) draws between the relative accuracy of perceptions and the relative accuracy of three drawings, where the drawing that is most inclusive of detail is the most accurate. In his example, the most accurate drawing is the one that does not merely get the color-shade right, but that also accounts for the lighting conditions.

[27] See Watzl 2014 for a discussion of such issues.

this second way, then a hallucination can have a gappy content and nonetheless be inaccurate. On this understanding of gappy contents, the fact that a content is gappy implies that the content is necessarily inaccurate insofar as a gappy content could never make an accurate claim about the world.[28]

On this view, there is nothing veridical about so-called "veridical hallucinations." In such a case, a subject is hallucinating, say, an apple, and there happens to be an apple where she hallucinates one to be. But she is not perceptually related to the apple because there is a wall between her and the apple. As a consequence, the content of her experience is gappy. Indeed, the content of hallucinations with the same phenomenal character will have the same content—even if one hallucination is non-veridical and the other is a so-called "veridical hallucination."

3.6. Advantages of Fregean particularism

The thesis that perceptual content is constituted by employing perceptual capacities allows for a substantive way of analyzing perceptual content as nonconceptual. After all, perceptual capacities can be understood as nonconceptual analogs to concepts. While I have argued that perceptual capacities are nonconceptual capacities, they could be understood as conceptual capacities. Thus, as argued in Chapter 2, understanding perceptual content as constituted by perceptual capacities allows for a way to bypass the largely terminological debate over whether perceptual content is conceptual or nonconceptual: whether or not one will understand perceptual content as conceptual will depend largely on how one understands concepts. If concept possession requires the ability to draw inferences, then it is wildly implausible that perceptual content is conceptual. However, if all perceivers possess concepts, even those that have no inferential abilities or any other such high-level cognitive abilities, then it is more plausible that perceptual content is conceptual.

A second advantage of Fregean particularism is that the thesis that perceptual content is constituted by employing perceptual capacities allows for a way to analyze the difference between perception and cognition as a difference in representational vehicle, where that difference in representational vehicle is explained in terms of a difference in the capacities employed. The representational vehicle of perceptual representation is the employment of perceptual capacities. The representational vehicle of cognition is the employment of cognitive capacities.

---

[28] For a dissenting view of the truth-value of gappy propositions, see Everett 2003. Recall that I analyzed perceptual capacities as having the function to discriminate and single out particulars (see Chapter 2). Now in formal discussion, functions are understood as necessarily requiring an input to have an output. As I am understanding perceptual capacities, one can employ a perceptual capacity and thereby be in a mental state with content, despite the fact that one is not perceptually related to anything. So one can employ a perceptual capacity and yield a content as output even if there is no input. So the notion of function in play is distinct from the one in formal discussion. Alternatively, the view presented here could be reformulated by arguing that in the case of a hallucination, the input is the empty set. This would allow being in tune with the use of "functions" in formal discussions, but would require accepting the existence of the empty set. For this reason, I argue that in the case of hallucination there is no input.

A third advantage is that the view neither implies that the experiencing subject stands in a propositional attitude to the content of her experience nor does it rely on there being such a relation between the subject and the content of an experience. So there is no need to say that the experiencing subject 'exes' that p,—to use Byrne's (2009) phrase.

A fourth advantage of Fregean particularism is that it does not imply that experiences have an attributional structure, such as "object o is F," where F is a property instantiated by o. In Chapter 3, we discussed how this is an advantage of content particularism. Fregean particularism is a species of content particularism, and so also has this advantage. Fregean particularism does not depend on the idea that we are perceptually related to objects. It depends only on the idea that we are perceptually related to particulars, which can be events or property-instances in addition to objects.

A fifth advantage is that Fregean particularism can easily account for hallucinations as of multiple objects. We rejected the Russellian gappy content view on the grounds that it cannot account for hallucinations as of multiple objects. How can Fregean particularism account for such hallucinations? In response, hallucinations as of multiple objects are unproblematic for Fregean particularism, since it is the mode of presentation that is gappy and so the content of a hallucination is not altogether gappy in the object-place. As a consequence, there is sufficient structure to account for hallucinations as of multiple objects.[29]

3.7. Fregean particularism, the particularity desideratum, and the phenomenal sameness desideratum

I have argued that the content of experiential states is constituted both by the perceptual capacities employed and the particulars (if any) thereby singled out. In this way, perceptual experience is constitutively both relational and representational. In this section, I will compare Fregean particularism to austere relationalism and austere representationalism. In doing so, I will show how it satisfies both the particularity and the phenomenal sameness desiderata.

Fregean particularism accepts the central relationalist insight that relations to particulars are constitutive of perceptual states. If perceptual content is constituted by perceptual capacities that function to discriminate and single out mind-independent particulars, then relations to particulars are implicated in the very nature of perceptual content. Moreover, if the fact that perceptual capacities single out mind-independent particulars in some environments but not others has any semantic significance, then

---

[29] We rejected the Russellian gappy content view moreover on grounds that it cannot account for hallucinations as of an object that seems to be instantiating a property that is in fact an uninstantiated property, such as supersaturated red or Hume's missing shade of blue, without making controversial phenomenological and metaphysical commitments. I discuss how the view I am suggesting can account for such hallucinations in Chapter 6, Section 4.

the content ensuing from employing perceptual capacities will be constituted at least in part by the perceived particulars.[30]

Since perceptual content is constituted by the particulars perceived, Fregean particularism allows for a straightforward way of accounting for the particularity desideratum. The particular to which the subject is perceptually related secures the relational particularity of her perceptual state. There is a difference between the token contents of perceptions of numerically distinct but qualitatively identical objects. To explain this, consider Percy who sees a white cup at time t_1. Without Percy noticing, the cup is replaced by a qualitatively identical cup, so that at time t_2, Percy sees a cup that is numerically distinct from the one he saw at t_1. The content of his perceptual state at t_1 and at t_2 is distinct despite the fact that the difference in content is not reflected in the phenomenal character of his perceptual states. The content of Percy's perceptual states is distinct since it is constituted by a singular mode of presentation of a different object before and after the switch. So what Fregean particularism shares with relationalism (that austere representationalism lacks) is the ability to satisfy the particularity desideratum.

However, in contrast to austere relationalism, Fregean particularism can easily account for the phenomenal sameness desideratum. Fregean particularism accepts the minimal representationalist commitment that perception is constitutively a matter of representing one's environment such that one's perceptual state is characterized by representational content. Employing perceptual capacities in a sensory mode constitutes both the representational content and the phenomenal character of experiential states. In experiential states with the same phenomenal character, the same perceptual capacities are employed in the same sensory mode. So in contrast to disjunctivists and austere relationalists, I am arguing that a hallucination, an illusion, and a perception with the same phenomenal character share a common element that explains their sameness in phenomenal character.

How does Fregean particularism make room for content that manifests phenomenological particularity while lacking relational particularity? In response, even if one happens to be hallucinating or suffering an illusion, the capacities employed do not cease to function to do what they do in the case of perception, namely, discriminate and single out particulars in the environment. Employing them is the basis for the intentional directedness at particulars in perception and accounts for the intentional directedness at a seeming particular in illusion and hallucination. Thus, employing perceptual capacities accounts for the fact that when we suffer an illusion or a hallucination, it seems to us as if a particular is present. In this way, employing perceptual capacities grounds phenomenological particularity. So while the gap in the token content of a hallucination marks the lack of relational particularity, the intentional directedness at an object is accounted for by the (gappy) mode of presentation. Even though in the case of illusion or hallucination, the experiencing subject fails to single out at least one

---

[30] For a defense, see Chapters 1 and 3. See also Schellenberg 2016a.

of the particulars that she purports to single out, the gappy token content is inherently related to external and mind-independent particulars of the type that the subject's perceptual capacities function to single out in the good case. Whether a perceptual capacity is employed baselessly will not affect the phenomenal character of the experience. Only if this is the case can the view satisfy the phenomenal sameness desideratum. For only if it is not revealed in phenomenal character whether a perceptual capacity is employed baselessly could a perception, an illusion, and a hallucination have the same phenomenal character.

So, with representationalists but against austere relationalists, I am arguing that the phenomenal character of a hallucination manifests phenomenological particularity without being characterized by relational particularity. However, with relationalists and against austere representationalists, I am arguing that the content of perception grounds relational particularity. Fregean particularism satisfies the particularity desideratum since it does not equate perceptual content with phenomenal content. Although content types remain the same across experiential states with the same phenomenal character, token contents are constituted by the particulars (if any) perceived. As a consequence, there can be differences in content that are not reflected in phenomenal character. While Fregean particularism rejects the austere representationalist thesis that perceptual content is phenomenal content, and consequently is not compatible with so-called strong representationalism, it is compatible with weak representationalism. That said, if the content type is the same between two experiences, the phenomenal character will be the same. So Fregean particularism holds that there is a kind of content that covaries with phenomenal character.

4. Fregean Particularism and Alternative Views

It has been argued that a content that purports to be of a particular object but fails to refer is best thought of as a general content (Burge 2010). It has, moreover, been argued that a singular content is object-dependent such that we cannot be in a mental state with a token content that purports to be of a particular, but fails to refer (Evans 1982, McDowell 1984).

Fregean particularism avoids the pitfalls of both approaches in that it makes room for a notion content that manifests phenomenological particularity but lacks relational particularity. According to Fregean particularism, the content of hallucination is structured by a content type and a token content, neither of which is a general content. The content type is a potentially particularized content schema. The token content is gappy. In contrast to a view on which *de re* modes of presentation are radically object-dependent such that there cannot be a token content if there is no object to be represented, Fregean particularism shows that *de re* modes of presentation are only partly constituted by the particulars perceived. Singular modes of presentation are constituted by the perceptual capacities employed and the particulars perceived.

While the perceptual capacities employed provide the general element of perceptual content, the objects, events, and property-instances singled out provide the particular element. If no particulars are perceived, as in the case of a total hallucination, the token content is constituted only by the perceptual capacities employed. While the token content of hallucination is defective in virtue of the perceptual capacities being employed baselessly, the mere fact that perceptual capacities are employed gives the token content enough structure to ground the phenomenal character and thus the phenomeno-logical particularity of hallucinatory states. So Fregean particularism makes room for hallucinations to have a token content, even though no mind-independent particular is perceived.

In contrast to the gappy Russellian view discussed earlier, Fregean particularism does not posit that the object-place is gappy in the case of a hallucination. It is rather the mode of presentation in the object-place that is gappy. So even if one hallucinates multiple objects, there is enough structure in the content to distinguish the various objects that one seems to be perceiving. The structure is provided by the gappy modes of presentation.

Now, one might argue that there is no reason to appeal to gaps to account for the content of hallucinations. An alternative solution is to say that the gaps are filled by intentional objects. On such a view, experience is a matter of representing properties that are attributed to intentional objects (see Lycan 1996 and Crane 1998). These intentional objects can be thought of as existing abstracta or as non-existing concreta. Such a view is less attractive than Fregean particularism for at least two reasons. One reason is that if hallucinations are construed as relations between subjects and intentional objects, then one is pressed to construe perceptions as relations between subjects and intentional objects as well. However, doing so leads to well-known problems.[31] A second reason is that positing intentional objects does not secure any explanatory advantage over Fregean particularism with regard to the phenomenal character of experience, and is furthermore less powerful in explaining both the relational particu-larity of perceptions and the absence of relational particularity in hallucinations. Finally, a difference in token contents between perceptions and hallucinations with the same phenomenal character can explain the epistemic difference between them.[32] An intentional object view does not have this benefit.

I have argued that perceptual content should be understood as serving multiple explanatory roles insofar as it grounds both phenomenal character and perceptual particularity. An alternative way of satisfying these two explanatory roles is to argue that experience has multiple layers of content. On such a multiple contents view, different layers of content satisfy the two explanatory roles. There are many reasons to introduce

---

[31] For a discussion of the skeptical problems that ensue if the content of mental states is understood as constituted by intentional objects or relations to intentional objects, see Brewer 1999. Loar (2003) argues that a view on which perception is construed as a relation to an intentional object is phenomenally implausible.

[32] See Schellenberg 2013a and Part III of this book.

multiple layers of content. My argument, if right, undermines at least one motivation for the multiple contents view, namely, the motivation that one layer grounds phenomenal character while another layer accounts for the reference-fixing role of perception. Chalmers (2006b) argues, for example, that one layer is a Fregean content that is associated with a primary intension that is a function from centered worlds to extensions (where the Fregean content is understood as *de dicto*), while the other layer is a Russellian content that is associated with a secondary intension, which is a function from uncentered worlds to extensions. What these views have in common is that one layer of content grounds phenomenal character, while the other determines the reference of the mental state.

Fregean particularism is motivated by many of the same concerns as the multiple contents view, but it does not entail the multiple contents view, and it is not a particular version of that view. The multiple contents view entails that experience has different sets of accuracy conditions associated with the different layers of content. The thesis that experience has multiple explanatory purposes involves no such entailment. While on Fregean particularism, any perception, hallucination, and illusion is characterized by a content type and a token content, the content type and token content do not constitute two distinct layers of content. After all, they do not determine two different sets of accuracy conditions. Only the token content determines accuracy conditions. The content type is no more than a content schema. So according to Fregean particularism, the content of a perceptual experience has only one set of accuracy conditions. Thus the view provides a way of satisfying the different explanatory roles of perceptual content without introducing a second layer of content. As the second difference between the two views will show, there are powerful reasons to resist introducing multiple layers of content to account for the different explanatory roles of perceptual content.

In contrast to the multiple contents view, Fregean particularism is a view of both the constituents of perceptual content and of what holds these constituents together. It takes seriously Frege's insight that modes of presentation play a dual role: they have a cognitive significance and they determine a reference—at least in the successful case. On the multiple contents view, the cognitive significance and the reference-determining roles of content are accounted for on different levels of content. Experiences with the same phenomenal character will have the same content on one level, but, depending on their environment, they may have a different content on the other level. The relation between the phenomenal content and the perceived object is simply the semantic relation of satisfaction.

Insofar as the multiple contents view analyzes perception as the co-instantiation of two independent elements it is a version of what I called conjunctivism. It is a version of conjunctivism on which the relational element is not simply a perceptual relation between a subject and an object, but rather constitutes an object-dependent layer of content. In contrast to the simple version of conjunctivism that I considered in Section 1, the multiple contents view can satisfy the particularity desideratum, since one level of content is constituted by the particulars perceived. However, since the layer of content that accounts for relational particularity is independent of the layer of content that grounds phenomenal character, the question arises as to how phenomenal contents are connected to what they are about. Consider Chalmers's epistemic two-dimensional semantics. As Chalmers notes, "primary intensions do not determine extensions in a strong sense (although they may still determine extension relative to context)" (2006b: 596). The layer of content that grounds the phenomenal character of the experience does not itself determine an extension. Chalmers considers the possibility of accounting for the reference-determining role of modes of presentation by stipulating that the content of an expression-token is an ordered pair of its primary intension and its extension (2006b: 596). Although such an ordered pair plays the role of determining reference, it does so trivially, given that the extension is part of the ordered pair. The question remains as to how the primary intensions, that is, the phenomenal contents, are connected to what they are about.

The notion of a singular mode of presentation that I have developed cannot be identified with an ordered pair of a *de dicto* mode of presentation and a referent. To deny that the content can be identified with such an ordered pair is not to deny that the content can be analyzed into two layers, one of which is constituted by the perceived particular (if any), the other of which is independent of the perceived particular (if any). However, the ability to analyze A in terms of B does not imply that A is identified with B.[33] Being in a perceptual state is not just a matter of being intentionally directed at a (seeming) mind-independent particular and, in the successful case, being causally related to that mind-independent particular. Content needs to be connected to its referent by some non-attributional means. On Fregean particularism, perceptual capacities fulfill the role of connecting mental states with the particulars perceived. Perceptual capacities both play a reference-fixing role and constitute content that grounds phenomenal character. Indeed, employing perceptual capacities constitutes singular modes of presentation, namely modes of presentation that are constituted by the perceptual capacities employed and the particulars thereby singled out. In this way, employing perceptual capacities constitutes representational content that accounts for the Fregean idea that modes of presentation both have a cognitive significance and are a means of referring to particulars.

5. Coda

If a distinction is drawn between what an experience is of and what one takes one's experience to be of, then we can drive a wedge between the content and the phenomenal character of an experience, without thinking of them as entirely independent. By driving a wedge between phenomenal character and content, one can account for the possibility that a perception, a hallucination, and an illusion can have the same phenomenal character while accounting for differences that are due to the experiencing

---

[33] For a critical discussion of two-dimensional semantics, see also Speaks 2009.

subject being perceptually related to different particulars (or not being perceptually related to any particulars). Content plays the dual role of grounding relational particularity in the case of an accurate perception and grounding phenomenological particularity regardless of whether the subject is perceiving, hallucinating, or suffering an illusion. Moreover, insofar as employing perceptual capacities constitutes phenomenal character and secures the reference of the perceptual state, Fregean particularism rejects all ways of factorizing perceptual content into internal and external components.[34] In this way, the suggested view combines the virtues of relationalism and representationalism, while avoiding the difficulties of the austere versions of these views. According to Fregean particularism, perceptual content is constituted by general elements, namely the perceptual capacities employed, and particular elements, namely the external, mind-independent particulars perceived.

---

[34] See Williamson (2000) for a discussion of factorizing mental content into internal and external components.

Chapter 5

In Defense of Perceptual Content

It used to be common ground that perception represents the environment. The thesis that perception is representational can be traced back to Kant.[1] With few interludes, it has been orthodoxy in the philosophy of perception ever since. It figures prominently in the work of thinkers as different as Evans (1982), Peacocke (1983), Searle (1983), McDowell (1994), Dretske (1995), Tye (1995), Chalmers (1996), and Byrne (2001). I will call the thesis that perception is constitutively a matter of representing the environment the content thesis.

> *Content Thesis:* A subject S's perceptual state M brought about by being perceptually related to a particular α is constituted by content c in virtue of S representing α.

This thesis has been questioned by Reid (1764), by sense-data theorists such as Russell (1913), Price (1932), and Moore (1953), and most recently by austere relationalists such as Campbell (2002), Travis (2004), Soteriou (2005), Brewer (2006), Fish (2009), Logue (2012), and Genone (2014) among others.[2] According to austere relationalists, perception is not representational, but rather constitutively a matter of a subject being perceptually related to mind-independent objects, properties, or events; alternatively, perception is understood as the event in which such relations obtain. Needless to say, one can endorse the content thesis while holding that, at least in the case of accurate perception, we are perceptually related to particulars in our environment. As I will explain in more detail, the question at stake is how much is built into the perceptual relation and, in particular, whether this relation is an acquaintance relation.

In this chapter, I will defend the content thesis against austere relationalists. The aim is twofold: to consider in detail the austere relationalist objections to the content thesis and to develop and defend a version of the content thesis that does not fall prey to these objections. I will argue that on a relational view of perceptual content, the fundamental

---

[1] In his famous Stufenleiter passage of the *Critique of Pure Reason*, Kant categorizes different kinds of representations: "The genus is representation in general (*representatio*). Subordinate to it stands representation with consciousness (*perceptio*). A perception which relates solely to the subject as the modification of its state is sensation (*sensatio*), an objective perception is knowledge (*cognitio*)" (A320/B377).

[2] For a recent discussion of Reid's direct realism, see Wilson 2013. Martin (2002a, 2004) argues against any view on which perception can be analyzed in terms of a propositional attitude toward a content, leaving open the possibility that perceptual states could have content without the subject standing in a propositional attitude to that content. Since he does not outright deny that perceptual states have content, I will discuss his view only to the extent that his positive view of perception is structurally similar to that of austere relationalists.

insights of austere relationalism do not compete with representationalism. I contend that the objections to the content thesis either do not pass muster or are objections only against austere representationalism—that is, the view on which perceptual relations to the particulars perceived make no constitutive difference to perceptual content.

Against austere relationalists, I argue that perceptual relations to particulars neither ground nor explain perceptual representations: being perceptually related to particulars in one's environment is neither metaphysically nor explanatorily more basic than representing those particulars. Nor is it the case, however, that perceptual representations ground or explain perceptual relations to the particulars perceived. I argue rather that perceptual relations and representations are mutually dependent: in being perceptually related to particulars in one's environment, one employs perceptual capacities, thereby yielding representational states. So with austere relationalists, I argue that perception is constitutively relational. But against austere relationalists, I argue that it is constitutively both relational and representational.

In Section 1, I discuss what is at stake in the debate over whether perception has content and critically examine one way in which one might attempt to argue for the content thesis. In Section 2, I distinguish three central choice points for any account of perceptual content. In Section 3, I identify the five main objections that austere relationalists have articulated against the content thesis. In Section 4, I defend the content thesis. In Section 5, I qualify the notion of content established by the argument for the content thesis by arguing that perceptual content is relational content. I defend the view that perceptual content is relational content by considering each austere relationalist objection in turn.

1. What is at Stake?

Why should we be concerned with defending the content thesis? There are at least seven intuitive reasons to think that perceptual states have content.

One reason is to account for the fact that our environment can either be or fail to be the way it seems to us. In other words, the way our environment seems to us is assessable for accuracy. If perceptual states have content, then we can explain this phenomenon in terms of the content of the perceptual state.

A second reason is to account for the fineness of grain of perceptual experience. The very same scene perceived from the very same angle can be perceived in a number of different ways. Take Mach's example of perceiving a shape first as a square and then as a diamond, with no change in vantage point. Arguably, in such a situation, the phenomenal character of the two perceptual states differs despite there being no difference in the perceiver's environment. If perceptual states have content, this difference in phenomenal character can be accounted for by appealing to differences in the way the subject represents her environment.[3] If all we had were the fact that we

---

[3] For an argument against a representationalist account of Mach's (1959) diamond, see Macpherson 2006.

were perceptually related to the shape, then it is not clear how we could explain this difference in phenomenal character. After all, there is no difference in the environment. There is only a difference in the way in which the environment is perceived.

A third reason is to explain how we can remember past perceptions. If perceptual states have content, then we can account for the memory of a perception in terms of recalling or reconstructing its representational content.

A fourth related reason is to explain the phenomena of fading and distorted memories. If perceptual states have content, then we can explain these phenomena in terms of changes in the stored perceptual content or changes in the way the stored content is retrieved or reconstructed. If perception is not understood as a matter of representing one's environment, this option is not available and it is not clear how else to explain these phenomena.

A fifth reason is to account for the phenomenal character of illusions and hallucinations. Austere relationalists argue that phenomenal character is constituted simply by (perceptual relations to) the particulars perceived. To recap: in orthodox cases of hallucination, we fail to be perceptually related to the mind-independent object that it seems to us we are perceiving. Likewise, in orthodox cases of illusion, we fail to be related to a property-instance that it seems to us we are perceiving. If phenomenal character is accounted for simply in terms of (relations to) perceived particulars, it is on the face of it mysterious how to account for the phenomenal character of illusions and hallucinations. If experiential states have content, however, we can account for the phenomenal character of illusions and hallucinations in terms of their content.

A sixth reason is to give a unified account of the phenomenal character of perception, hallucination, and illusion. An elegant way to do so is to argue that all three experiential states have content and that this content grounds their phenomenal character.

A seventh reason is to account for the phenomenal impact of top-down effects on perception. A sentence uttered in Urdu sounds different to a native speaker than it does to somebody unfamiliar with the language. Arguably if I possess the concept of a skyscraper then tall buildings look different than if I lack the concept.[4] If perceptual states have content, then these differences can be accounted for in terms of the impact of possession of such concepts on perceptual content.

2. Perception and Representation

As austere relationalists point out, the content thesis is often assumed, but rarely argued for. Representationalists typically do not bother to defend the thesis that perception is representational, but rather immediately proceed to develop a specific way of understanding the nature of perceptual content. I use the label "representationalism" for any view that endorses the content thesis. So as to avoid terminological confusion, it is

---

[4] See Siegel 2006, Macpherson 2012 for different arguments for this thesis.

important to distinguish this view from the more specific view according to which phenomenal character is grounded in perceptual content. Such views are sometimes labeled "representationalism" rather than the more traditional "intentionalism." I will reserve "representationalism" for any view that endorses the content thesis irrespective of how the view conceives of the relationship between perceptual content and phenomenal character.

As mentioned in Chapter 4, the most minimal representationalist commitment is that perception is a matter of a subject representing her environment. There are many different ways of understanding the nature of content given this constraint. More specifically, there are three critical choice points for any view of perceptual content.

One choice point concerns how to understand the nature of perceptual content. Any view of perceptual content must take a stance on at least four questions. One is whether the content is understood in terms of a Russellian proposition, a possible world proposition, a Fregean sense, an indexical content, a map of the environment, an image-like representation, or in some other way. A second is whether perceptual content is conceptually or nonconceptually structured.[5] A third is whether or not perceptual content is propositionally structured. A fourth is whether the content is constituted by the particulars perceived, or whether it is only internally individuated and so in no sense constituted by the particulars perceived.

I will consider the fourth question in more detail, since it is crucial to the debate on whether perception is representational, relational, or constitutively both representational and relational.[6] According to austere representationalism, perceptual content is internally individuated—internally individuated in the sense that it is not in any way constituted by the mind-independent particulars perceived.[7] The view is austere since it leaves no room for perceptual relations to make a constitutive difference to perceptual content. The only difference between subjectively indistinguishable experiences in distinct environments is a difference in the causal relation between the experiencing subject and her environment; and this difference in causal relation has no repercussions for the content of the experiencing subject's mental state. On such a view, perceptual content can be analyzed in terms of existentially quantified content of the form that there is an object x that instantiates a certain property F: $(\exists x)Fx$. So perceptual states represent only that there is an object with the relevant properties in the perceiver's environment. No element of the content constitutively depends on

---

[5] The debate about whether perceptual content is conceptually or nonconceptually structured is sometimes understood as a debate about whether perceptual content is structured by Fregean concepts and not just by properties and objects. On this understanding, the first and second questions about the nature of perceptual content distinguished above are conflated. As argued in Chapter 4, one can understand perceptual content as constituted by modes of presentation and as nonconceptually structured. Therefore, the two questions should be treated separately.

[6] Nanay (2013) argues that the debate between representationalists and relationalists is best understood as a debate not about what is constitutive of perceptual states, but rather as a debate about the individuation of perceptual states.

[7] McGinn (1982), Davies (1992), Tye (1995), Lycan (1996), and Byrne (2001) among others have defended views that are committed to perceptual content being, in this way, independent of the perceiver's environment.

whether such an object is in fact present. Austere representationalism has it that the content lays down a condition that something must satisfy to be the object determined by the content. The condition to be satisfied does not constitutively depend on the object that satisfies it. Of course, the object perceived does not fall out of the picture altogether on an austere representationalist view. The content of a perceptual state is accurate only if there is an object at the relevant location that instantiates the properties specified by the content. But the important point is that whether an object of the right kind is present has a bearing only on the accuracy of the content, not on the content proper.

We can contrast such a generalist view of perceptual content with a relational content view. While general content is the very same regardless of the perceiver's environment, relational content differs depending on which environmental particulars (if any) the subject perceives. The token relational content covaries with the environment of the experiencing subject. In the case of a successful perception, the token content determines a referent and is constituted by the particular perceived. Thus, it is singular content. As previously, when I say that A is constituted by B, I mean always partial constitution, allowing that A may be constituted by both B and C. Moreover, if A is constituted by B that does not imply that A is materially constituted by B.[8]

So far, we have distinguished different ways of understanding the nature of perceptual content. A second choice point for any view of perceptual content concerns how to understand the relationship between the content of a perceptual state and its phenomenal character. One might argue that any facts about phenomenal character are facts about content.[9] Alternatively, one might maintain either that content is grounded in phenomenal character or that phenomenal character is grounded in content. Or, one might treat content and phenomenal character as independent elements of perceptual states, thereby denying that there is any grounding relation between them.[10]

A third choice point concerns how to understand the relationship between the perceiver and the content of her perceptual state. To avoid verbal disputes, this choice point is critical in the discussion of whether perceptual states have content. Therefore, I will address the different options in some detail.

The content thesis must be distinguished from a thesis on which the relation between the perceiver and the content of her perceptual state is one of mere association. We can call this the association thesis.

Association Thesis: Every perceptual state can be associated with content in the sense that sentences can be articulated that describe how the environment seems to the subject. The content so expressed need not be constitutive of the perceptual state.

---

[8] For a more detailed discussion of constitution, see Chapter 1.

[9] This strong representationalist view is sometimes formulated as the view that content and phenomenal character are identical (see e.g. Tye 2009). Any such identity claim commits a category mistake. After all, phenomenal character is a property that captures what it is like to perceive one's environment, while representational content has semantic and perhaps linguistic properties.

[10] Papineau (2014, 2016) defends a view on which conscious sensory qualities are not intrinsically representational.

Any account of perception can accept the association thesis. After all, any account can accept the fact that a perceptual experience can be at least partially described. But this fact does not entail that the perceptual state has the content that is expressed with the description. Likewise, a painting can be described, but it does not follow from this that the painting has the content that is expressed with the description.[11] So the association thesis does not entail the content thesis. According to the content thesis, perceptual content is not merely associated with a perceptual state, but is constitutive of a perceptual state.

To explain in more detail how the content thesis and the association thesis differ, consider the following attempt to establish the content thesis by appealing to the relation between sensory awareness, accuracy conditions, and perceptual content.[12]

The Association Argument

1. If a subject S perceives a particular α (while not suffering from blindsight or any other form of unconscious perception), then S is sensorily aware of α.

2. If S is sensorily aware of α, then α sensorily seems a certain way to S due to S perceiving α.

3. If α sensorily seems a certain way to S due to S perceiving α, then S is in a perceptual state M with content c, where c corresponds to the way α sensorily seems to S.

From 1–3: If S perceives α (while not suffering from blindsight or any other form of unconscious perception), then S is in a perceptual state M with content c, where c corresponds to the way α sensorily seems to S.

4. α is either the way it sensorily seems to S or it is different from the way it sensorily seems to S.

5. If S is in a perceptual state M with content c, where c corresponds to the way α sensorily seems to S, then the content c of S's perceptual state M is either accurate or inaccurate with regard to α.

From 1–5: If S perceives α (while not suffering from blindsight or any other form of unconscious perception), then S is in a perceptual state M with content c, where c corresponds to the way α sensorily seems to S, and the content c of S's perceptual state M is either accurate or inaccurate with regard to α.

Note that the conclusion of this argument is not the content thesis. The association argument establishes that if the environment seems a certain way to a perceiver, then she is in a perceptual state that can be characterized with content where that content corresponds to the way the environment seems to her. So while the argument establishes

---

[11] For a discussion of the relation between the content of pictures and the content of perceptual states and mental states more generally, see Hopkins 1998 and Crane 2009.

[12] For similar arguments highlighting the relation between sensory awareness, accuracy conditions, and perceptual content, see also Byrne 2001, Pautz 2010, and Siegel 2010. As I will show such arguments do not establish more than the association thesis.

that there is a link between phenomenal character and perceptual content, it does not establish the content thesis.

We can accept that there is a notion of content on which perceptual content corresponds to the phenomenal character of the relevant perceptual state. Let's call this connection between perceptual consciousness and content the *consciousness-content link*. While we can accept that there is such a consciousness-content link, accepting such a consciousness-content link does not show that perception is constitutively representational. Accepting such a consciousness-content link is compatible not only with almost any view of the nature of perception, it is compatible with almost any notion of perceptual content. Indeed, the notion of perceptual content established by the association argument is compatible with accepting only the association thesis. So it does not give support to the thesis that perception is constitutively a matter of representing the environment.

Any account that endorses the content thesis needs to explain not only the structure and nature of perceptual content, but also in virtue of what this content is a constitutive aspect of the the relevant perceptual state. A view of perceptual content that fails to give an account of what it is about perception such that the perceptual state is characterized by content does not establish more than the association thesis.

Now, there are different versions of the content thesis, some more controversial than others. A controversial version of the content thesis has it that the relationship between the perceiver and the content of her perceptual state is that of a propositional attitude:

Propositional Attitude Thesis: A perceiver stands in a propositional attitude to the content of her perceptual state.

The propositional attitude thesis posits both that perceptual content is a proposition and that perception is a matter of standing in a certain attitudinal relation to this proposition, analogous to the sense in which one might say that belief is a matter of standing in the believing relation to the propositional content of the belief. English does not have a word to denote such a perceptual attitudinal relation. Byrne (2009: 437) calls the relation the ex-ing relation; Pautz (2010: 54) calls it the sensorily entertaining relation; Siegel (2010: 22) calls it the A-relation. While the propositional attitude thesis is a version of the content thesis, we can accept the content thesis without accepting the propositional attitude thesis. The content thesis is committed neither to perceptual content being a proposition nor to the perceiver standing in a propositional attitude to that content.

An even more controversial version of the content thesis has it that the relation between the perceiver and the content of her perceptual state is an awareness relation:

Awareness Thesis: A perceiver stands in an awareness relation to the representational content of her perceptual state.

The awareness thesis originates with Russell (1913), who argued that a perceiver is acquainted with particulars that are constituents of the representational content of her perceptual state.[13] While Russell did not explicitly argue that a perceiver is aware of representational content, some representationalist views that claim descent from Russell are formulated in a way that suggests a commitment to the awareness thesis. As in the case of the propositional attitude thesis, the awareness thesis entails the content thesis, but not vice versa: we can accept the content thesis without accepting that perceivers stand in any kind of awareness relation to the content of their perceptual states, or indeed the constituents of that content.

It is important to emphasize that endorsing the content thesis does not commit one to endorsing either the awareness or the propositional attitude theses, since at least some austere relationalist arguments against the content thesis make the mistake of assuming exactly that (e.g. Travis 2004). Once one recognizes that the content thesis does not in fact entail these controversial versions of the thesis, those arguments lose their force.

To establish the association thesis is to establish almost nothing. To commit to the awareness or propositional attitude thesis is to commit to too much. Fortunately, there is a middle way between these two options. Perceptual states can be understood as representing the subject's environment where the representational content is constitutive of the perceptual state, without the subject either being aware of that content or bearing a propositional attitude to it. We can call this middle way the *representation thesis*.

There are several possible ways of precisifying this thesis. One such way is the following: representing perceived particulars is a matter of employing perceptual capacities by means of which one discriminates and singles out those particulars. More precisely, the content of the perceptual state is constituted by the perceptual capacities employed and the particulars thereby singled out. So far there is no need to say that one is either aware of that content or bears a propositional attitude to it.

What happens in the case of hallucination or illusion? In those cases, one employs the very same perceptual capacities that one would employ in a perception with the same phenomenal character, but one fails to discriminate and single out a mind-independent particular. The content of the relevant state is constituted by the perceptual capacities employed. As in the perceptual case, there is no need to say that one is aware of this content. Rather, one is intentionally directed at what seems to one to be a particular in one's environment in virtue of employing perceptual capacities. Moreover, the version of the representation thesis that I will defend is not committed to any version of the propositional attitude thesis. It is neither committed to the experiencing subject bearing a propositional attitude to the content of her experiential state, nor indeed is it committed to that content being a proposition. It is committed merely to the thesis that perceivers represent particulars under a mode of presentation.[14]

---

[13] One can argue that on Russell's view, acquaintance with particulars and universals is more basic than any mental content insofar as such acquaintance explains how it is possible to entertain the relevant content.

[14] It should be noted that the bar for being a proposition could be set so low that on any notion of content, perceptual content will be a proposition (see e.g. King 2007). Moreover, there are ways of understanding propositional attitudes such that any mental state characterized by content will also include a propositional

In what follows, I will take a stance on all three choice points. I will argue that while some accounts of perceptual content fall prey to the austere relationalist objections, a view on which perceptual content is constituted by relational Fregean modes of presentation does not (1st choice point). On this view, the phenomenal character of a subject's perceptual state is grounded in its content (2nd choice point) and perceptual content is constitutive of perceptual states (3rd choice point).[15] First, however, let's take a closer look at the nature of perceptual relations and the austere relationalist objections to the content thesis.

3. Perception and Relations

Austere relationalists have formulated at least five different objections to the content thesis. They can be summarized as follows:

The Phenomenological Objection:	Representationalist views misconstrue the phenomenological basis of perceptual states insofar as they detach the phenomenal character of perceptual states from relations to qualitative features of the environment (e.g. Campbell 2002, Martin 2002a, Brewer 2007).
The Epistemological Objection:	Representationalist views do not properly account for the epistemological role of perception. Only if perception is itself not representational can it constitute the evidential basis for perceptual knowledge of particulars (e.g. Campbell 2002, Johnston 2014).
The Semantic Grounding Objection:	Representationalist views cannot adequately account for the fact that perception grounds demonstrative thoughts and singular thoughts about particulars in the environment. Moreover, they cannot adequately account for the fact that perceptual relations to the environment provide the ground for the possibility of thought and language (e.g. Campbell 2002, Brewer 2006).

attitude toward that content. If that is all that is meant by a propositional attitude and if perceptual content is always a proposition, then any view that endorses the content thesis will also endorse the propositional attitude thesis.

[15] It should be noted that there are many further issues beyond these three choice points that bear on the notion of perceptual content. One concerns how much of our environment we represent. Consider the case in which you are perceiving the scene in front of you. As it happens, there is a little bug in your line of sight that you do not notice. Are you perceptually related to the bug? If so, do you represent the bug such that it plays a role only at the level of unconscious perception? Or is it the case that you represent the bug such that it plays a role at the level of conscious perception, but you lack access to that aspect of your conscious perception? If my argument holds, it holds regardless of what stance one takes on these questions. For a discussion of conscious and unconscious perception, see Phillips and Block 2016.

The Accuracy Condition Objection: Perception is a relation between a perceiving subject and her environment or, alternatively, an event in which such a relation obtains. Relations and events do not have accuracy conditions. So perception is not the kind of thing that can be accurate or inaccurate. If accounting for accuracy conditions is the reason for introducing content, then denying that perception has accuracy conditions undermines at least this reason for accepting the content thesis (e.g. Brewer 2006).

The Indeterminacy Objection: If perceptual states have representational content, then the way an object looks on a given occasion must fix the representational content of the perceptual state. The way an object looks on a given occasion does not, however, fix the representational content of the perceptual state. Therefore, perceptual states do not have representational content (e.g. Travis 2004).[16]

In light of these five objections, austere relationalism rejects the content thesis. The central positive idea of austere relationalism is that perception is constitutively a matter of a subject standing in an awareness or an acquaintance relation to a particular: a mind-independent object, a property that this object instantiates, an event, or a combination thereof (Campbell 2002, Brewer 2006). Alternatively, perception is analyzed as an event in which such relations obtain (Martin 2002a). Austere relationalist views differ further on whether perceivers are perceptually related only to objects in their environment (Brewer 2006, 2011) or whether they are also related to the properties that these objects instantiate (Campbell 2002). Views differ moreover on how the perceptual relation is understood: it can be understood as a sensory awareness relation

---

[16] One could formulate a sixth objection, namely, a particularity objection: representationalist views cannot adequately account for perceptual particularity, that is, they cannot account for the constitutive difference that particulars perceived make to the relevant perceptual states. I will not treat this as an independent objection, since it is folded into the epistemological objection and the semantic grounding objection.

Naturally, different austere relationalists emphasize different objections. For example, Travis emphasizes the indeterminacy objection, while Martin emphasizes the phenomenological objection. The accounts that Travis targets are committed to "first, that a perceptual experience has a particular representational content... second, that the perceiver can recognize this feature of it... third, that this is a content the perceiver may accept or reject" (2004: 82). Brewer specifies the views he targets as committed to two principles: "The first is that contents admit the possibility of falsity, and that genuine perception is therefore to be construed as a *success*, in which the way things experientially seem to the subject to be is determined as *true* by the way things actually are in the world around him... The second is that contents involve a certain kind of *generality*, representing some object, or objects, as being a determinate *way*, that a range of qualitatively distinct such things in general may be" (2006: 166).

or as an epistemic acquaintance relation.[17] Finally, views differ on how they oppose representationalism: while all austere relationalists agree that appeals to content are unnecessary to give a satisfying account of perception, some go a step further and argue that relationalism explains certain phenomena better than representationalism can. Some argue moreover that representationalism is flat-out incapable of accounting for certain phenomena that the relationalist can readily explain (e.g. Brewer 2006, 2011).

What austere relationalist views have in common is that they endorse the negative thesis that no appeal to representational content is necessary in a philosophical account of perception, in conjunction with the positive thesis that any perception constitutively involves at least three components: a subject, the environment of the subject, and a perceptual relation between the subject and particulars in that environment.

For the sake of specificity, I will focus on the simple case of a subject being acquainted with a mind-independent object that instantiates only one perceivable property. Everything I will say about this case needs to be modified only slightly to fit other versions of austere relationalism. I will specify these modifications where required to establish my argument. The case of a subject being acquainted with a mind-independent object that instantiates only one perceivable property is a model that requires making the simplifying assumption that there can be a perception of an object as instantiating only one perceivable property. Typical cases of perception are more complex: any visual perception of an object arguably involves perceiving at least a color and a spatial property that this object instantiates along with situation-dependent properties correlating with these color and spatial properties.[18] Further, it is arguably possible to perceive a property-instance without perceiving an object that instantiates the relevant property. Finally, many perceptions are crossmodal in that they involve interactions between two or more different sensory modalities.

Given this simplifying assumption, the austere relationalist thesis can be articulated in the following way: a subject perceives a particular white cup only if she is acquainted with that particular white cup. Being acquainted with a white cup may in turn be analyzed in terms of being acquainted with a cup instantiating whiteness, where the relevant object and property-instance are (roughly) co-located. More generally, subject S perceives object o and any property-instance F only if S is acquainted with o and F, where o and F are (roughly) co-located.[19]

[17] Arguably, understanding the perceptual relation as a mere causal relation will not do for austere relationalist purposes.

[18] For a defense of situation-dependent properties, see Schellenberg 2008. For a discussion of how austere relationalism can exploit situation-dependent properties, see Genone 2014.

[19] Byrne (2009: 436f.) argues that austere relationalists face the problem of what binds the relevant objects with the relevant properties: "In an ordinary situation in which one sees a yellow lemon and a red tomato, one is 'simply presented' with the lemon, the tomato, yellowness, and redness—perhaps that amounts to the fact that one sees the lemon and the tomato and sees yellow and red. But that is not all: the lemon is 'simply presented' *as* yellow, not as red...How does the fact that the lemon is yellow get into the perceptual story?" This problem of what unifies the relevant objects and properties can be dealt with in an austere relationalist account by arguing that the properties that an object instantiates are necessarily (roughly) co-located with the object. The qualification "roughly" leaves room for the color of the object

Three clarifications are in order. First, austere relationalists do not deny that beliefs and judgments are formed on the basis of perception. So what is contentious is not whether perception brings about mental states with content. What is contentious is rather whether this content is constitutive of perceptual states.

Second, austere relationalists do not contest that perception involves information processing. As Campbell argues (using the term "cognitive" rather than "information processing"), "[o]n a Relational View of perception, we have to think of cognitive processing as 'revealing' the world to the subject" (2002: 118). Austere relationalists do not deny that perception involves information processing, but rather insist that no appeal to representational content is necessary to explain the nature of the awareness of our surroundings that we have as a consequence of this processing. So while, for example, Campbell allows that representations play a role on a subpersonal level, he denies that any appeal to representational content is necessary to explain perception on a personal level.[20]

Finally, austere relationalists need not deny that we can articulate propositions to express what we perceive. Acknowledging that a subject can articulate such propositions entails no commitment to her perceptual state being constituted by the content thereby articulated. It might be that the propositions articulated are merely associated with the perceptual state. In other words, austere relationalists can accept the association thesis.[21]

4. The Perceptual Content Argument

As noted above, the content thesis is typically taken for granted and rarely argued for. To be sure, many views have been defended that rely on the content thesis. But more often than not such views simply assume that perception is representational and proceed to argue for one particular way of understanding its content. There are many ways one might argue that perception is constitutively representational. I will develop an argument in support of the content thesis drawing on the view that perception

---

being only a surface property of the object, rather than a property that encompasses the three-dimensional shape of the object. This strategy of co-location deals with another criticism of austere relationalism. Siegel (2010) argues that the thesis that subjects are related to objects and the properties these objects instantiate implies that subjects are related to facts such as that *o* is *F*, which in turn implies that subjects are related to propositions. So she argues that austere relationalists are committed to treating perception as factive and thus as propositionally structured. If the thesis that subjects are related to objects and the properties these objects instantiate is analyzed in terms of co-location of the relevant particulars, then no appeal to facts is necessary to make sense of the austere relationalist thesis.

[20] For a recent discussion of the personal/subpersonal distinction, see Drayson 2014.

[21] For an argument that disposing of perceptual representations is inconsistent with empirical findings about dorsal perception and about the multimodality of perception, see Nanay 2014. For a discussion of how the ventral and the dorsal stream work together in visual experience, see Wu 2014 and Schwenkler and Briscoe 2015. For a critical discussion of recent representationalist views on empirical grounds, see Ganson et al. 2014.

is constitutively a matter of employing perceptual capacities—that is, discriminatory, selective capacities.

The Perceptual Content Argument

I.   If a subject S perceives a particular α, then S discriminates and singles out α.

II. If S discriminates and singles out α, then S is employing perceptual capacity C_α by means of which S discriminates and singles out α.

III. If S is employing C_α by means of which S discriminates and singles out α, then S's perceptual state M brought about by being perceptually related to α and employing C_α is repeatable and has accuracy conditions.

IV. If S's perceptual state M brought about by being perceptually related to α and constituted by employing C_α is repeatable and has accuracy conditions, then S's perceptual state M is constitutively a matter of representing α in virtue of employing C_α.

V.   If S's perceptual state M is constitutively a matter of representing α in virtue of employing C_α, then S's perceptual state M brought about by being perceptually related to α is constituted by content c in virtue of S representing α.

From I–V: If S perceives α, then S's perceptual state M brought about by being perceptually related to α is constituted by content c in virtue of S representing α.

Premise I of the perceptual content argument is the same as Premise I of the particularity argument. So we have already given support for Premise I in Chapter 1. To recap: discriminating and singling out a particular from its surround is a minimal condition on perceiving the particular. For example, when Kim sees a white cup, she employs her capacity to discriminate white from other colors and to single out white in her environment. Similarly, she employs her capacity to differentiate and single out cup-shapes from other shapes in her environment. Such discriminatory activity allows for scene segmentation, border and edge detection, and region extraction.[22] It is not clear how one could perceive a particular without at the very least discriminating and singling it out from its surround. For this reason, we can say that discriminating and singling out a particular from its surround is a minimal condition on perceiving the particular. If this is right, then perception is constitutively a matter of discriminating and singling out particulars.

Now, discriminating and singling out particulars requires employing perceptual capacities—namely, discriminatory, selective capacities (Premise II). As argued in Chapter 2, a perceptual capacity is repeatable and, in employing a perceptual capacity, one either singles out the particular one purports to single out or one fails to do so. I will give support to each part of this claim in turn.

First, perceptual capacities are repeatable in that the very same perceptual capacity can be employed to single out particular α or to single out particular β, where α and β

---

[22] For a more detailed defense of the thesis that perception is constitutively a matter of discriminating and singling out particulars, see Schellenberg 2016a. See also Chapter 1. Singling out a particular is a proto-conceptual analogue of referring to a particular. While referring may require conceptual capacities, singling out particulars does not.

are both particulars of the type that the perceptual capacity functions to single out. For example, the perceptual capacity RED functions to single out any perceivable instance of red. So the same perceptual capacity can be employed in distinct environments. Moreover, the same perceptual capacity can be employed to single out α at time t_1 and at time t_2 and thus yield the same perceptual state at t_1 and t_2. If this is right, then there is a repeatable element that is constitutive of perceptual states, namely, the perceptual capacities employed. And with repeatability comes generality—for what it is for a capacity to be general simply is for it to be applicable across a variety of temporal and situational contexts. As a consequence, perceptual states have a general element. This general element is due to the nature of the perceptual capacities the employment of which constitute the perceptual state.

Being a repeatable capacity is, of course, not a sufficient condition for yielding a mental state characterized by representational content. After all, many things in the world have repeatable capacities without those capacities yielding mental states characterized by content. Being repeatable is, however, a necessary condition on yielding a mental state that is characterized by representational content. And the necessary condition is what we need.

When one is perceptually related to a scene, one employs perceptual capacities which may or may not function to single out the particulars present. If I employ my capacity to discriminate and single out red from other colors in an environment in which there is no instance of red, the content of my experiential state will be inaccurate in that respect.

Insofar as a perceptual capacity is repeatable and insofar as one either singles out the particular one purports to single out or one fails to do so, employing perceptual capacities generates a perceptual state that is repeatable and has accuracy conditions (Premise III). Now, being repeatable and having accuracy conditions are jointly key features of representational content. So employing perceptual capacities yields perceptual states that exhibit key features of representational content: it yields a perceptual state that is repeatable and that can be accurate or inaccurate with regard to the particulars in the environment of the perceiver. If this is right, then the perceiver's perceptual state represents particulars in her environment in virtue of employing perceptual capacities (Premise IV).

So far, we have established that the perceiver's perceptual state is constitutively a matter of representing the particulars perceived in virtue of employing perceptual capacities. If that is right, then that perceptual state is constituted by content in virtue of employing those perceptual capacities (Premise V). Thus, our perceiver bears the representation relation to the content rather than the mere association relation. As a consequence, the notion of content established by Premises I–V goes beyond that established by the argument for associative content. Since S is arbitrarily chosen, the conclusion holds for any perceiver and so characterizes perception generally. Therefore, the argument establishes the content thesis.

5. The Relational Content Argument

How does the content thesis fare with regard to the five austere relationalist objections? Austere relationalists present us with a dilemma: either deny that perception has content or fail to adequately account for its epistemological, phenomenological, and representational role. In the rest of this chapter, I will argue that we need not accept this dilemma since there is a view of perceptual content that circumvents the austere relationalist's objections. In doing so, I will argue that the content of perception should be understood as relational content.

More specifically, I will argue that if the phenomenological, epistemological, and semantic grounding objections carry any weight, then any austere representationalist is vulnerable to these objections. However, as I will argue, if content is understood to be relational content (and not general content as the austere representationalist holds), then the content thesis emerges unscathed. I will then argue that the indeterminacy objection and the accuracy condition objection are not objections to the content thesis, regardless of how perceptual content is understood.

So I will contend that the defender of the content thesis should embrace that content is relational content—be it the content of perception, hallucination, or illusion. Not only does such a view avoid objections to which the austere representationalist falls prey, such a view moreover accommodates the phenomenological, epistemological, and semantic grounding insights of austere relationalism. As I will show, such a view can explain phenomenal character in terms of perceptual relations to particulars and can explain how perception provides us with knowledge of particular objects, grounds demonstrative reference, yields singular thoughts, fixes the reference of singular thoughts, and more generally grounds language in the world.

The relational content argument goes as follows:

The Relational Content Argument

From I: If a subject S perceives particular α, then S discriminates and singles out α.

VI.   If S discriminates and singles out α, then S is perceptually conscious of α in virtue of discriminating and singling out α.

VII.   If S is perceptually conscious of α in virtue of discriminating and singling out α, then S is perceptually conscious of α in virtue of employing perceptual capacity C_α by means of which she discriminates and singles out α.

VIII. Perceptual capacities are by their nature linked to what they single out in the case of an accurate perception.

From I–IV: If S perceives a particular α, then S's perceptual state M is constitutively a matter of representing α in virtue of employing C_α.

IX.   If S's perceptual state M is constitutively a matter of representing α in virtue of employing C_α and if perceptual capacities are by their nature linked to what they single out in the case of an accurate perception, then S's perceptual state M is constituted by relational content rc in virtue of S being perceptually related to α and of S representing α.

From I–IX: If S perceives α (while not suffering from blindsight or any other form of unconscious perception), then S's perceptual state M is constituted by relational content rc in virtue of S being perceptually related to α and of S representing α.

I will give support to the premises of this argument by discussing the austere relationalist objections to the content thesis.

5.1. The phenomenological objection

Austere relationalists argue that phenomenal character is constituted by the very mind-independent objects and properties of which one is aware when perceiving. As Campbell succinctly puts it:

On a Relational View, the phenomenal character of your experience, as you look around the room, is constituted by the actual layout of the room itself: which particular objects are there, their intrinsic properties, such as colour and shape, and how they are arranged in relation to one another and to you.   (2002: 116; similarly, Martin 2002a: 393 and Brewer 2007: 92f.)

Austere relationalists diverge regarding whether phenomenal character is constituted by mind-independent particulars *tout court* or by awareness or acquaintance relations to these particulars. They agree, however, that phenomenal character is externally determined.

The phenomenological objection has it that a view on which phenomenal character is grounded in content (rather than in the actual layout of the perceiver's surroundings) faces the problem that what constitutes the phenomenal character of the perceptual state is distinct from that of which the perceiver is aware—at least on representationalist views that deny that perceivers are aware of the content of their perceptual states. Moreover, any view that accounts for phenomenal character in terms of intentional objects, qualia, sense-data, or propositions faces the problem of why and how such peculiar entities bring about phenomenal states. In short, the objection is that explaining phenomenal character in terms of relations to anything other than the particulars perceived severs phenomenal character from that of which we are aware.

One could question how serious a problem the phenomenological objection is for austere representationalism. I will not pursue that matter here. Rather, I will, for the sake of argument, grant that phenomenal character should be analyzed in terms of perceptual relations to mind-independent particulars. I will argue that the phenomenological objection only threatens views on which phenomenal character is determined by its content, where that content is general. It does not threaten views on which phenomenal character is grounded in relational content. As I will show, if content is relational content, then the phenomenological objection can be circumvented and we can recognize the austere relationalist insight that phenomenal character is grounded in perceptual relations to mind-independent particulars.

By arguing that the phenomenal character of perception, hallucination, and illusion is grounded in relational content, I go beyond austere relationalists: the view I defend does not only analyze the phenomenal character of perception in terms of relations to perceived particulars, it defends the more radical thesis that the phenomenal character of hallucination and illusion should be understood in this way as well.

Doing justice to the austere relationalist insight will require constraining the content thesis in two respects. First, the content of a perception is constituted at least in part by (perceptual relations to) the particulars perceived. Second, the content of an illusion or a hallucination is derivative of the content of perception insofar as it can be specified only with reference to the structure of the content of a perception with the same phenomenal character.

In Chapter 4, we saw that while austere relationalists argue that perceptual relations to the environment should be taken as explanatorily primary in an account of perceptual consciousness, austere representationalists instead take the content of the perceptual state to be explanatorily primary. Against both views, I argue that perceptual content and perceptual relations to the environment should be recognized to be mutually dependent in any explanation of what brings about perceptual consciousness. In other words, I argue that perceptual experience is constitutively both relational and representational: when we perceive, we employ perceptual capacities by means of which we discriminate and single out particulars in our environment, where the relevant particulars are external and mind-independent objects, events, and property-instances. When we suffer an illusion or a hallucination, we employ the same perceptual capacities baselessly that we would employ in a perception with the same phenomenal character in virtue of being perceptually related to the relevant particulars. Given that in cases of illusion, we fail to single out one or more mind-independent property-instances that we purport to single out, illusions are treated on a par with hallucinations. After all, in both cases, the subject fails to single out a particular in her environment. The difference between illusion and hallucination is simply this: in an illusion, the particular we fail to single out is a property-instance; in a hallucination, the particular we fail to single out is an object.

Taking into account that perception is constitutively a matter of employing perceptual capacities, we can specify the second constraint as follows: the content of an illusion or a hallucination is derivative of the content of perception insofar as the perceptual capacities employed in illusion or hallucination can only be specified with reference to their role in a perception with the same phenomenal character. There are explanatory and metaphysical aspects to this primacy of the employment of perceptual capacities in perception. We cannot explain the employment of perceptual capacities in illusion and hallucination without appealing to what would be the case if the subject were perceiving. Licensing this explanatory primacy, there is a metaphysical primacy: while perceptual capacities can be employed in illusions and hallucinations, they function to do what they do in perception.

The key idea is that employing perceptual capacities in a sensory mode, for example, a mode such as seeing, hearing, touching, smelling, or tasting, constitutes the phenomenal character of the perceptual state.[23] If a subject's environment sensorily seems to contain the particular α, then she is in a phenomenal state that is constituted by employing a perceptual capacity that functions to single out particulars such as α. An example will help illustrate the idea. Let's say I am perceptually related to a red flower growing in a thicket of green foliage. Parts of the flower are a gorgeous shade of crimson. So among other things, I am perceptually related to an instance of crimson. Let's call the particular patch of crimson to which I am perceptually related α. To be perceptually conscious of α, I need to discriminate and single out α from its surround: for example, I need to discriminate it from the green foliage in the background. Engaging in this kind of discriminatory activity is what it means to be perceptually conscious of α. I can employ a variety of perceptual capacities to discriminate and single out α. I can employ my capacity to discriminate red from other colors. Alternatively, I can employ more fine-grained capacities, such as my perceptual capacity to discriminate crimson from other colors, including other shades of red. If I employ this capacity to discriminate and single out α, then my phenomenal character will be more fine-grained than if I employ only my capacity to discriminate red from other colors. After all, I am now not only discriminating α from the green background, but moreover discriminating α from the darker shade of red on the tip of the petal and from the more orange shade of red of the adjacent petal. Either approach allows me to be perceptually conscious of the patch of crimson amidst the green foliage. The fact that I can discriminate in more or less detail, thereby changing the phenomenal character of my perceptual state, is evidence in support of the thesis that employing discriminatory, selective capacities constitutes phenomenal character.

On the suggested view, experiences in which the same perceptual capacities are employed in the same sensory mode have the same phenomenal character. More specifically, phenomenal character corresponds one-to-one with the employment of perceptual capacities in a sensory mode. If phenomenal character is constituted by employing perceptual capacities, whether the subject succeeds or fails to single out a particular has no effect on phenomenal character (Premise VI). Insofar as discriminating and singling out a particular is a matter of employing perceptual capacities, the subject is perceptually conscious of α in virtue of employing such capacities (Premise VII). In Chapter 6, I will argue in more detail for the view that phenomenal character is constituted by employing perceptual capacities. Here I will restrict my focus to how such a view entails a relational account of perception—albeit not an austere relational account.

To show why the thesis that perception is a matter of employing perceptual capacities supports the view that perception is constitutively not just representational but moreover relational, it is crucial to take a closer look at perceptual capacities. A perceptual capacity is systematically linked to particulars of a specific kind, in that

---

[23] I will defend this thesis in Chapter 6.

it functions to differentiate and single out such particulars. For example, my perceptual capacity to discriminate and single out instances of red in my environment is systematically linked to red particulars, in that the function of the capacity is to discriminate and single out red particulars.[24] It is unclear what it would mean to possess a perceptual capacity—the very function of which is to single out particulars of a specific kind—without being in a position to single out such a particular when perceptually related to one and nothing else is amiss. Consider again the capacity to discriminate and single out red from other colors. Were we not in a position to use our capacity to single out red in our environment when we are perceptually related to an instance of red and nothing else is amiss, then it is unclear how we could possibly count as possessing the capacity to discriminate red. Thus, being in a position to single out a particular of the kind that the capacity functions to single out (when perceptually related to such a particular and nothing else is amiss) is a minimal condition for possessing a perceptual capacity.

If we possess a perceptual capacity, then we can employ it not only in perception, but also in hallucination and illusion. When we suffer an illusion or a hallucination, we employ the very same perceptual capacities that we would be employing were we enjoying a perception with the same phenomenal character—albeit while failing to single out the relevant particulars. The perceptual capacities are, even when employed in hallucination or illusion, systematically linked to what they function to single out in perception. After all, they still function to do what they do in perception, namely, to discriminate and single out particulars in the environment. The problem is simply that the environment is not playing along. Now it might be that we are always unlucky and, like Jackson's Mary prior to leaving her black and white room, are never perceptually related to red things and so never in a position to single out anything red in our environment (Jackson 1986). Even so, the minimal condition would still hold. While perceptual capacities can be employed in illusion or hallucination, they are determined by relations between perceivers and their environment insofar as the function of the capacity is to discriminate and single out mind-independent particulars. This is to say that there is a metaphysical priority of perception over hallucination and illusion.[25]

Regardless of whether one is perceiving, hallucinating, or suffering an illusion, the perceptual capacities employed are systematically linked to what they function to single out in perception. After all, perceptual capacities function to single out particulars; they do not function to fail to single out particulars. It is not only parsimony that dictates that the capacities employed in hallucination or illusion are the same as the ones employed in perception. A second reason is that it would be odd to say that hallucinations or illusions are brought about by capacities that function to bring about hallucinations or illusions. As the argument above shows, perceptual capacities

---

[24] I will argue for this in more detail in Chapter 7.

[25] For a more detailed discussion of the metaphysical primacy of perception over hallucination and illusion, see Schellenberg 2013a and 2014b. See also the discussion in Chapter 7.

are by their nature linked to what they single out in the case of an accurate perception (Premise VIII).

Insofar as perceptual capacities are systematically linked to particulars, the phenomenal character constituted by employing perceptual capacities is systematically linked to particulars. This is to say that phenomenal character is systematically linked to what the relevant perceptual capacities single out in perception. If the fact that perceptual capacities single out particulars in some situations but not others has any semantic significance, then the token content ensuing from employing perceptual capacities in perception will be constituted by the perceptual capacities employed and the particulars thereby singled out.[26] Employing perceptual capacities yields a content type that perceptions, illusions, and hallucinations with the same phenomenal character have in common. So individuating perceptual states by their content type amounts to individuating them with regard to the experiencing subject's phenomenal character. The token content of a perceptual state ensues from employing perceptual capacities in a particular environment, thereby either singling out particulars or failing to do so. In the case of a perception, the token relational content will be a singular content. Insofar as at least some of the perceptual capacities that constitute the content of an illusion or a hallucination are employed baselessly, the token content of such mental states is gappy. The ensuing content of an illusion or a hallucination has the form of a singular content, but fails to be a token singular content.

By analyzing phenomenal character as constituted by employing perceptual capacities that function to discriminate and single out particulars (and in perception do just that), we can recognize the austere relationalist insight that phenomenal character can and should be explained in terms of (perceptual relations to) the very particulars of which we are aware in perception. This insight demystifies phenomenal character insofar as it analyzes it in terms of (relations to) concrete, mind-independent particulars, rather than say qualia, sense-data, phenomenal properties, intentional objects, or any other peculiar entities. However, by arguing for the radical thesis that all there is to being in a perceptual state with a certain phenomenal character is being perceptually related to the environment, austere relationalists leave mysterious how one could be in a mental state with phenomenal character if one is not perceiving, but rather suffering an illusion or hallucination. By introducing perceptual capacities that ground our ability to single out particulars, we can reject this radical thesis. And, by rejecting that thesis, we can not only hold on to the content thesis, but we can moreover give a straightforward explanation of what accounts for the phenomenal character of illusions and hallucinations.[27]

The view suggested is constitutively representational insofar as perceptual content is constituted by employing perceptual capacities. It is constitutively relational insofar as

---

[26] For a development of this idea and the view of perceptual content presented in this paragraph, see Chapter 4.

[27] For a discussion of how to account for aspects of phenomenal character that are not a matter of the environment seeming a certain way (e.g. blurriness) within the framework provided, see Chapter 6.

perceptual capacities function to single out particulars—and in perception fulfill this function. Since the content of an experiential state is constituted by employing perceptual capacities that function to single out particulars, relations to particulars are implicated in the very nature of experiential content. As a consequence, the content yielded by employing perceptual capacities is relational content (Premise IX). In virtue of recognizing that perception is constitutively both relational and representational, the suggested view rejects all ways of factorizing perceptual content into an internal and an external component.[28]

I have presented a way of accounting for phenomenal character that both recognizes the content thesis and respects the austere relationalist insight that phenomenal character is grounded in perceptual relations to the particulars perceived. While I have argued that phenomenal character is constituted by employing perceptual capacities in a sensory mode, these perceptual capacities have in turn been analyzed in terms of the particulars they function to single out (and in fact single out in perception). So on the account presented, phenomenal character is analyzed in terms of mind-independent particulars.

5.2. The epistemological objection

Austere relationalists argue that perception can provide us with knowledge of particulars only if those particulars make a constitutive difference to the relevant perceptual states. I will argue that this epistemological objection does not undermine the content thesis. If perceptual content is constituted by the particulars perceived, we can endorse the content thesis while acknowledging the epistemological insights of austere relationalists. Thus, I will argue that a view on which perception is constitutively both relational and representational is at least as well suited as austere relationalism to account for perception providing us with knowledge of particulars.

Before I show why the epistemological objection is not a threat to the content thesis, we should explain what motivates the objection. It is widely accepted that by perceiving a particular, a subject can gain perceptual knowledge of that particular. After all, if we cannot gain knowledge of particulars via perception, it is unclear how we could ever gain such knowledge. Consider again Kim, who sees a coffee cup at time t_1. Let's call the cup she sees cup_1. In virtue of seeing cup_1, Kim gains perceptual knowledge of that particular cup. If her perceptual state were the same whether or not she were perceiving cup_1, then it is not clear how her perceptual state could ground knowledge of cup_1.

Switching cases bring out the point particularly clearly. Let's suppose Kim closes her eyes briefly and, unbeknownst to her, cup_1 is replaced with the qualitatively identical cup_2. So, when Kim reopens her eyes at time t_2, she is causally related to a numerically

---

[28] For a helpful discussion of the problems of factorizing mental content into internal and external components, see Williamson 2000, 2006. See also Burge 2010. For an alternative way of avoiding the pitfalls of both austere representationalism and austere relationalism, see Dorsch 2013.

distinct cup. Even though she cannot tell, she is perceiving different cups at t_1 and at t_2. Before the switch, she gains perceptual knowledge of cup$_1$. After the switch, she gains perceptual knowledge of cup$_2$. Moreover, her belief that the cup she sees at t_2 is the same as the cup she saw at t_1 is false. So despite it seeming to her as if they are the same cup, she does not know that the cup she sees at t_2 is the same as the cup she saw at t_1. If the cup had not been replaced, then her belief would have been true.

Another way of motivating the idea that perception grounds knowledge of particulars is with regard to the role of perception in grounding knowledge of the referent of demonstratives. Perception grounds our ability to know to which particular a demonstrative term refers (Campbell 2002: 22). If perceptual states were not constituted by the particulars perceived, it is not clear how perception could play this epistemological role. Campbell argues that only a view "on which experience of an object is a simple relation holding between perceiver and object, can characterize the kind of acquaintance with objects that provides knowledge of reference" (2002: 115). To motivate this, consider Kim who says "that cup of coffee is the one with sugar in it." If Kim's perceptual state were exactly the same regardless of whether she were seeing cup$_1$ or cup$_2$, then what would ground Kim's knowledge that "that" refers to the cup she is perceiving, rather than some other cup? The idea is that when Kim says, "that cup of coffee is the one with sugar in it," my ability to know to which cup she is referring requires knowing to which particular cup "that" refers. This knowledge is grounded in being perceptually related to the particular cup to which "that" refers in the specific situation.

Austere relationalism is ideally structured to give an account of perceptual knowledge insofar as it posits that one can perceive o's Fness if and only if one is perceptually related to o and o is F. By contrast, if the content and phenomenal character of a perceptual state are in no way constituted by the particulars perceived—as the austere representationalist holds—then one's perceptual state can have the same phenomenal character and the same existentially quantified content $(\exists x)Fx$ regardless of what particular (if any) one perceives. The austere representationalist posits that two experiences with the same phenomenal character do not differ in content. So according to the austere representationalist, Kim who sees cup$_1$ at t_1 and cup$_2$ at t_2 will *ceteris paribus* have the same perceptual content at t_1 and at t_2. Another way of bringing out the contrast between austere relationalism and austere representationalism is to say that an environment-independent representation that o is F does not entail that o is F. By contrast, austere relationalism has it that perceiving o's Fness entails that o is F.

The austere representationalist could argue that it is the causal relation between the perceiver and the particulars perceived that grounds knowledge of those particulars: if the subject is related to cup$_1$, the content of her perceptual state is caused by cup$_1$. If she is related to cup$_2$, the content of her perceptual state is the very same, but it is caused by cup$_2$. The brute difference in causal relations accounts for any difference in knowledge. The problems with this causal strategy are the same as the ones that face any causal view of perception in general and any causal view of knowledge in particular. I will not rehearse these here, but will just mention that the most salient problem is that—although causal relations may play an important role in transmitting information—the possibility of deviant causal chains prevents knowledge and perception from being straightforwardly analyzed in terms of causal relations to mind-independent particulars.[29]

If causal relations cannot do the job, what accounts for the constitutive difference between Kim's perception of cup$_1$ at t_1 and her perception of cup$_2$ at t_2? Assuming that perceptual knowledge is a perceptual state, the critical question is: what is the constitutive difference between Kim's perceptual state at t_1 and her perceptual state at t_2, such that her perceptual state at t_1 grounds knowledge of cup$_1$ and her perceptual state at t_2 grounds knowledge of cup$_2$?[30] There are at least two ways of understanding the relevant difference: in terms of phenomenal character or in terms of perceptual content.[31]

Austere relationalists pursue the first option. As Campbell argues, the object of perception is a constituent of the perceptual state insofar as attending to it brings about an unrepeatable phenomenal aspect of the perceptual state. If phenomenal character is constituted by perceived objects and not multiply realizable, then the phenomenal character of perceiving numerically distinct objects necessarily differs, even if those objects are qualitatively identical. Campbell commits himself to this radical consequence in his discussion of the following inference:

P1:   That woman is running.
P2:   That woman is jumping.
Conclusion: That woman is running and jumping.[32]

As he argues, "[r]ecognizing the validity of the inference requires that your experience should make the sameness of the object transparent to you" (2002: 129). If the woman running were in fact the qualitatively identical twin of the woman jumping, then Campbell would have to say that one's experience should make the difference of the objects transparent or phenomenally accessible, such that one could recognize the inference as invalid. It is, however, counterintuitive that the distinctness of the objects would be phenomenally accessible via perception—assuming that the two women are indistinguishable to the perceiver and she does not notice that there are two different women present.[33]

---

[29] For a detailed criticism of causal theories of perception, see Hyman 1992.

[30] For a defense of the thesis that knowledge is a mental state, see Williamson 2000. In Chapter 9, I discuss how understanding perception in terms of employing perceptual capacities allows for a way to analyze what it means for perceptual knowledge to be a mental state.

[31] For a discussion of more options, see Chapter 3.

[32] It should be noted that the inference is in fact only valid if "that" refers to the same woman in all three instances.

[33] Campbell acknowledges that "it may be impossible to tell, simply by having the experience, which sort of experience it is—whether it is one that involves a single object, or if it is, rather, an experience that involves a multiplicity of objects" (2002: 130). The question is how acknowledging this is compatible with positing that "[r]ecognizing the validity of the inference [cited above] requires that your experience should make the sameness of the object transparent to you." For a more detailed discussion of this point, see Chapter 3.

The obvious solution to the problem is to argue that it is not phenomenal character, but rather perceptual content that tracks the difference between perceptions of numerically distinct but qualitatively identical objects.[34] Since austere relationalists deny that perceptual states have content, this solution is not open to them. If we accept that perceptions of distinct objects differ in content, then we can accept that Kim's perception of cup$_1$ at t_1 and her perception of cup$_2$ at t_2 are phenomenally the same, while acknowledging a difference in the perceptual state that grounds knowledge of the distinct objects.

Austere relationalism has it that for perception to ground knowledge of particulars, there must be a phenomenal difference between perceptions of qualitatively identical but numerically distinct objects. If we accept that perceptual content is relational, we can avoid this unfortunate consequence, while recognizing the austere relationalist insight that relations to particulars bring about a constitutive difference in perceptual states that grounds knowledge of the particulars perceived. Any epistemological reason there is to hold that perceptual states are constituted by the particulars perceived can be accommodated if perceptual content is constituted by those particulars. To be sure, I have not argued that this is the only or the best way to account for perceptual knowledge.[35] My aim in this chapter was more modest. It was to show that a view that endorses the content thesis while analyzing perceptual content as relational content can account for the epistemological role of perception in much the same way as austere relationalism.

5.3. The semantic grounding objection

Perception grounds demonstrative reference, fixes the reference of singular terms, and yields *de re* mental states such as singular thoughts. One could argue that, in virtue of playing these roles at the intersection of mind and language, perception grounds language in the world. Indeed, austere relationalists have it that only if perceptual states are understood as not having content can we explain how perception grounds concepts and, more generally, language in the world. As Campbell puts it, "[t]he fundamental objection to the common factor approach is that on the common factor approach, experience cannot play its explanatory role; we cannot understand how experience, so conceived, could be what provides us with our concepts of the objects around us" (2002: 123). The austere relationalist idea is that while we have singular thoughts and so beliefs that put us in contact with mind-independent particulars, perception puts us in contact with such particulars more directly. This contact with particulars is, according to austere relationalists, why perception grounds concepts and, more generally, language in the world.

---

[34] By arguing that phenomenal character is constituted only by the perceptual capacities employed (rather than being constituted also by the particulars thereby singled out), the view I am suggesting allows that perceptions of numerically distinct yet qualitatively identical objects differ in content while having the same phenomenal character.

[35] For a detailed discussion of perceptual knowledge, see Chapter 9.

Again, austere relationalists present us with a dilemma: either perception grounds language or perceptual states have content. Again, this is a false dilemma. I will argue that we need not choose between perception grounding language and perceptual states having content, as long as perceptual content is relational content.

There are at least two ways to think of language as grounded in perception. A radical perceptual grounding view has it that all concepts need perceptual grounding (e.g. Barsalou 1999, Prinz 2002, for criticism see Machery 2007). A modest perceptual grounding view has it that at least some of our concepts need perceptual grounding (e.g. Dove 2009). I will here assume a modest perceptual grounding view, but everything I say about that view generalizes to the radical view.

If employing perceptual capacities constitutes perceptual content and if those capacities are analyzed in terms of the particulars they function to single out, then we can accept that perception has content while recognizing the empiricist insight that "[e]xperience is what explains our grasp of the concepts of objects" (Campbell 2002: 122). So we can recognize the semantic grounding insight without rejecting the content thesis.

Brewer suggests that any representational account of perception would amount to a descriptive view of perception: all we get in perception of an object is a qualitative specification of the way things stand with that object, a specification that could hold equally well of any other numerically distinct yet qualitatively identical object (2011: 32–41). So according to Brewer, if the content thesis were correct, perception could only offer descriptions of objects that may equally well be satisfied by any number of distinct particulars.

In response, while many views of perceptual content are no doubt committed to a form of descriptivism, this is not true if perceptual content is relational. Singular modes of presentation do not constitute descriptions of environmental particulars that may equally well be satisfied by any number of distinct particulars; they are rather the semantic counterpart of singling out particulars in virtue of employing perceptual capacities.

Brewer's central argument against perception being representational hinges on a version of the semantic grounding objection:

If S sees a mind-independent physical object o, then there are certainly (perhaps indefinitely) many true sentences of the form 'o looks F', but I would...deny that S's seeing o itself consists in the truth of those sentences or can be fruitfully illuminated by listing the facts that o looks F_1, o looks F_2,..., o looks F_i, etc., or the fact that it visually seems to S that o is F_1, o is F_2,..., o is F_i, etc. S's seeing o, her perceptual experiential relation with that particular mind-independent physical object is more basic than any such facts and is what grounds the truth of all those sentences...   (2011: 62f.)

Brewer argues here that perceptual relations between a perceiver and an object are more basic than the sentences that express how the object looks to the perceiver. We can agree with Brewer that truthmakers are more basic than the sentences they make true. So we can agree with him that "S's seeing o, her perceptual experiential relation with that particular mind-independent physical object is more basic than any such facts and is what grounds the truth of all those sentences," where these sentences express how the environment looks to a person. However, what is at issue in the debate about whether perception has content is not the relation between sentences and their truthmakers. The thesis that perception is a matter of representing the environment is neither a thesis about sentences nor a thesis about sentential truth. It is a thesis about mental content. No one thinks that perception is constitutively a matter of expressing true sentences that report how the object looks to perceivers.[36]

While everyone can accept that perception is not constitutively a matter of expressing sentences, there is an argument in the vicinity of Brewer's argument that strengthens his case against representationalism. This argument has the same form as Brewer's and preserves the intuitions guiding his argument, but it is about mental content rather than sentences:

If S sees a mind-independent physical object o, then there are certainly (perhaps indefinitely) many accurate mental contents of the form 'o looks F', but S's seeing o itself does not consist in the accuracy of those mental contents, nor can it be fruitfully illuminated by listing the facts that o looks F_1, o looks F_2,..., o looks F_i, etc., or the fact that it visually seems to S that o is F_1, o is F_2,..., o is F_i, etc. S's seeing o, her perceptual experiential relation with that particular mind-independent physical object is more basic than any such facts and is what grounds the accuracy of all those mental contents.

In response to this amended version of Brewer's argument, we can acknowledge that S seeing o is more basic than the accuracy of the content of her perceptual state. However, accepting this does not commit us to accepting that S seeing o is more basic than S representing o. So we can accept that S seeing o is more basic than the accuracy of the mental content, while acknowledging that S seeing o is *not* more basic than S representing o. As argued above, S seeing o entails that S represents o: S cannot see o without employing perceptual capacities by means of which she discriminates and singles out o and employing such perceptual capacities constitutes representational content.

5.4. The accuracy condition objection

Austere relationalists argue that perceptual experience is not the kind of thing that can be accurate or inaccurate. Brewer articulates the idea in the following way:

[I]n perceptual experience, a person is simply presented with the actual constituents of the physical world themselves. Any errors in her worldview which result are products of the subject's responses to this experience, however automatic, natural or understandable in retrospect

---

[36] For a discussion of the relation between mental content and linguistic meaning, see Speaks 2006. On perceptual reports, see Brogaard 2015.

these responses may be. *Error*, strictly speaking, given how the world actually is, is never an essential feature of experience itself.   (2006: 169)

No doubt neither events nor relations are assessable for accuracy. So if perceptual experience is simply a perceptual relation to the environment or an event in which such a relation obtains, then perceptual experience cannot be assessable for accuracy. On the austere relationalist approach, it is trivially true that perceptual experience itself is not assessable for accuracy. When representationalists say that perceptual experience is accurate or inaccurate, they must be understanding perceptual experience either as something other than a perceptual relation or an event, or they must be using the phrases "this perceptual experience is accurate" or "this perceptual experience is inaccurate" as elliptical for "the content of this perceptual state is accurate" or "the content of this perceptual state is inaccurate."

How should we understand the claim that perceptual content is assessable for accuracy? In virtue of a subject perceiving her environment, she is perceptually conscious of the environment. The phenomenal character of her perceptual state specifies the way the environment would have to be for the content of her perceptual state to be accurate. The environment is either the way it seems to her or it is different from the way it seems to her. If the environment is the way it seems to her, then the content of her perceptual state is accurate. In all other cases, the content is inaccurate. So if a subject is in a perceptual state with a particular content, then this content is either accurate or inaccurate.

Accepting this is compatible with accepting that any given scene can be perceived in many different ways, and it is compatible with accepting that any given perception can be articulated in many different ways. To motivate this, consider again Norway's jagged coastline: as argued in Chapter 4, while Norway's coastline has one objective length, we can attribute different numeric lengths to it depending on how detailed our method of measurements are.[37] The results of these measurements may seem to be incompatible, they are, however, compatible as long as one factors in the differences in the methods of measurement by which one arrived at the different measurements. The important point is that the fact that we can arrive at different measurements is not to deny that there is only one way the coast of Norway is. Travis ties his indeterminacy objection to issues about accuracy conditions. So I will here connect the two issues as well: even though the results of our measurements are different, any given measurement either succeeds in accurately representing the coastline or fails to do so. Although the measurements are incompatible that does not imply that only one of them is accurate. It implies only that the accuracy of the measurement must be assessed relative to the chosen method of measurement. Indeed, the measurements can all be accurate relative to the method of measurement chosen.

---

[37] For a more detailed discussion of this analogy, see Chapter 4, Section 3.5.

Similarly, a scene can be photographed with different lenses. Although the representations of the scene will differ, this does not imply that at least one of them must be inaccurate. Again, just because there is only one way the scene in fact is, it does not follow that there can be only one accurate representation of the scene. Our perception is accurate only if we represent the way our environment is, but any given environment can be represented in many different ways. So even if we recognize the non-comparative use of appearance words and thus reject the second premise of the indeterminacy argument, we can nonetheless accept the indeterminacy thesis that many propositions can be associated with any given perception.

Now, one could argue that if there are all these different representations of the same scene, then some representations must be more accurate than others. In response, consider again measuring the coast of Norway. If ten people measure the coast of Norway, they are likely to come up with different numbers. But as argued, each number can be an accurate representation of the length of Norway's coast relative to the method of measurement chosen.

Before moving on, it should be noted that the accuracy condition objection could be understood as implying that the way the environment sensorily seems to one is necessarily the way the environment is. The idea is that if the environment is necessarily the way it seems to one in perceiving that environment, then perceptual experience does not have accuracy conditions.

There are at least two ways to understand the idea that the environment is necessarily the way it seems. On one understanding, the idea relies on the alleged factivity of seeming: if α seems a certain way to you, then α must exist. One might argue that a particular in the environment cannot seem a certain way to one, without that particular existing such that it can seem to you to be a certain way. While it is widely accepted that awareness is factive in that one being aware of α implies that α exists, it is more controversial to accept that seemings are factive. In response to this argument: even if "α seeming a certain way" were factive in this way, it does not follow that perception is not representational. It follows only that the perceptual content is necessarily accurate.

On a second understanding, the idea is that perception is infallible. This idea may be argued to follow from a certain understanding of what it means for perception to be a matter of being perceptually related to the environment. Let's assume for the sake of argument that perception is indeed infallible. Even if we make this controversial assumption, there is no reason to think that perceptual content does not have accuracy conditions. Like factivity, infallibilism about perception implies that perceptual content is necessarily accurate. It does not imply lack of accuracy conditions.

5.5. The indeterminacy objection

Austere relationalists argue that when we see an object, there are many ways that the object can look. Let's assume for a moment that it is clear what it means for an object to look a certain way. Given this assumption, the indeterminacy objection can be formulated in terms of the following argument:

The Indeterminacy Argument

1. If perception has representational content, then the way an object looks on a given occasion must fix what representational content the perception has.[38]

2. The way an object looks on a given occasion does not fix what representational content the perception has.

From 1 & 2: Perception does not have representational content.

The second premise needs explaining. As Travis points out, there are different and incompatible ways an object can look to be: "A peccary…may look exactly like a pig…It may also look like a tapir, a clever dummy pig, a wax imitation peccary, and so on. Experience cannot coherently represent it to us as both a peccary and wax (and a pig, and so on)" (2004: 73). He argues, moreover, that no one way an object can look to be should be given primacy. So one and the same peccary—with one and the same look—may bring about perceptions with different representational contents.

I will argue against the indeterminacy objection, by showing that on at least one understanding of "looks" the second premise must be rejected. As I will show, the force of the indeterminacy objection relies on a particular understanding of "looks," namely, on what Chisholm calls the comparative use of appearance words.[39] Austere relationalists do not deny that a subject is sensorily aware or perceptually conscious of a particular in her environment when she is perceptually related to that particular (while not suffering from blindsight or any other form of unconscious perception). On the face of it, a subject's being sensorily aware of a particular entails that the particular sensorily seems a certain way to her. Now, austere relationalists argue that perception is simply openness to the environment, and by doing so may be read as questioning this connection between being sensorily aware of a particular and the particular seeming a certain way to her. As Travis formulates the idea:

[P]erception, as such, simply places our surroundings in view; affords us awareness of them. There is no commitment to their *being* one way or another. It confronts us with what is there, so that, by attending, noting, recognizing, and otherwise exercising what capacities we have, *we may*…make out what is there for what it is—or, again, fail to…[I]n perception things are *not* presented, or represented, to us as being thus and so. They are just presented to us, full stop.

(2004: 65; see also Brewer 2006: 174)

---

[38] As Travis puts it: "If perception is representational, then, for any perceptual experience, there must be a way things are according to it…things looking as they do on a given occasion must fix *what* representational content experience then has" (2004: 71).

[39] See Chisholm 1957 and also Jackson 1977. Travis focuses on the case of visual perception and therefore focuses on looks-locutions, but his point arguably generalizes to other sensory modes. In the interest of generality, I will talk of the environment seeming a certain way in one or more sensory modes, rather than the environment looking a certain way. This section draws on Byrne 2009, which provides a detailed discussion of Travis's argument against the thesis that experience is looks-indexed.

One can accept both that perception simply affords us awareness of our surroundings and that if one is sensorily aware of a particular in one's environment, then that particular seems a certain way. The thesis that a particular seems a certain way implies only that it seems this way, rather than that way. To give an example: I am perceptually related to a desk. In virtue of being perceptually related to that desk, I am sensorily aware of the desk. I am not perceptually related to a chair and I am not sensorily aware of a chair. Were I sensorily aware of a chair, the phenomenal character of my perceptual state would be different. If one can accept that perception affords us awareness of our surroundings, while also accepting that awareness of the environment implies that the environment seems a certain way, then there is no obvious reason why austere relationalists should deny the connection between being sensorily aware of a particular and the particular seeming a certain way to her.

Let's assume that the austere relationalist accepts that if one is perceptually related to a particular and so sensorily aware of that particular, then the particular will seem a certain way to one. Even so, they would reject that a particular seeming a certain way to a perceiver implies that she is in a perceptual state with content, where that content corresponds to the way the particular seems to her. Travis argues against the thesis that perceptual content corresponds to how the environment sensorily seems to a perceiver by arguing against the idea that experience is looks-indexed, that is, the idea that "the representational content of an experience can be read off of the way, in it, things looked" (2004: 69). He considers the comparative and epistemic senses of looks, although he does not use these labels to distinguish them. Following Chisholm (1957: 43–52), we can understand the comparative sense of appearance words as pertaining to cases in which appearance words are used to compare the ways things look, as when an object is said to look like a typical member of some category. Examples of this use are "That looks as if it is a coffee cup" and "That sounds as if it is a cello." The epistemic sense of appearance words pertains to cases in which appearance words are used to express evidence in support of a proposition. One might say, for example, when confronted with a puddle of coffee and a broken cup, "It looks like someone dropped their coffee cup"; or, when hearing a beautiful rendition of Brahms's cello trio, "It sounds like someone has been practicing."

For the sake of argument, let's accept Travis's reasons for rejecting the thesis that perceptual content is looks-indexed on the epistemic and comparative use of appearance words. This leaves the option that perceptual content corresponds to how the environment looks (or more generally seems) on a non-comparative use of appearance words. Following Chisholm (1957: 50–3), we can understand the non-comparative use as pertaining to cases in which appearance words are used to single out or refer to particulars, such as objects or property-instances, without thereby making comparisons to other particulars. Cases include uses of demonstratives, such as, "that shade of blue," "that shape," and "this high pitch." Arguably, the epistemic and comparative uses are parasitic on such demonstrative, non-comparative uses of appearance words. After all, how the environment seems in such cases provides the basis on which comparisons are drawn and thus provides the basis for the environment to seem a certain way comparatively. Moreover, how the environment seems non-comparatively provides the evidence that allows for the environment to seem a certain way in the epistemic sense of "seems." The force of the indeterminacy objection relies on understanding "looks" comparatively. If "looks" is understood non-comparatively, then the second premise of the indeterminacy objection is false.

By denying that representational content plays any fundamental role in perception, austere relationalism amounts to a view on which the way the environment seems to a perceiving subject is matched by a contentful mental state only at a second stage when judgments or beliefs are formed on the basis of perception. Austere relationalism thus relies on a distinction between a state of awareness that lacks content and a (causally downstream) state of awareness that possesses content, namely, the state one is in when one judges and believes certain things about one's environment on the basis of perception.

The critical question is what it can be for the environment to seem a certain way to a subject without her being in a mental state with content. As I have argued, one cannot be sensorily aware of a particular without employing perceptual capacities by means of which one discriminates and singles out the particular. But employing perceptual capacities by means of which one discriminates and singles out the particular just is to be in a mental state with representational content.[40]

Accepting this is compatible with accepting that any given scene can be perceived in many different ways and any given perception can be articulated in many different ways. Even if there are many ways that the world can be perceived as being, there is only one way the world is. Recall again Norway's jagged coastline: it has exactly one objective length, but we attribute very different numeric lengths to it depending on how detailed our measurements are. Although the results of these measurements are different, they are not incompatible as long as one factors in the differences in the methods of measurement deployed. The important point is that the fact that we can arrive at different measurements is not to deny that there is only one way the coast of Norway is. Travis ties his indeterminacy objection to issues about accuracy conditions. So I will here connect the two issues as well: even though the results of our measurements are different, any given measurement either succeeds in accurately

---

[40] One might object that this notion of content simply amounts to what Travis calls autorepresentation, which he understands in the following way: "To take things to be thus and so just *is* to represent them to oneself as that way. Such representing is *all* in the attitude...one might find such [auto]representation in embedded propositions, 'mock speech'." He contrasts auto- with allorepresentation, which "represents such-and-such as *so*." Travis argues that, in contrast to autorepresentation, allorepresentation is "*committed* representation" (2004: 60f.). Allorepresentation is the notion of representation that Travis targets with his criticism. The notion of content in play amounts to allorepresentation given that how one's environment seems to one does not simply amount to taking it to be some way, but, moreover, to being committed to it being that way. While autorepresentation may be the kind of representation at play in "mock speech," I do not take it to be a kind of representation that plays any role in perception. Travis admits as much (p. 65). So, we can safely assume that what is at stake is whether experience involves what Travis calls allorepresentation, not what he calls autorepresentation.

representing the coastline or fails to do so. Although the measurements are different, that does not imply that only one of them is accurate. It implies only that the accuracy of the measurement must be assessed relative to the chosen method of measurement. Indeed, the measurements can all be accurate relative to the method of measurement chosen.

Now, one could argue that if one scene can be represented in many different ways, then it must be the case that some of these representations are more accurate than others. In response, suppose that we make ten distinct measurements of the coast of Norway. Each number can be an accurate representation of the length of Norway's coast relative to the method of measurement chosen.

To take an example closer to home: a scene can be photographed once with a standard lens and once with a wide-angle lens. Although the representations of the scene will differ, this does not imply that at least one of the representations must be inaccurate. Again, just because there is only one way the scene in fact is, it does not follow that there can be only one accurate representation of the scene. Our perception is accurate only if we represent the way our environment is, but any given environment can be represented in many different ways. So even if we recognize the non-comparative use of appearance words and thus reject the second premise of the indeterminacy argument, we can nonetheless accept that there are many different ways to accurately represent the same scene. So the representationalist can accept one of the motivations driving the indeterminacy objection.

Not only are there many different ways to accurately represent the same scene, we can accept that there is indeterminacy in the way we represent our environment in perception. Consider the case in which we perceive two lines and notice that they are different in length. One line being longer than the other implies that it is some specific length longer. This, however, does not imply that any representation of a difference in length is a representation of some specific difference in length. We can simply represent the two lines as being different in length. In the same way, we can perceive the rim of a cup as round despite the fact that it is not perfectly round. Perception is often a rough guide to the world.[41]

The way the environment seems to a perceiver may change from moment to moment, even as her gaze remains steady. Say she is looking at a pig. She can direct her attention at its shape, its color, the texture of its skin, or any combination of these features. As her attention shifts, the phenomenal character of her perceptual state will change. One or more propositions can be associated with every one of these phenomenal states and, thus, with every one of these ways that the environment may seem to her. All these propositions are equally legitimate. Nevertheless, at any given moment, the environment will non-comparatively seem to her to be one specific way.

[41] See Stazicker 2016 for an argument against the traditional assumption that we represent maximally determinate properties, rather than just determinable properties.

Travis considers, but immediately dismisses, the idea that perceptual content is looks-indexed on a non-comparative use of "looks." He does so on the grounds that a non-comparative use presupposes a comparative use of "looks"—though, again, he does not use Chisholm's labels to distinguish between the different uses (2004: 81). In response, we can say that, no doubt, perceptual reports involve concepts the meaning of which abstract from the richness of what is perceived. Typically we abstract from the particular shape of a perceived object by using concepts such as "round" or "square" to express what shape the object seems to us to have. But although the content of perceptual reports may be coarse-grained in this way, there is no reason to think that the content of the relevant perception is similarly coarse-grained. If perceptual content is understood as corresponding to how the environment seems to us, then the content can be understood to be as fine-grained as our phenomenal character.

I argued that if "looks" is understood non-comparatively, then the way things look fixes the content of a perceptual state. The indeterminacy objection depends on a comparative or an epistemic understanding of appearance words. If appearance words are understood non-comparatively, then the second premise of the indeterminacy argument is false and the indeterminacy objection can be rejected. So I showed that even if we accept Travis's argument that neither epistemic nor comparative looks fix perceptual content, we can still reject the indeterminacy objection. Moreover, if we reject Travis's argument that looks—in the comparative or epistemic sense—fixes the content of a perceptual state, then the scope of my argument for the content thesis can be understood as pertaining not only to the way the environment seems non-comparatively, but also to the way it seems comparatively and epistemically.

6. Coda

I have defended the view that perceptual states have content by critically discussing what I identified as the five main austere relationalist objections against the content thesis. While austere relationalists have good reasons to criticize many views that rely on the content thesis, I aim to have shown that any reason there is to argue that perception is constitutively relational can be accommodated by understanding perceptual content to be relational content. Thus, I argued that perception is constitutively both relational and representational. More specifically, I argued that if perceptual content is understood to be relational, then we can take on board the phenomenological, epistemological, and semantic grounding insights of austere relationalists without rejecting the content thesis.

I conclude that we can accept the austere relationalist thesis that perception puts us in direct contact with particulars in our environment, while acknowledging that perception is representational. Indeed, if we recognize the role that perceptual capacities play in bringing about our perceptual states, we must accept that perception is representational. Moreover, contrary to what austere relationalists would have us believe, we are always constrained by our perceptual tools: there is always a way in which we perceive the world to be. Austere relationalism wants us to have a kind of immediate contact with the world that simply is not available to us. Denying that we are always in some respect constrained by our perceptual tools is not only epistemically arrogant: it undermines the role that perception plays in our cognitive lives.

The mind is constitutively a matter of employing mental capacities in virtue of which we represent our environment. These mental capacities can take the form of concepts or low-level discriminatory capacities. Understanding the mind in this way allows for a clear way of understanding the content of mental states, and moreover allows for a clear way of understanding how mental states are grounded in the physical.

PART III

Consciousness

Chapter 6

Perceptual Consciousness as a Mental Activity

When a subject sees an object, it is natural to say that it seems to her that the object is present because she is perceptually related to that very object. Consider again Percy who is perceptually related to a white cup. When Percy sees a white cup, he is perceptually conscious of a white cup because he is perceptually related to that very white cup. By definition, when a subject is hallucinating, she is not perceptually related to the external, mind-independent object that it seems to her is present. Consider again Hallie who suffers a non-veridical hallucination as of a white cup at a location where there is no such cup. Since Hallie is not perceptually related to a white cup, the fact that it seems to her that a white cup is present cannot be explained in virtue of a perceptual relation to an external, mind-independent object and the properties it instantiates. So how should we explain the phenomenal character of hallucinations? We can call this the hallucination question. Many differences between views of perceptual experience can be traced back to how this question is answered.

There are two standard ways of answering the hallucination question. One standard response is to argue that a hallucinating subject stands in a sensory awareness relation to a peculiar entity. This peculiar entity has been understood in a multitude of ways. It has been understood to be an abstract entity, such as a property-cluster, an (uninstantiated) universal, a phenomenal property, a proposition, or an intentional object. It has also been understood to be a strange particular, such as a sense-datum, a quale, or a Meinongian object.[1] As Dretske formulates the idea: "hallucinations are experiences in

---

[1] For views according to which hallucinating subjects stand in awareness or acquaintance relations to property-clusters, see Johnston 2004; for (uninstantiated) universals, see Dretske 1995, Byrne 2001, Tye 2002; for phenomenal properties, see Chalmers 2006a, Block 2007; for propositions, see Russell 1913; for intentional objects, see Harman 1990, Lycan 1996; for sense-data, see Robinson 1994; for qualia, see Levine 1983, Chalmers 1996, Block 2003, McLaughlin 2007; for Meinongian objects, see Parsons 1980. It is important to note that one could argue that hallucinating subjects represent intentional objects without arguing that perceivers stand in awareness or acquaintance relations to such objects. For a defense of such a view, see Crane 1998. There are ways of understanding qualia on which they are simply identified with phenomenal character, such that any phenomenological state necessarily instantiates qualia. This understanding of qualia implies that experiences trivially instantiate qualia. But if that is all that is meant with qualia, then introducing qualia just amounts to a reformulation of the fact that experiences are phenomenal states. For a discussion of this set of issues, see Stoljar 2004. Ned Block analyzes qualia in terms of neural states. So for Block the final level of analysis is not qualia but rather neural states. In that sense his

which one is aware of properties. . . . Can we really be aware of (uninstantiated) universals? Yes, we can, and, yes, we sometimes are" (2000: 163). By "peculiar entity" I mean any object that is not an external, physical, mind-independent particular.[2] An external, mind-independent particular could be an object, such as a cat, a cup, or a carrot; an event, such as a cat eating a carrot out of a cup; or a property-instance, such as the specific color instantiated by a particular cat. Let's call a view according to which a hallucinating subject stands in a sensory awareness relation to an entity that is not a material, mind-independent object or property-instance, a *peculiar entity view*. Peculiar entity views have it that since Hallie is seemingly sensorily aware of something, she must stand in a sensory awareness relation to something that accounts for the phenomenal character of her hallucinatory state. Since she is not standing in a sensory awareness relation to the material, mind-independent particular that seems to her to be present, she must be standing in a sensory awareness relation to something else. The idea that perceptual consciousness is constituted by entities or particulars of which the experiencing subject is sensorily aware is akin to the phenomenal principle, that is, the principle that if it sensibly seems to a subject that there is something that possesses a particular sensible quality, then there is something of which the subject is aware and which does possess that sensible quality (Robinson 1994: 32). The phenomenal principle was explicitly endorsed by sense-datum theorists. Price, for example, stated that "When I say 'this table appears brown to me' it is quite plain that I am acquainted with an actual instance of brownness" (Price 1932: 63; see also Broad 1923: 240). By arguing that subjects suffering a hallucination or illusion are aware of peculiar entities, peculiar entity views uphold the phenomenal principle.[3]

A second way of responding to the hallucination question is to stipulate that a hallucination could be subjectively indistinguishable from a perception, but to leave unexplained what accounts for the phenomenal character of hallucination beyond this

---

view is more powerful than views on which the final level of analysis is qualia. It should be noted that it has been argued that if inverted spectrum scenarios are empirically possible, then introducing qualia is necessary, where qualia are understood as more substantive than simply what can be identified with phenomenal character (Shoemaker 1982). However, as Egan (2006) has argued convincingly, it can be ruled out on conceptual grounds that inverted spectrum scenarios are empirically possible. Finally, one can argue that the content of a hallucination is a Russellian proposition without arguing that hallucinating subjects stand in awareness or acquaintance relations to these propositions or their constituents. Byrne (2001) and Pautz (2007) defend versions of such a view. Arguably, any view that aims to explain phenomenal character in virtue of properties or objects that constitute perceptual content is committed to holding that the experiencing subject stands in an awareness or acquaintance relation to these properties or objects. For a defense of this thesis, see Crane 2006: 128ff. It would lead too far afield to discuss here to what extent such views are peculiar entity views. I will reserve this for another occasion. For the purposes of this chapter, any view that denies that subjects stand in awareness or acquaintance relations to peculiar entities is not my target. I will address such views only to the extent that they face the same problems as peculiar entity views.

[2] Some early sense-datum theorists had it that sense-data are external and mind-independent particulars. But given that they understood sense-data as non-physical particulars, sense-data qualify as peculiar entities even on such understandings.

[3] See Kriegel 2011 for an argument that any attempt to account for hallucination in terms of intentional relations to properties will ultimately draw a "veil of abstracta over the concrete world."

stipulated indistinguishability (e.g. Snowdon 1981, Campbell 2002, Martin 2002a).[4] We can call such a view *negativism* about hallucinations. Negativist views avoid introducing peculiar entities of which hallucinating subjects are aware, but at the cost of leaving unexplained just what accounts for the phenomenal character of hallucinations.[5] Such views are motivated by analyzing perceptual consciousness in terms of sensory awareness relations to the mind-independent particulars to which we are perceptually related in perception. Since we are not perceptually related to a mind-independent particular in hallucination—or at least not the one of which we seem to be sensorily aware—this analysis of the phenomenal character of perceptual states does not carry over to an analysis of the phenomenal character of hallucinatory states.

So while peculiar entity views analyze the phenomenal character of a hallucination in terms of (sensory awareness relations to) peculiar entities, negativists stipulate that a hallucination could be subjectively indistinguishable from a perception, but leave unexplained what accounts for the phenomenal character of hallucination. What the views have in common is that they analyze perceptual consciousness in terms of (sensory awareness relations to) some entity, be it a mind-independent, external particular or a peculiar entity. So the orthodoxy that perceptual consciousness is constituted by the entities or particulars of which we are sensorily aware is a commitment of otherwise radically different views. Indeed, the idea is endorsed by views that disagree on almost everything else. Naïve realists, qualia theorists, sense-data theorists, intentionalists, and most representationalists all endorse this orthodoxy.

There are deep problems with this orthodoxy. Therefore, I propose that we make a fresh start in our thinking about perceptual consciousness. I will present a radically different account of perceptual consciousness: I will argue that perceptual consciousness is constituted by a mental activity, namely, the mental activity of employing perceptual capacities. This is a radical thesis, but I hope to make it plausible. The thesis that perceptual consciousness is constituted by a mental activity marks a profound break from the orthodoxy that perceptual consciousness is to be analyzed in terms of (sensory awareness relations to) peculiar entities. I will show how this new way of understanding perceptual consciousness is not only more in tune with the empirical

---

[4] Of course, it need not be a positive part of the view that the possible subjective indistinguishability of a hallucination and a perception is not something that requires explanation. What characterizes negativism is the fact that the view does not explain possible subjective indistinguishability. Negativist views could fail to explain this due to neglect or because the defender of the view holds that possible subjective indistinguishability does not require explanation.

Martin (2002a) argues that a hallucination that is subjectively indistinguishable from a perception instantiates an indistinguishability property, in virtue of which it is subjectively indistinguishable from the perception. More specifically, he argues that our epistemic situation with regard to our experience is the same regardless of whether we are perceiving or hallucinating. Arguably, this does not constitute an explanation of what accounts for the phenomenal character of hallucination.

It should be noted that Campbell (2002), among others, denies that a hallucination has the same phenomenal character as a perception in the metaphysical sense. However, even he concedes that a hallucination could be subjectively indistinguishable from a perception in the epistemic sense, given that the experiencing subject may not be able to detect the metaphysical difference between her experiences.

[5] See Millar 2007 for a discussion of the epistemological considerations that motivate disjunctivism.

sciences, but is moreover able to avoid a whole range of problems that bedevil the orthodox philosophical views of perceptual consciousness. While the view I will develop generalizes to non-perceptual forms of consciousness, I will, so as to keep the discussion tractable, focus on the case of perceptual consciousness.

So far I have distinguished between two ways of answering the hallucination question: peculiar entity views and negativism. Most peculiar entity views are common factor views and most negativist views are versions of disjunctivism. *Disjunctivists* and *naïve realists* characterize hallucinations in terms of a deficiency of an accurate perception and argue that perceptions and hallucinations do not share a common element.[6] By contrast, *common factor views* have it that perceptions and hallucinations can have the same phenomenal character that is grounded in a common element. While most peculiar entity views are common factor views and most negativist views are versions of disjunctivism, the fault line between disjunctivism and common factor views does not coincide with the fault line between negativism and peculiar entity views. There are views on which hallucinations—but not perceptions—are a matter of being related to a peculiar entity (e.g. Johnston 2004). So there are peculiar entity views on which hallucinations and perceptions do not share a common element. However, with the aim of giving a common account of both perception and hallucination, most peculiar entity views hold that a perceiving subject is related to the very same (or the very same kind of) peculiar entity that she would be related to, were she hallucinating. Thus, most peculiar entity views are common factor views. Moreover, with the aim of analyzing perceptual consciousness in terms of a sensory awareness relation to something other than the material, mind-independent particulars present in perception, most common factor views analyze the common factor in terms of (a sensory awareness relation to) a peculiar entity. So, most common factor views are peculiar entity views.

The distinctions between negativist and peculiar entity views, as well as disjunctivism and common factor views, allow us to formulate the aim of this chapter more precisely: I will develop a common factor view that does not amount to a peculiar entity view and I will argue that this common factor grounds perceptual consciousness. I avoid analyzing the common factor in terms of (a sensory awareness relation to) a peculiar entity by showing that hallucinations exhibit a deficiency that can only be explained with reference to accurate perceptions. Thus, I will present a positive account of the phenomenal character of hallucinations without arguing that hallucinating subjects stand in a sensory awareness relation to a peculiar entity—thereby avoiding both the negativist and peculiar entity approaches to answering the hallucination question.

In Section 1, I will critically discuss orthodox views of perceptual consciousness. In Section 2, I will develop the view that perceptual consciousness is constituted by

---

[6] Naïve realism is a new-fangled version of disjunctivism. By contrast to most traditional disjunctivists, naïve realists deny not only that hallucinations have content, but are typically also skeptical that perceptions have content. Campbell (2002), Travis (2004), and Brewer (2006) argue explicitly that perceptions do not have content. For ease of presentation, I will speak only of disjunctivism, but everything I say about disjunctivism generalizes to naïve realism.

a mental activity. I call this view *mental activism*.[7] In Section 3, I will show that mental activism is a version of Fregean representationalism. Finally, in Section 4, I will show that mental activism does not require that a subject must have a history of employing perceptual capacities successfully in perception to employ a capacity in hallucination or illusion.

Throughout, I will operate with the ideal case of a so-called perfect hallucination, that is, a hallucination that has the same phenomenal character as a perception. Similarly, I focus on illusions that have the same phenomenal character as a perception. It is not relevant for my purposes whether a hallucination or an illusion could in fact have the same phenomenal character as a perception. I will assume for the sake of argument that such hallucinations and illusions exist and will explain how to understand their phenomenal character given this assumption. I focus on the case of such perfect hallucinations and illusions since they are the hardest cases to explain. The analysis of the phenomenal character of perfect hallucinations and illusions generalizes to an analysis of the phenomenal character of hallucinations and illusions that the experiencing subject would not mistake for a perception. So while I focus on the case of perfect hallucinations and illusions, the view of perceptual consciousness I develop holds for all forms of perception, illusion, and hallucination.

1. Disjunctivism and the Common Factor View

Disjunctivists take as their starting point the perceptual relation between subject and object in the case of an accurate perception and argue that perception is fundamentally an acquaintance or a sensory awareness relation to an external, mind-independent particular, such that the particular constitutes the phenomenal character of the subject's perceptual state. So when a subject S perceives a particular α, she stands in a perceptual relation R to that α, such that her perception has the form $RS\alpha$. Since a hallucinating subject is not perceptually related to the particular to which it seems to her she is related, a hallucination could not possibly share the $RS\alpha$-form of perception. So disjunctivists conceive of the basic structure of perception in a way that cannot possibly accommodate hallucination. As a result, they argue that there is no common element between hallucinations and perceptions.

Naïve realists build on disjunctivism and argue that perceptual consciousness is best analyzed in terms of sensory awareness relations to the very mind-independent objects, property-instances, and events to which we are perceptually related.[8] Given that in hallucination we are not perceptually related to mind-independent particulars, this analysis of perceptual consciousness cannot be applied to hallucinations. Thus, like disjunctivists, naïve realists argue that there is no common element between hallucinations and perceptions.

---

[7] This chapter builds on and develops the ontological minimalist view in Schellenberg 2011b.
[8] For a detailed discussion of naïve realism or more generally austere relationalism, see Chapter 5.

In contrast to disjunctivism, common factor views argue that a perception and a hallucination can have a metaphysically substantial common element that grounds their phenomenal character. They take this common element as their starting point, conceiving of the basic structure of perception as this common element plus an additional element that secures the relation to the particulars perceived. Typically, this additional element is understood to be a causal relation between the perceiver and the perceived particular. The basic structure of hallucination is simply the common element, without the additional element.

There are many different versions of this view. Indeed, there are at least as many different versions as there are different ways of conceiving of the common element, multiplied by the different possible ways of understanding the additional element that distinguishes perceptions from hallucinations. Adverbialists conceive of the common element as being appeared to F-ly (Chisholm 1957). Adverbialism is a view according to which hallucinations and perceptions share a common element, without that common element constituting a peculiar entity. Sense-datum theorists conceive of the common element as a sense-datum, that is, a concrete particular that has just the properties of which the experiencing subject is sensorily aware (Price 1932, Moore 1953, Jackson 1977, Robinson 1994). Qualia theorists argue that the common element is a quale (Block 1990, Chalmers 1996). Another version of the common factor view is the property-cluster view. According to the property-cluster view, an experiencing subject is related to a property-cluster. This is the case regardless of whether she is perceiving, hallucinating, or suffering an illusion. The property-cluster (or the awareness relation to it) constitutes the phenomenal character of the subject's mental state. There are at least three versions of this view. On what we can call a *pure property-cluster view*, experience does not have content. It is simply a matter of being related to a property-cluster. A more orthodox alternative is the view that an experiencing subject is related to a Russellian proposition that is constituted by a property-cluster and possibly one or more objects. We can call this the *content property-cluster view*. There are two versions of this view. On the standard version, a perception and a hallucination that have the same phenomenal character are analyzed in terms of relations to the very same (or the very same kind of) Russellian proposition. On a gappy version of the view, the content of a hallucination is gappy in the object-place because an object is missing, while the gap is filled by an object in the case of a perception.[9] I will argue that the common element is constituted by the perceptual capacities employed by means of which we discriminate and single out particulars in our environment. As I argued in Part II, employing such perceptual capacities constitutes the representational content of perceptual experience.

---

[9] For the pure property-cluster view, see Johnston 2004; for the content property-cluster view, see Tye 2000, Byrne 2001, and Pautz 2007 among others; for the gappy content property-cluster view, see Bach 2007 and Tye 2007. For a defense of a gappy content view that is not a version of the property-cluster view, see Chapter 4; see also Schellenberg 2006 and 2010.

Adverbialism, sense-datum views, and qualia views have all been criticized widely (e.g. Strawson 1979, Smith 2002, Johnston 2004, Crane 2006) and I have nothing substantial to add to those criticisms. I will focus on what is currently the most orthodox view of perceptual consciousness, namely, the view that perceptual consciousness is constituted by (a sensory awareness relation to) properties or a property-cluster.[10] In doing so, I will critically discuss the orthodox version of the peculiar entity view. I will first address the problematic commitments of the pure property-cluster view and will then discuss the extent to which the problems facing this view arise for content property-cluster views.

Since the pure property-cluster view is most famously associated with Johnston, it will be helpful to first make a few clarifying remarks about his account. Johnston's view is summed up in the following passage:

When we see we are aware of instantiations of sensible profiles. When we hallucinate we are aware merely of the structured qualitative parts of such sensible profiles. Any case of hallucination is thus a case of "direct" visual awareness of less than one would be "directly" aware of in the corresponding case of seeing.   (2004: 137)

As Johnston argues, when we hallucinate, we are aware of an uninstantiated property-cluster, that is, a structured qualitative part of a sensible profile. When we perceive, we are aware of a property-cluster instantiated by an external, mind-independent object, that is, an instantiated sensible profile. Instantiations of sensible profiles and structured qualitative parts of sensible profiles are distinct. Given that they are distinct, they do not amount to a common factor. If they do not amount to a common factor, then Johnston's view is a version of disjunctivism.[11]

For the sake of presentation, I will work with an idealized version of a property-cluster view on which an experiencing subject is related to the very same property-cluster regardless of whether she is hallucinating or perceiving. Consider a subject S who has a non-veridical hallucination as of a material, mind-independent object o that seems to be instantiating property P at location L. Since there is no object o at location L, there is no object that could be instantiating P. Therefore, what the subject is aware of cannot be the material, mind-independent object o, nor can it be the properties instantiated by a material, mind-independent object. The property-cluster view has it that hallucinating subjects stand in a sensory awareness relation to properties that are not instantiated where the subject experiences them to be instantiated. Since these properties are not instantiated where they are experienced to be, they are conceived of as universals.

Such a view faces a range of problematic commitments. The view is phenomenologically controversial since universals are abstract entities. Abstract entities are

---

[10] Versions of this view have been endorsed by Dretske (1995), Tye (2000), Byrne (2001), Chalmers (2004, 2006a), Johnston (2004), Siegel (2006, 2011), Hill (2006, 2009), Pautz (2007), Mendelovici (2013), and Stazicker (2016), among others.

[11] For a critical discussion of Johnston's view, see also Pautz 2007.

neither spatially nor temporally extended, they are not spatio-temporally located, and are not causally efficacious. I will show how each of these three properties of abstract entities causes problems for the thesis that we could be sensorily aware of abstract entities. Arguably, a minimal condition of something that one can be sensorily aware of is that it is either spatially or temporally extended. If that is right, then the property-cluster thesis that in hallucination we are sensorily aware of abstract entities turns out to be implausible. To be clear, I am not here arguing that there is a problem with the idea that we are cognitively aware of abstract entities.[12] I can, for example, be cognitively aware of the concept of world peace. When I am cognitively aware of WORLD PEACE, I am not cognitively aware of something that is either spatially or temporally extended. But while it is unproblematic to say that we are cognitively aware of something that is not spatially or temporally extended, it is not clear what it would be to be *sensorily* aware of something that is neither spatially nor temporally extended. A second way to cast doubt on the possibility of sensory awareness of abstract entities is to argue that one can only be sensorily aware of something that is spatio-temporally located, where being located goes beyond being merely extended. Universals are not spatio-temporally located. So one cannot be sensorily aware of universals. Yet a third way to question the possibility of sensory awareness of abstract entities is by arguing that one can be sensorily aware only of something that is causally efficacious: universals are not causally efficacious and so one cannot be sensorily aware of universals. For our present purposes, we need only focus on the fact that abstract entities are neither spatially nor temporally extended, since that suffices to undermine the idea that we are sensorily aware of universals. I will argue that when one experiences a white cup, one is aware of an instance of whiteness, not an abstract entity.[13]

There are several possible ways for the property-cluster theorist to respond to the criticism that her view is phenomenologically controversial. She might lean on the distinction between sensory and cognitive awareness to argue that in hallucination we are cognitively aware of properties, while in perception we are sensorily aware of the mind-independent property-instances to which we are perceptually related. While this might be a way to circumvent the first phenomenological problem, it brings out a second phenomenological problem. Being cognitively aware of α is phenomenally distinct from being sensorily aware of α; moreover, a property is distinct from a property-instance. So if one holds that in hallucination we are cognitively aware of a property, while in perception we are sensorily aware of a mind-independent property-instance, it is not clear how one could explain why a perception and a hallucination have the same phenomenal character. Indeed, any such account would be committed to a disjunctivist view of phenomenal character.

The property-cluster theorist could circumvent this second phenomenological problem by arguing that regardless of whether the subject is perceiving or hallucinating,

---

[12] For example, see Chudnoff 2012 for a defense of the view that a kind of conscious cognitive awareness, namely mathematical intuitions, makes subjects aware of abstract objects.

[13] For a classic elaboration of this worry, see Williams 1953.

she is cognitively aware (rather than sensorily aware) of abstract entities. This way of dealing with the problem faces several worries. One worry is how such a view can account for the specific phenomenal character of perceptual states, in virtue of which they phenomenally differ from other, non-perceptual mental states in which we are cognitively aware of abstract entities. A second worry is that perceptual experience is now assimilated to thought. If perceptual experience is assimilated to thought, it is not clear what accounts for the cognitive and epistemological roles that perception plays, such as its role in grounding demonstrative reference, fixing the reference of singular terms, yielding perceptual knowledge of particulars, and justifying beliefs about particulars. If perception does not provide us with direct sensory contact with particulars in our environment it is not clear how it can fulfill these roles. A third worry is that while non-rational animals can perceive, arguably they cannot be cognitively aware of abstract entities. So if perception is understood in terms of cognitive awareness of abstract entities, then it is an open question how non-rational animals can be sensorily aware of their environment.

This is not the end of the road for the property-cluster theorist. There are several possible paths for her to take at this point in the dialectic, but all paths will involve positing that hallucinating subjects are either cognitively or sensorily aware of abstract entities. Arguably, this controversial commitment is reason enough to be wary and seek alternative options.

The property-cluster view not only entails phenomenologically problematic commitments, but also metaphysically problematic commitments. To show why, let's assume for a moment an Aristotelian view of types, that is, a view that is committed to the principle that the existence of a type depends on its tokens, where these tokens depend in turn on concrete entities of the physical world. We can call this the *Aristotelian principle*. This principle implies that any type must be tokened somewhere and that it must be possible to analyze any token in terms of concrete entities of the physical world. Applied to properties, the Aristotelian principle implies that any property must be instantiated somewhere in the physical world.

A property-cluster theorist who accepts the Aristotelian principle will have to constrain possible illusions to illusions of properties that are instantiated somewhere in the actual world. But by doing so her view faces a whole range of counterexamples. It is easy to conceive of illusions of uninstantiated properties, that is, properties that are not instantiated anywhere. Examples are illusions of Hume's missing shade of blue and illusions of supersaturated red. Not only are such illusions conceivable, it is possible to induce them.[14]

The property-cluster theorist could account for illusions of uninstantiated properties by rejecting the Aristotelian principle and by arguing that hallucinating subjects are

---

[14] See Ffytche and Howard 1999 and Ffytche 2008. See Manzotti 2011 for an argument that such illusions are actually a kind of perception.

at least sometimes related to uninstantiated universals.[15] However, by doing so, she commits herself to a controversial metaphysics of types. Accepting the existence of uninstantiated universals requires a Platonic 'two realms'-view on which there is more to reality than what can be analyzed in terms of what exists in the concrete physical world. After all, uninstantiated universals cannot be analyzed in terms of their instances in the concrete physical world. The rival Aristotelian view that requires universals to be analyzable in terms of concrete physical entities can make do without such a Platonic heaven. By understanding abstract entities such as universals in terms of their instances, the Aristotelian view can accept the existence of abstract entities, while denying that subjects are ever sensorily aware of anything other than the instances of these abstract entities.[16]

The property-cluster theorist could aim to circumvent the metaphysical problem by arguing that supersaturated red, for example, actually is instantiated, namely, by the mental state of a subject in the grips of an illusion as of supersaturated red.[17] In response, while this would avoid the metaphysical problems associated with accepting the existence of uninstantiated universals, it would amount to one of the following two undesirable views. On the first view, the phenomenal character of the illusion is constituted by the (phenomenal) properties of which the mental state is stipulated to be constituted. But such an approach fails to provide a non-circular explanation of what accounts for the phenomenal character of the hallucination, since the phenomenal character is now explained in terms of the properties of the mental state, the nature of which was the explanandum.[18] Such an approach simply reformulates the fact that experiences are phenomenal states. On the second view, phenomenal character is explained in terms of awareness or acquaintance relations to concrete, mind-dependent entities, such as phenomenal properties, sense-data, qualia, or Meinongian objects.

---

[15] When I speak of an uninstantiated universal, I mean—following common use—a universal that is not instantiated anywhere. It is important to distinguish an uninstantiated universal from a universal that is instantiated somewhere, but not instantiated where a subject who suffers an illusion or hallucination experiences it to be instantiated.

[16] For a critical discussion of uninstantiated universals, see Armstrong 1989. Armstrong restricts the Aristotelian principle to so-called sparse properties. By contrast, I aim to vindicate the Aristotelian principle for all perceivable properties. One might object that the metaphysical problem articulated over-generalizes in that it would work just as well against Russellian accounts of the content of false beliefs. However, the metaphysical problem articulated is specific to accounts of perceptual consciousness that analyze perceptual consciousness in terms of awareness relations to (uninstantiated) abstract entities. If perceptual consciousness is analyzed in terms of awareness relations to (uninstantiated) abstract entities, then these (uninstantiated) abstract entities must exist such that we could stand in sensory awareness relations to them. The same is not true of beliefs as of abstract entities, since there is no reason why a belief as of o must be analyzed in terms of a sensory awareness relation to o. If, however, beliefs are analyzed in terms of awareness relations to (uninstantiated) abstract entities, then the phenomenological and metaphysical problems articulated would indeed arise for such an account of beliefs as well. As I will show in Section 2, any view that analyzes perceptual consciousness in terms of a sensory awareness relation to (uninstantiated) abstract entities can and should be avoided.

[17] Thanks to Adam Pautz for a helpful email exchange on this set of issues.

[18] It could be stipulated that these properties are in fact very different from the explanandum, but such a stipulation would be at best *ad hoc*.

This approach, however, is simply a version of the peculiar entity view and faces all the problems of that view, with the only difference to the property-cluster view being that the peculiar entities in question are not abstract entities, but rather concrete, mind-dependent entities.[19]

To what extent does the content property-cluster view inherit the phenomenological and metaphysical problems of the pure property-cluster view? Any content property-cluster view is committed to accepting the existence of uninstantiated universals to avoid restricting possible hallucinations to hallucinations of properties that are instantiated somewhere. Insofar as the view is committed to rejecting the Aristotelian principle and accepting a Platonic 'two realms'-view, it inherits the metaphysical problem of the pure property-cluster view.

Does the content property-cluster view inherit the phenomenological problems of the pure property-cluster view as well? The answer to this question depends on how one understands the relation between the experiencing subject and the content of her experience. Russell argued that subjects stand in acquaintance relations to the objects and properties that constitute propositions. He used the terms "acquaintance" and "awareness" synonymously (1913: 35), and indeed the standard reading of Russell has it that his acquaintance relation is a particular kind of awareness relation.[20] If we stand in awareness relations to the properties and objects that constitute the content of our experience, then the Russellian view inherits all the phenomenological problems of the pure property-cluster view. After all, the view is committed to the phenomenologically controversial thesis that hallucinating subjects are either sensorily or cognitively aware of abstract entities.[21] Byrne (2001) and Pautz (2007) argue that perceptual content is a Russellian proposition, but posit that experiencing subjects sensorily entertain the content of their experience rather than stand in acquaintance or awareness relations to the proposition or its constituents. We can, however, reject this distinction and argue that to sensorily entertain a proposition or its constituents just is to stand in an acquaintance or awareness relation to the proposition or its constituents. If that is right, then these views entail the phenomenologically controversial thesis that hallucinating subjects are either sensorily or cognitively aware of abstract entities. But for the sake of argument, let's assume that sensorily entertaining a proposition or its constituents would not amount to standing in an acquaintance or awareness relation to the proposition or its constituents. Given this assumption, such a view inherits only the metaphysical problem of the pure property-cluster view. For the reasons given above,

---

[19] See Strawson 1979, for a classic critical discussion of such views.

[20] For an interpretation of Russell's acquaintance relations along these lines, see Campbell 2009.

[21] For content property-cluster views that are committed to the thesis that subjects are either sensorily or cognitively aware of abstract entities, such as (uninstantiated) universals, propositions, or their constituents, see McGinn 1982, Harman 1990, Davies 1992, Lycan 1996, Dretske 2000, and Tye 2002. It is important to note that such views are not committed to the thesis that we are aware of abstract entities or any other peculiar entities *as such*, that is, the thesis that we are aware of abstract entities does not entail that we are aware that the entities are abstract.

I take the metaphysical problem to be sufficiently serious to merit rejecting any such view in favor of one that accommodates the Aristotelian principle.

2. Mental Activism

I propose that we do away with the old debates and approach the problem of consciousness in a radically different framework. The problems of peculiar entity views are avoided if hallucinating subjects are understood not as related to abstract entities or strange particulars, but rather as engaging in a mental activity. I will argue that perceptual consciousness is constituted by engaging in a mental activity, namely, the mental activity of employing perceptual capacities in a sensory mode, that is, modes such as seeing, hearing, touching, smelling, or tasting among others.[22] We can call this view *mental activism*. The argument for this view goes as follows.

The Argument for Mental Activism

I. If a subject S perceives a particular α, then S is employing a perceptual capacity C_α by means of which she discriminates and singles out α.

II. If S is employing C_α by means of which she discriminates and singles out α, then S's phenomenal character is constituted by employing C_α by means of which she discriminates and singles out α.

From I–II: If S perceives α, then S's phenomenal character is constituted by employing perceptual capacity C_α by means of which she discriminates and singles out α.

III. If S suffers an illusion or a hallucination as of α, then S's phenomenal character is constituted by employing C_α by means of which she purports to discriminate and single out α.

IV. If S perceives α or suffers an illusion or a hallucination as of α, then S's phenomenal character is constituted by employing C_α, by means of which she (putatively) discriminates and singles out α.

V. Employing a perceptual capacity is a mental activity.

VI. If S perceives α or suffers an illusion or a hallucination as of α, then S's phenomenal character is constituted by a mental activity.

From I–VI: Phenomenal character is constituted by a mental activity.

Mental activism builds on the thesis that when we perceive, we employ perceptual capacities by means of which we discriminate and single out particulars in our

---

[22] For a discussion of the notion of perceptual capacities, see Chapter 2. As before, here and throughout, 'constituted' is understood in the sense of at least partially constituted. This leaves open whether there might be other determinants. There are many sensory modes that are not perceptual sensory modes. For example, kinesthesia is a sensory mode, but arguably not a perceptual sensory mode. I am here focusing on those sensory modes that are relevant for perception, though my argument would have to be adapted only slightly to generalize to phenomenal states that are not perceptual states.

environment. As argued in Chapter 1, discriminating and singling out a particular from its surround is a minimal condition on perceiving the particular. After all, it is unclear what it would be to perceive a particular without at the very least discriminating and singling it out from its surround. Say that I perceive a red apple hanging from a tree. In perceiving the red apple, I will discriminate at least some of its properties from its surround. I may discriminate its red color from the green of the leaves around it. I may discriminate its round shape from the ovate shapes of the leaves around it. Or I may discriminate the smooth and shiny surface of the apple from the rougher, matte texture of the leaves. As noted in Chapter 1, such discriminatory activity allows for scene segmentation, border and edge detection, and region extraction. If there were no discriminatory activity, it is unclear how I could be perceptually aware of the apple. If this is right, then when we are perceptually related to a particular, we employ perceptual capacities by means of which we discriminate and single out the particular (Premise I).

The relevant particulars are external and mind-independent objects, events, property-instances, and instances of relations. The notion of property-instance in play is best illustrated with an example: when one sees two qualitatively identical white cups, the cups instantiate the same property, but the property-instances are distinct. When one suffers a hallucination as of a white cup, it seems to one that there is a white cup present, but since one is not perceptually related to the object that seems to be present, one is not perceptually related to any instance of whiteness.

I will argue that if a subject S's environment sensorily seems to contain F particulars (regardless of whether it in fact does), then S is in a phenomenal state that is consti-tuted by employing perceptual capacities that function to single out F particulars, where a phenomenal state is a perceptual state that is characterized by a specific phenomenal character. Consider Percy who perceives a white cup on a desk. He employs his capacity to discriminate white from other colors and to single out white in his environment. He may also employ his capacity to differentiate and single out cup-shapes from other shapes in his environment. He may even employ his capacity to differentiate and single out cups from, say, computers and lamps, or whatever other objects may be in his environment. By employing such capacities, he is dis-criminating and singling out actual particulars in his environment. Engaging in this discriminatory activity allows him to detect the edge of the cup and segment the scene in front of him.

Percy can see the very same scene while employing perceptual capacities that are more or less fine-grained. For example, he may initially not attend to the fact that the rim of the cup is chipped, and so he may not employ his perceptual capacity to discriminate the grayish color of the part that is chipped from the white color of the unchipped parts of the rim. But then he might employ his more fine-grained perceptual capacity to discriminate between the various shades of white and gray on the cup. By employing perceptual capacities that are more fine-grained, the phenomenal character of his perceptual state will be more fine-grained in turn, and he will be sensorily aware of more details in his environment. So even if everything in the environment remains exactly the same, the phenomenal character of Percy's perceptual state may differ insofar as he employs more or less fine-grained perceptual capacities to single out the particulars in his environment.

As these examples illustrate, discrimination and perceptual consciousness are in lockstep. Indeed, we can say that any change in perceptual consciousness is either due to a change in the perceptual capacities employed or due to a change in the sensory mode in which those perceptual capacities are employed. Being sensorily aware of particulars in our environment is to discriminate those particulars. More precisely we can say that phenomenal character is constituted by employing perceptual capacities in a sensory mode by means of which we discriminate and single out the particulars to which we are perceptually related (Premise II).

How can we extend this analysis of perceptual consciousness to hallucinations and illusions? As argued in Chapter 2, although perceptual capacities are determined by functional connections between perceivers and their environment, they can be employed even if one is misperceiving, hallucinating, or suffering a hallucination. If this is right, then we can say that when we hallucinate or suffer an illusion, we employ the very same capacities that we would employ in a perception with the same phenomenal character. Since in cases of illusion and hallucination, we are not perceptually related to at least one of the particulars that we purport to single out, we fail to single out at least one particular. We merely purport to single out that particular. As a consequence, at least one of the perceptual capacities is employed baselessly, in the sense that the target of discrimination and selection—an external, mind-independent particular—is absent. Analogously, if we employ a concept but fail to refer, the concept employed remains empty. If one employs a perceptual capacity in an environment in which no particular that the capacity functions to single out is present, then one fails to single out what the perceptual capacity purports to single out. As in the case of concepts, the failure occurs at the level of singling out a particular. There is no failure at the level of employing the capacity (Premise III).

Consider Hallie who suffers a hallucination as of a white cup on a desk. Like Percy, she employs the capacity to discriminate and single out white from other colors and she employs the capacity to differentiate and single out cup-shapes from, say, computer-shapes and lamp-shapes. Since she is hallucinating rather than perceiving, and so is not perceptually related to a particular white cup, she employs these capacities baselessly. Yet even though she fails to single out any particular white cup, she is in a phenomenal state that is as of a white cup, in virtue of employing perceptual capacities that purport to single out a white cup. As in the case of perception, employing these perceptual capacities constitutes her phenomenal character. So what perception, hallucination, and illusion have in common is that perceptual capacities are employed that constitute the phenomenal character of the relevant experiential states.

The difference between Hallie and Percy is simply that while Hallie fails to single out what she purports to single out, Percy succeeds. There is no reason to think that whether we succeed in singling out what our perceptual capacities function to single out has any repercussions for the phenomenal character of our experiential state. We can distinguish the employment of a capacity—what perceptions, hallucinations, and illusions have in common—from discriminating and singling out a particular—the matter on which perceptions, hallucinations, and illusions differ. It is the employment of the capacity that constitutes perceptual consciousness. The capacities employed account for the fact that in hallucinations or illusions we can purport to single out particulars: from a first-person perspective it can seem as if we were perceptually related to particulars in our environment. Whether a particular is singled out does not affect perceptual consciousness. Only if this is the case, can the view explain how a perception, a hallucination, and an illusion could have the same phenomenal character and thus avoid a disjunctivist view of phenomenal character. For only if it is not revealed in perceptual consciousness whether a perceptual capacity is employed baselessly can a perception and a hallucination have the same phenomenal character. Since perceptual consciousness is constituted by employing perceptual capacities, it is not revealed in perceptual consciousness whether the capacities are employed baselessly and so whether we are perceiving, hallucinating, or suffering an illusion (Premise IV). Furthermore, insofar as employing perceptual capacities is a kind of mental activity, this implies that phenomenal character is constituted by a mental activity (Premises V and VI).

If it is right that two experiential states in which all the same perceptual capacities are employed in the same sensory mode have, *ceteris paribus*, the same phenomenal character, then there is a metaphysically substantial common factor between perceptions, hallucinations, and illusions. That common factor is constituted by the perceptual capacities that the subject employs in a sensory mode. As I will show, the fact that there is such a common factor neither implies that we are aware of a common factor, nor does it imply that the good case is to be analyzed as a conjunction of a common factor and some additional element, such as a causal perceptual relation.

Before I show how mental activism amounts to a modestly externalist view about perceptual consciousness, I will address two potential misconceptions. First, we possess and make use of many discriminatory, selective capacities that are not phenomenally relevant—even when we perceive. I am not arguing that all capacities employed in perception have repercussions for our phenomenal states. The visual system makes use of many capacities on a subpersonal level. The thesis in play is rather that the nature of phenomenal states is best understood in terms of employing perceptual capacities, rather than in terms of awareness relations to strange particulars, such as sense-data or qualia, or abstract entities, such as properties or propositions. We can accept this thesis while acknowledging that there are many capacities—including discriminatory, selective capacities—the employment of which has no repercussions for our phenomenal lives.

Second, as argued in Chapter 3, it is crucial that employing discriminatory, selective capacities is not just a matter of differentiating particulars, but also of singling out particulars. Due to this, the phenomenal character of perceiving an instance of red is distinct from the phenomenal character of perceiving an instance of blue. Both cases may include differentiating red and blue, but in the former case an instance of red is singled out, while in the latter case an instance of blue is singled out. So the capacities employed are distinct and the phenomenal states differ.

2.1. *Mental activism and modest externalism about perceptual consciousness*

So far I have shown how mental activism posits a common element shared by perception, hallucination, and illusion at the level of *employing* perceptual capacities. Now I will argue that at the level of the *function* of perceptual capacities, there is a primacy of the employment of capacities in perception over their employment in hallucination or illusion. In virtue of this primacy, mental activism is an externalist view of perceptual consciousness.

I have argued that perceptual consciousness is constituted by employing perceptual capacities in a sensory mode. These capacities are, however, in turn analyzed in terms of the external, mind-independent particulars that they function to single out. Thus, perceptual consciousness is inherently related to the particulars that these perceptual capacities single out in the good case. So given the properties of perceptual capacities, perceptual consciousness is externally determined.

This approach allows us to recognize the austere relationalist insight that perceptual consciousness can and should be explained in terms of perceptual relations to the very external, mind-independent particulars of which a perceiver is aware. Austere relationalists argue that perceptual consciousness should be understood in terms of a sensory awareness or acquaintance relation to particulars in the perceiver's environment. This insight demystifies perceptual consciousness. However, by arguing for the radical thesis that all there is to perceptual consciousness is to be perceptually related to one's environment, austere relationalists leave mysterious how one could be in a phenomenal state if one is not perceiving, but rather suffering an illusion or a hallucination.[23]

By recognizing that a minimal condition on perception is that the perceiving subject discriminates particulars in her environment, we open the door to acknowledging that perceiving particulars is a matter of employing perceptual capacities that function to discriminate and single out particulars. By introducing such perceptual capacities, we can reject the radical austere relationalist thesis. By rejecting the radical austere relationalist thesis, the presented view constitutes a positive account of hallucinations on which a perception and a hallucination can have a common factor that constitutes their phenomenal character.

---

[23] For a defense of this radical austere relationalist thesis, see Campbell 2002, Brewer 2006, and Fish 2009. Martin (2004) argues for a more moderate version of austere relationalism.

So, against austere relationalists, I have argued that perceptions and hallucinations share a common element that constitutes their phenomenal character. However, with austere relationalists, I have argued that hallucinations exhibit a deficiency that can only be explained with reference to accurate perceptions. Hallucinations are derivative of perceptions insofar as the perceptual capacities employed in hallucinations can only be specified with reference to their possible role in perception. I have argued that to possess a perceptual capacity is to be in a position to discriminate and single out particulars that the capacity functions to single out in the good case, that is, when one is perceptually related to such a particular. Since perceptual capacities are analyzed in terms of perceptual relations to external, mind-independent particulars, mental activism amounts to a naturalized view of perceptual consciousness.[24]

2.2. Intensional perceptual consciousness and extensional sensory awareness

While standard views analyze perceptual consciousness in terms of awareness relations to peculiar entities, mental activism allows acknowledging that a hallucinating subject does not stand in a sensory awareness relation to anything despite being in a phenomenal state that purports to be of mind-independent particulars. To defend the conjunction of these two theses it will be helpful to uncover a key structural difference between perceptual consciousness and sensory awareness. For a subject to be sensorily aware of a particular implies that the subject stands in a sensory awareness relation to that very particular. So a subject cannot be sensorily aware of the particular α without standing in a sensory awareness relation to α. Indeed, being sensorily aware of α entails the existence of α. In this sense, sensory awareness is factive. Peculiar entity views analyze perceptual consciousness in terms of that of which we are sensorily aware. Such views take it that a hallucinating subject must be sensorily aware of some entity, where that entity constitutes the phenomenal character of the hallucination. Since she is not sensorily aware of any external, mind-independent particular that she seems to be seeing, such views conclude that she must be sensorily aware of a peculiar entity. Similarly, naïve realists analyze perceptual consciousness in terms of sensory awareness relations to particulars. The difference between the peculiar entity view and naïve realism is simply that the former has it that we are sensorily aware of peculiar entities, while the latter has it that we are sensorily aware of external, mind-independent particulars.

If we recognize that perceptual consciousness need not be analyzed in terms of that of which we are sensorily aware, we can circumvent any commitment to both naïve realism and the peculiar entity view. Consider a subject who is in a phenomenal state, that is, an experiential state that is characterized by perceptual consciousness. We can

---

[24] I am not arguing that externalism about perceptual consciousness is the only way of developing a naturalized account of perceptual consciousness—though there are good reasons to think that it is the best such approach. However, see Robinson 2004 for an argument that dualism, which often goes hand in hand with phenomenal internalism, is not in conflict with a naturalistic approach to the mind.

all agree that for a subject to be in a phenomenal perceptual state is for her to be in an experiential state that purports to be of something. So far there is no reason to say that she is sensorily aware of something. After all, for a phenomenal state to purport to be of α does not imply that the subject is aware of α (or of anything else). Indeed, being in a phenomenal state does not entail the existence of that which the mental state purports to be of. Moreover, being in a phenomenal state does not entail the existence of some other entity to which the subject stands in a sensory awareness relation. It follows that a subject can be in a phenomenal state without standing in a sensory awareness relation to any entity. So there is a structural difference between awareness of, on the one hand, and being in a phenomenal state, on the other. While awareness of is extensional, being in a phenomenal state is intensional.

Austere relationalist and peculiar entity views are structurally similar in that they both analyze perceptual consciousness extensionally.[25] By doing so both views conflate perceptual consciousness with sensory awareness. Some views go so far as to equate that which constitutes perceptual consciousness with that of which the experiencing subject is sensorily aware.[26] The idea that perceptual consciousness is extensional goes back to at least Moore, who assumed that all sensory awareness involves an object of awareness (Moore 1925: 54).

It is important to note that denying that a hallucinating subject stands in a sensory awareness relation to an object (or some other particular) is not to deny the linguistic fact that the expression "I hallucinate" takes a grammatical object. Even so, there is no need to take this grammatical object to correspond to an ontological existent of which the hallucinating subject is sensorily aware. The grammatical object merely marks what the hallucinating subjects takes to be present and what she would be sensorily aware of, were she perceiving an external, mind-independent object.

This structural difference between sensory awareness and perceptual consciousness is analogous to the distinction between relational and phenomenological particularity.[27] To recap, a mental state is characterized by relational particularity if and only if the experiencing subject is perceptually related to the particular perceived. A mental state exhibits phenomenological particularity only if it seems to the subject as if there is a particular present. Every experience that is subjectively indistinguishable from a perception exhibits phenomenological particularity. After all, it is unclear what it would be to have an experience that seems to be as of an external, mind-independent particular without it seeming to the subject that there is a particular present. Since the hallucinating subject is not perceptually related to the mind-independent particular that it seems to her is present, hallucinations are not characterized by relational particularity. More generally, we can say that if a subject has an experience that is

---

[25] It should be noted, however, that austere relationalists only analyze the phenomenal character of perception extensionally (not the phenomenal character of hallucination).

[26] See e.g. Harman 1990, Dretske 1995, Lycan 1996, Tye 2000, Noë 2004, Brewer 2006, Fish 2009, and Hill 2009.

[27] For the distinction between phenomenological and relational particularity, see Chapter 1.

intentionally directed at a particular, it will seem to her as if she is experiencing a particular—regardless of whether there is in fact such a particular present. If this is right, then any view on which a perception, illusion, or hallucination is intentionally directed at the experiencer's environment is committed to saying that such experiences exhibit phenomenological particularity.

Now, one may wonder how such an account can secure the identity of hallucinated objects across hallucinations. It cannot, but this is a desirable consequence of the view. A hallucinating subject may form false judgments on the basis of her hallucinations and believe that the unicorn it seemed to her she saw yesterday is the very same unicorn as the one that it seems to her she is seeing today. But the identity postulated here is within the scope of how things seem to the subject and thus based on mere phenomenological particularity. There is nothing in the world that corresponds to how things seem to the hallucinating subject, and thus there is nothing in the world that corresponds to this phenomenological particularity. In other words, the phenomenological particularity of her experience is not coupled with any relational particularity. Since the subject is not sensorily aware of any unicorn, no identity of the hallucinated objects can be secured.

Recognizing the distinction between sensory awareness and perceptual consciousness makes it possible to accept the Aristotelian principle without forfeiting a positive account of hallucinations. Recall that the Aristotelian principle has it that the existence of a type depends on its tokens, which depend in turn on concrete entities of the physical world. As I will argue in Section 4 of this chapter, any given perceptual capacity is necessarily employed successfully to single out a particular at some point by someone. The notion of perceptual capacities in play vindicates the Aristotelian principle since employing a perceptual capacity tokens the perceptual capacity and these tokens are in turn individuated by the particulars that the perceptual capacity functions to single out. Thus, any commitment to a Platonic 'two realms'-view can be avoided. So recognizing the distinction between sensory awareness and perceptual consciousness makes it possible to understand types in terms of their tokens, but nonetheless to give a positive account of the phenomenal character of hallucinations. The entities a subject stands in a sensory awareness relation to are always material, mind-independent objects, property-instances, or events. So according to mental activism, subjects are only ever sensorily aware of external, mind-independent particulars. Insofar as mental activism accounts for perceptual consciousness without having to appeal to awareness relations to peculiar entities, and insofar as the view vindicates the Aristotelian principle, mental activism is ontologically minimalist.

2.3. Blurriness and afterimages

The discussion so far has focused exclusively on perceptual consciousness (as) of particulars that are either located in the environment of the perceiving subject, or which merely seem to be so located, as in the case of an illusion or a hallucination. There are, however, aspects of perceptual consciousness, such as blurriness and afterimages, that do not pertain to (seemingly) material, mind-independent particulars.[28] For example, upon removing a pair of prescription glasses, one experiences blurriness. It will not, however, necessarily seem to one as if the environment is blurry (though, of course, that can happen). Similarly, if one presses against one's closed eyes, one can experience color patches in one's visual field—even after reopening one's eyes. As in the case of experiencing blurriness, it will not necessarily seem to one that the color patches are colors instantiated in one's material, mind-independent environment (though, again, that may happen). How can mental activism account for such aspects of perceptual consciousness that do not seem to the experiencing subject to pertain to the material, mind-independent environment?

A blurry experience of a white cup can be analyzed in terms of employing the perceptual capacity that functions to single out instances of blurriness (along with employing the perceptual capacity that functions to single out instances of white and the perceptual capacity that functions to single out the relevant shapes in one's environment, and so forth). The perceptual capacity that functions to single out blurriness is grounded in perceptions of instances of blurriness: when I look out of the window on a rainy day, the tree in front of my window is presented blurrily to me because of the raindrops on the window.[29] Now, seeing something as blurry is of course distinct from seeing something blurrily, but the very same perceptual capacity $C_{blurriness}$ can be understood to be employed in both experiences. The difference between seeing something as blurry and seeing something blurrily can be accounted for in virtue of what blurriness is attributed to. If one experiences an object as blurry, blurriness is attributed to that object. If one experiences blurrily, blurriness is attributed to one's experience. In this way, mental activism undermines the need to appeal to qualia, sensations, phenomenal properties, or any other peculiar entities to account for aspects of perceptual consciousness that do not pertain to particulars that are either located in the environment or that seem to be located in the environment of the experiencing subject.

3. Mental Activism is a Version of Representationalism

So far, I have argued that perceptual consciousness is constituted by a mental activity. Now I will show how this view is in fact a version of representationalism. Any view on which perceptual consciousness is said to be grounded in representational content needs to explain what it is about representational content such that it can ground perceptual consciousness. As I argued in Part II, employing perceptual capacities just is to be in a perceptual state with content. After all, perceptual capacities are repeatable and constitute a phenomenal state that either accurately or inaccurately accounts for how

---

[28] Visual blur is often posed as a problem for the transparency thesis. For more discussion on blur, see Tye 2000, Schroer 2002, Smith 2008, Speaks 2009, Allen 2013, and French 2014. For other challenges to the transparency thesis, see Kind 2003 and Howell 2016.

[29] For a discussion of how such properties can be analyzed as mind-independent, external properties, see Schellenberg 2008.

the environment really is. Insofar as employing perceptual capacities just is to be in a perceptual state with content, mental activism is a version of representationalism.

So mental activism is both a view of perceptual consciousness and a specific interpretation of the thesis that perceptual consciousness is grounded in representational content. On most representationalist views, it is either left mysterious how the representational content could in fact ground the perceptual consciousness of the representational state, or perceptual consciousness is ultimately explained in terms of awareness relations to peculiar entities. Recall, for example, how Dretske (2000)—the ultimate representationalist—argues that in hallucination we are aware of universals. As I have argued, this view is deeply problematic insofar as it is not clear what it would be to be sensorily aware of properties, given that properties are not spatio-temporally extended, not spatio-temporally located, and not causally efficacious. In contrast to such views, I am arguing that perceptual consciousness is grounded in representational content in that representational content is yielded by employing perceptual capacities which constitute perceptual consciousness.[30]

I have argued that both perceptual consciousness and perceptual content are constituted by employing perceptual capacities. One might object that since perceptual consciousness and perceptual content are different in kind, they cannot both be constituted by the same activity. In response, no doubt, perceptual consciousness and perceptual content are different in kind. The latter, but not the former, is propositionally structured. We can honor this even if we accept that both are constituted by employing perceptual capacities. After all, perceptual content is only partially constituted by employing perceptual capacities. It is constituted also by the particulars singled out. Similarly, perceptual consciousness is constituted not only by the perceptual capacities employed but also by the sensory mode in which those perceptual capacities are employed. But even if it were the case that both perceptual content and perceptual consciousness were constituted exclusively by employing perceptual capacities that would not be a problem. After all, A and B can be different in kind, even if A and B are each constituted by C; just as the truth of pvq differs from the truth of $\sim\sim p$, even if the truth of pvq and the truth of $\sim\sim p$ are each grounded in the truth of p. In short, there is no problem in endorsing the thesis that both perceptual consciousness and perceptual content are constituted by employing perceptual capacities.

4. Grounded and Ungrounded Perceptual Capacities

Now, how should we understand the relation between being perceptually related to external, mind-independent particulars, such as white cups, and employing perceptual

---

[30] Orlandi (2010, 2014) has argued that there is little empirical ground to suppose that sensory properties, such as color, are represented in perceptual experience. If true, this would not present any challenge to mental activism, whereas it would pose a *prima facie* challenge to views according to which in perception a subject represents properties.

capacities that merely purport—but ultimately fail—to single out any such particulars? To address this question, it will be necessary to distinguish three possible ways of analyzing perceptual capacities.

On a first way of analyzing perceptual capacities, a perceptual capacity need not in any way be grounded in perception. So on this version, hallucinations or illusions as of particulars are possible even if no one has perceived the relevant particulars (perhaps because the relevant particulars do not exist). We can call this version *ungrounded perceptual capacities*. On this version, one can employ a perceptual capacity in hallucination or illusion that has never been employed to successfully discriminate and single out an external, mind-independent particular of the kind that the capacity functions to single out.

On a second way of analyzing perceptual capacities, any perceptual capacity is grounded in perceptions of the very perceiver employing the perceptual capacity derivatively in hallucination or illusion. So it is necessary to have employed any given perceptual capacity in perception to be in a position to employ that same perceptual capacity derivatively in hallucination or illusion. We can call this version *radically grounded perceptual capacities*. This version of mental activism posits that the content of hallucination or illusion is derivative of the content of perception insofar as it ensues from reemploying and possibly recombining perceptual capacities employed in past perceptions. A view that is committed to radically grounded perceptual capacities faces the problem that one can only have a hallucination or an illusion as of a particular if one has perceived such a particular in the past.

On a third way of analyzing perceptual capacities, any perceptual capacity is grounded in perception, but it is not necessary that perceptual capacity is grounded in perceptions of the very perceiver employing the perceptual capacity derivatively in hallucination or illusion. The perceptual capacity can be grounded in perceptions of some perceiver somewhere. So a perceiver can have hallucinations or illusions as of particulars even if she has no past perceptions of the relevant particulars. While the perceptual capacity is grounded in perception, it need not be grounded in past perceptions of the very subject who is suffering a hallucination or an illusion as of the particulars that the capacity functions to single out. We can call this version *modestly grounded perceptual capacities*. This version allows that a subject could have a hallucination or an illusion as of a particular unlike anything she has seen before. However, some bridge must exist between my hallucination or illusion as of a particular that I have never seen and someone else's perception of a relevant particular. Only if some such bridge exists can the perceptual capacity I employ in hallucination or illusion be plausibly understood to be grounded in accurate perceptions. The perceptual capacities employed in such hallucinations or illusions could be acquired via testimony from a perceiver who has used the capacity in perception. As I will show, mental activism is committed to perceptual capacities being modestly grounded.

On both ungrounded and modestly grounded perceptual capacities, a subject need not have had perceptions of particulars to have hallucinations or illusions as of such particulars. So both ways of analyzing perceptual capacities posit that a brain in a vat could have hallucinations as of white cups. If perceptual capacities are ungrounded, then an isolated brain in a vat could have such hallucinations. By contrast a view on which perceptual capacities are modestly grounded entails that a brain in a vat could only have hallucinations as of particulars if the brain acquired the relevant perceptual capacities from subjects who have perceived sufficiently similar particulars.

The Aristotelian principle posits that any given perceptual capacity is grounded in perception insofar as the existence of a perceptual capacity depends on perceptions of the particulars that the perceptual capacity functions to single out.[31] If this is right, then it follows that there cannot exist a perceptual capacity that is not grounded in perception. It does not, however, follow that an individual subject could only employ a perceptual capacity in hallucination or illusion if she has employed that very capacity in perception. It follows only that there cannot exist a perceptual capacity that has not been employed successfully by someone, somewhere. A subject can acquire a perceptual capacity through testimony and thus employ that perceptual capacity in hallucination or illusion without having perceived any particulars that the perceptual capacity functions to single out. If this is right, then any given individual perceiver can have hallucinations as of particulars that she has not perceived. It follows that there cannot be a world in which there are only and have only ever been brains in a vat suffering hallucinations or illusions.

Can Jackson's Mary hallucinate a red object?[32] Mary is a color scientist who knows everything about colors but who lives in a black and white world and so has never seen any colors. So she could not have acquired the perceptual capacity to discriminate and single out red through perceptions of instances of red. According to mental activism it is not necessary to have perceived instances of red to hallucinate a red object. It is plausible, however, that perceptions of at least some colors are necessary for a person to imagine what it would be like to experience red. If this is right, then Mary could not hallucinate a red object. Her sister, Anna, however, could. Anna is a color scientist who knows everything about colors and who lives in a world with all the colors except red. She has seen all colors, except for red.[33]

A question waiting in the wings is how mental activism can account for illusions as of uninstantiated properties while respecting the Aristotelian principle. In response, an illusion as of, say, supersaturated red could be analyzed as a result of jointly employing the perceptual capacity that functions to single out instances of red and the perceptual capacity that functions to single out instances of saturatedness, thereby inducing an experience of a particularly saturated shade of red. By contrast to the property-cluster

---

[31] For a defense of the thesis that perceptual concepts are grounded in perceptions, see Peacocke 1992 and Prinz 2002. This thesis is famously challenged by Fodor (1998). Any argument that perceptual concepts are grounded in perceptions carries over to an argument that perceptual capacities are grounded in perceptions.

[32] See Jackson 1982, 1986.

[33] For a discussion of experiences of novel colors, see Macpherson 2003.

view, this approach does not require that experiences of uninstantiated properties be analyzed in terms of awareness or acquaintance relations to the relevant uninstantiated properties. Since the content of hallucination is constituted by employing perceptual capacities rather than the bare properties that the experience is seemingly of, the content can be analyzed without any appeal to uninstantiated properties. So on mental activism, there is no reason to think that one must stand in an awareness or an acquaintance relation to the property of being supersaturated red when having a hallucination as of an object that seems to be instantiating supersaturated red.

Now, it could be argued that the property-cluster theorist can analyze illusions of uninstantiated properties such as supersaturated red in an analogous way, thereby avoiding the metaphysical problems that I have argued a property-cluster theorist faces. The property-cluster theorist could argue that supersaturated red is a complex property and that while supersaturated red is uninstantiated, the properties that the cluster consists of are instantiated. So illusions of supersaturated red can be analyzed in terms of (awareness) relations to instantiated properties.

In response, we can agree that hallucinating a unicorn may be analyzable in terms of standing in a sensory awareness relation to an uninstantiated property-cluster that consists of the instantiated properties of being white, having a single horn, and being horse-shaped, among others. By contrast to hallucinating a unicorn, it is contentious that suffering an illusion as of supersaturated red can be analyzed in terms of standing in a sensory awareness relation to the uninstantiated complex property that consists of the instantiated properties of redness and saturatedness. After all, color properties are phenomenally basic and can therefore not be analyzed in terms of more basic color properties.[34] Since perceptual capacities are not properties this problem does not arise for mental activism. Even if uninstantiated color properties could be analyzed as composites of instantiated color properties, and the property-cluster theorist could avoid the metaphysical problem, the phenomenological problem would remain. A subject who suffers a non-veridical hallucination as of a cat by definition does not stand in a sensory awareness relation to a material, mind-independent cat or any properties such a cat might instantiate. Since the properties that subjects who are suffering an illusion or a hallucination are said to be aware of are not actually instantiated where they seem to be, the revised version of the property-cluster view analyzes the phenomenal character of illusions and hallucinations in terms of awareness relations to universals. Given that universals are not spatio-temporally extended or causally efficacious, it is unclear how one could be sensorily aware of them.

In contrast to the property-cluster view, mental activism is not committed to positing the existence of uninstantiated universals. In contrast to the revised property-cluster view, mental activism is not committed to the contentious thesis that uninstantiated color properties are composites of instantiated color properties. By analyzing perceptual

---

[34] See Mizrahi 2009 for an argument that color properties are phenomenally basic. See Sundström 2013 for an argument that they might not be.

capacities as modestly grounded, mental activism satisfies the Aristotelian principle while allowing that a subject can have illusions and hallucinations as of particulars unlike any she has seen. By accepting that illusions and hallucinations are derivative of perceptions insofar as we reemploy and possibly recombine perceptual capacities that have previously been employed by someone, somewhere, the defended view allows for illusions and hallucinations as of uninstantiated properties while satisfying the Aristotelian principle.

5. Coda

I developed the view that perceptual consciousness is constituted by a mental activity. According to mental activism, perceptual consciousness is constituted by employing perceptual capacities, that is, low-level mental capacities that function to discriminate and single out particulars in our environment. Insofar as employing perceptual capacities constitutes perceptual content, mental activism is a version of representationalism. The perceptual capacities employed in hallucination or illusion are the very same perceptual capacities that in a perception with the same phenomenal character are employed as a consequence of the perceiving subject being related to the external, mind-independent particulars that the perceptual capacity functions to single out. As a consequence, mental activism is a common factor view: perceptions, hallucinations, and illusions with the same phenomenal character have a metaphysically substantial common factor that is constituted by the perceptual capacities employed. Thus mental activism avoids any commitment to disjunctivism.

As I showed, there is no need to think that employing perceptual capacities entails the existence of the particulars that the perceptual capacities purport to single out. So mental activism allows that we can be in a mental state that is characterized by perceptual consciousness without being sensorily aware of any external, mind-independent particulars. A subject who is suffering a hallucination or an illusion as of what seems to her to be a mind-independent particular α employs a perceptual capacity that functions to single out mind-independent particulars under which α falls. Employing such a perceptual capacity accounts for the fact that it seems to the subject that α is present and accounts for her being intentionally directed at what seems to be an external, mind-independent particular without in fact being sensorily aware of α. Thus, mental activism avoids analyzing perceptual consciousness as constituted by (sensory awareness relations to) peculiar entities—be they phenomenal properties, external mind-independent properties, propositions, sense-data, qualia, or intentional objects. In avoiding analyzing perceptual consciousness as constituted by sensory awareness relations to peculiar entities, mental activism avoids the problems of orthodox common factor views.

So mental activism reconciles the following four theses. First, the view does not require positing that hallucinating or perceiving subjects stand in a sensory awareness relation to peculiar entities. In this respect, the view is ontologically more minimalist than any view that must appeal to such entities and thus upholds Quinean commitments to ontological minimalism. Second, the view satisfies the Aristotelian principle according to which the existence of any type depends on its tokens that in turn depend on concrete entities of the physical world. In this respect, the view is at an advantage over any view that must assume a Platonic 'two realms'-view. Third, the view gives a positive account of the phenomenal character of hallucinations and, in this respect, is an improvement over naïve realism or austere relationalism. Finally, the view analyzes perceptual consciousness, in terms of employing perceptual capacities, where perceptual capacities are in turn individuated by the mind-independent particulars they function to single out. Thereby, mental activism amounts to a naturalized view of perceptual consciousness.

PART IV

Evidence

Chapter 7

Perceptual Evidence

What evidence does perceptual experience provide us with? Why heed the testimony of our senses? To motivate these questions, consider a perceiver and a hallucinator. Percy, the perceiver, accurately perceives a white cup on a desk. Hallie, the hallucinator, suffers a subjectively indistinguishable hallucination as of a white cup on a desk; that is, it seems to her that there is a white cup where in fact there is none. What evidence do Percy and Hallie have for believing that there is a white cup on a desk? I will argue that Hallie has some evidence for her belief, but that Percy has more evidence than Hallie.

While standard internalist views have it that Hallie has as much evidence as Percy (e.g. Feldman and Conee 1985), standard externalist views have it that Hallie has only introspective evidence, but no evidence provided directly through experience (e.g. Williamson 2000).[1] In contrast to both approaches, I will argue that perceptual experience provides us with both phenomenal and factive evidence and that both kinds of evidence have the same rational source. To a first approximation, we can understand *phenomenal evidence* as determined by how our environment sensorily seems to us when we are experiencing. To a first approximation, we can understand *factive perceptual evidence* as necessarily determined by the perceived particulars such that the evidence is guaranteed to be an accurate guide to the environment. As I will argue, Percy and Hallie both have phenomenal evidence for believing that there is a white cup on a desk, but Percy has additional factive evidence. In this sense, Hallie has some evidence, but not as much as Percy. In showing that the rational source of both kinds of evidence lies in employing perceptual capacities, I will develop a unified account of perceptual evidence.[2]

I will proceed as follows. In Section 1, I distinguish perceptual evidence from introspective evidence. In Section 2, I argue that experience provides us with phenomenal evidence. In Section 3, I argue that an accurate perception provides us with factive evidence. In Section 4, I show that phenomenal and factive evidence have the same rational source. The view of perceptual evidence that I develop is the epistemological side of capacitism: the rational source of perceptual evidence is grounded in

---

[1] It should be noted that 'introspective evidence' is not Williamson's term. I will clarify it in Section 1 below. Also Conee and Feldman (2008) are open to there being differences in evidence derived from beliefs in cases like the one described.

[2] The view developed in this chapter draws heavily on Schellenberg 2013a and 2014b. For a critical discussion of the view developed in those papers, see Byrne 2014.

properties of perceptual capacities, the employment of which constitutes the relevant perceptual state.

My project is purely positive. I mention competitor views only to the extent that it helps motivate and situate capacitism. With internalists, I argue that we have at least some evidence provided directly through experience regardless of whether we are perceiving, hallucinating, or suffering an illusion. However, against internalists, I argue that if we accurately perceive, we have more evidence, where that evidence is of a distinct kind. So while I develop an externalist view of perceptual evidence, I am in disagreement with externalists like Williamson (2000), according to whom we have only introspective evidence when we hallucinate, but no evidence provided directly through experience.

Others have developed hybrid views on which evidence has both internal and external elements.[3] What is new about the account developed here is that, if right, it establishes that perceptual experience provides us with two kinds of evidence that have the same rational source: both factive and phenomenal evidence have their rational source in the perceptual capacities employed in experience. So I give a unified account of the internal and external elements of perceptual evidence and their common rational source. Although my focus is on perceptual evidence, the lessons I wish to draw are more general. I believe that my arguments generalize to a bilateral view of evidence that is not restricted to perceptual evidence. But to keep the discussion tractable I focus on perception.

Before I embark on this project, it is worth pausing to clear up a few potential misconceptions. The thesis that perceptual experience provides us with evidence is neutral on what connection there is between having evidence and being justified.[4] More specifically, the thesis is neutral on the relationship between the evidence that experience provides and any beliefs formed on the basis of that evidence. The arguments of the chapter could be accepted regardless of what stance one takes on how and why experience justifies beliefs. So accepting that perceptual experience yields evidence does not commit one to any form of evidentialism. According to evidentialists, what one is justified in believing is entirely determined by one's evidence (Feldman

---

[3] Alston (1986) integrates the internalist condition that we have direct access to the grounds of our beliefs within an externalist view of justification. Sosa (1991) integrates internal and external dimensions of epistemic appraisal by distinguishing between animal knowledge and reflective knowledge. Comesaña (2010) and Goldman (2011) defend views on which justification has both an external, reliabilist and an internal, evidential component, which jointly yield justification, where the internal and external components are attributed to different aspects of experience. The internal component derives from phenomenal character, while the external component derives from the alleged reliability of perception. Hellie (2011) argues that being perceptually justified is a matter of accepting externally individuated sentences that cohere with one's stream of consciousness. By contrast to these views, I argue that the internal and external components are grounded in the very same aspect of experience.

[4] One might argue that having perceptual evidence is sufficient for an experience to justify a belief about the external world (Pollock 1974, Feldman and Conee 1985, and Pryor 2000). Alternatively, one might argue that background beliefs necessarily play a role when an experience justifies a belief about the external world (Cohen 2002).

and Conee 1985). While an evidentialist could adopt many of the ideas I will argue for, they could be equally well adopted by someone who rejects the basic commitments of evidentialism.

The thesis that experience yields evidence is neutral not only on the relationship between having evidence and being justified, but also on the relationship between having evidence and what is rational to believe. Indeed, it is neutral on whether being justified and being rational are one and the same. After all, the thesis that experience provides us with evidence is compatible with there being many other features that affect what would be rational to believe. One might, for example, be a foundationalist about justification, but think that additional coherence considerations come into play when assessing what it would be rational to believe. Moreover, one might have some justification in believing p, but due to having non-evidential defeaters it might not be rational to believe p. Suppose a subject has negligently 'buried her head in the sand' and failed to gather easily accessible evidence against p. Such a subject can retain good evidence for p and so have at least some justification for believing p. Nevertheless, it would arguably not be rational for her to believe that p.

Finally, the thesis that perceptual experience provides us with evidence is neutral on the connection between having evidence and having knowledge. That said, the view of perceptual evidence that I will defend is incompatible with the Williamsonian thesis that all evidence is factive, and so is incompatible with the idea that all evidence is knowledge. In this chapter, I am not concerned with whether we are doxastically justified when we have evidence, nor am I concerned with what, if any, further conditions are required for knowledge. Here, I am concerned only with what evidence perceptual experience furnishes and why it is rational to heed the testimony of our senses.

1. Perceptual Evidence and Introspective Evidence

Perceptual evidence is evidence provided by perceptual experience. Insofar as perceptual experience is directed at our environment, the evidence that perceptual experience provides us with is of (or as of) our environment. The idea that perceptual evidence is of (or as of) our environment is neutral on a whole range of vexed questions. It is neutral on whether perceptual evidence has content. It is neutral on what the nature of that content is—assuming there is evidential content. Moreover, it is neutral on the relation between the content of perceptual evidence (if any) and the perceptual experience that provides us with perceptual evidence. Finally, it is neutral on whether all aspects of our perceptual evidence are accessed or even accessible.[5] While I take a stance on all these questions, the arguments in this chapter can, for the most part, be accepted irrespective of one's stance on them.

---

[5] For the view that all evidence is propositional, see Williamson 2000; for the view that evidence can be nonpropositional, see Plantinga 1993. For the view that evidence is necessarily accessible, see Chisholm 1966; for the view that evidence is not necessarily accessible, see again Williamson 2000.

Regardless of how perceptual evidence is understood, it must be distinguished from introspective evidence. Introspective and perceptual evidence differ in what they are of: while perceptual evidence is of (or as of) one's environment, introspective evidence is of (or as of) one's experience or some other mental state. They differ in their source: while perceptual evidence stems from perception, introspective evidence stems from introspection. They differ in what one attends to: while one gains perceptual evidence by attending to one's environment, one gains introspective evidence by attending to one's experience or some other mental state (which may be of one's environment). When I speak of experience as providing us with evidence *directly*, I mean that we need not attend to our experience to have the evidence. So we need not introspect our experience to gain evidence: we have evidence simply in virtue of experiencing.[6]

I am not denying that when we experience we can introspect our experience and thereby gain introspective evidence. However, as I will argue in Section 2, experience yields evidence without us having to introspect our experience. Indeed, I will argue— contra Williamson—that even when we are hallucinating, our experience yields at least some evidence without having to resort to an appearance proposition. On Williamson's view, the evidence one has when one hallucinates is an appearance proposition of the form "it seems to me that p" and so is provided by attending to the fact that it seems to one that the environment is a certain way. Appearance propositions involve appearance concepts—for example "it seems" or "it appears"—and entertaining such a proposition requires the ability to refer to oneself. One can only arrive at such an appearance proposition by introspecting one's experience.

One problem with this view is that it over-intellectualizes evidence. Animals that do not possess appearance concepts and that are not capable of self-reference can hallucinate. The fact that they act on their hallucinations suggests that they gain evidence from their hallucinations—despite the fact that they are not capable of entertaining appearance propositions.[7] While it is a fact that the environment seems a certain way to us when we experience, we should distinguish between this fact and the phenomenal state we are in when such a fact holds. If we gain evidence in hallucination only by attending to the fact that it sensorily seems to us as if our environment is a certain way, and so only by attending to our experience (rather than by attending to our environment,

---

[6] This constraint is neutral on a whole range of ways of thinking of direct and indirect perception. For a discussion of the notions of 'direct' and 'indirect' perception, see Jackson 1977 and Snowdon 1992. It should be noted that on a radical view of the transparency of experience, we are never aware of properties of our experience, but only ever of what our experience is about. There are both empirical and philosophical reasons to deny that experience is radically transparent in this way. One reason is that when our epistemic access to our environment changes—for instance, because we remove our glasses—our experience changes. The difference is due to how we experience our environment. While we are not necessarily aware of the fact that the difference in experience is due to a change in the experience rather than the environment itself, we can be. The fact that we can be aware of this is sufficient reason to reject the thesis that experience is radically transparent. For a discussion of this set of issues, see Smith 2002 and Martin 2002a.

[7] Williamson (2000: 199) denies that such animals gain evidence through their hallucination. Such a view requires an independent explanation of why animals act on their hallucinations. For a more detailed discussion of the over-intellectualization worry, see Chapter 10, Section 1. On conditions for self-representation and self-reference, see Kriegel 2009.

THE PHENOMENAL EVIDENCE ARGUMENT

albeit failing to perceive), then the evidence we gain in hallucination is not provided directly through experience. I will present a view of perceptual evidence on which evidence need not be understood as propositionally or conceptually structured, and on which phenomenal evidence need not involve appearance concepts.

2. The Phenomenal Evidence Argument

The basic argument for the thesis that perceptual experience provides us with phenomenal evidence goes as follows:

The Basic Phenomenal Evidence Argument

I.   If a subject S perceives α or suffers an illusion or a hallucination as of α (while not suffering from blindsight or any other form of unconscious perception), then it sensorily seems to S as if α is present.

II. If it sensorily seems to S as if α is present, then S is in a phenomenal state that provides phenomenal evidence for the presence of α.

From I–II: If S perceives α or suffers an illusion or a hallucination as of α (while not suffering from blindsight or any other form of unconscious perception), then S is in a phenomenal state that provides phenomenal evidence for the presence of α.

Premise I makes a claim about what is the case when we are perceptually directed at our environment. We can be perceptually directed at our environment without being perceptually related to it: when suffering a hallucination that is subjectively indistinguishable from a perception, we are perceptually directed at our environment, but fail to be perceptually related to it. The premise states that if we are perceptually directed at our environment, then it sensorily seems to us as if our environment is a certain way.[8] It is neutral on whether our environment could sensorily seem the very same to us regardless of whether we are perceiving, hallucinating, or suffering an illusion. So it is compatible with a range of views about the nature of sensory seemings. Moreover, Premise I is neutral on whether experience has content. So it is compatible with a range of views about the nature of experience. Since the relevant sensory seemings are restricted to those in which our environment seems a certain way to us, the scope of the premise does not extend to non-sensory seemings, such as a joke seeming funny, a proof seeming valid, or the ways things seem to us when we imagine.[9]

---

[8] It is controversial whether blindsighters are perceptually directed at their environment. One could argue that they do not perceive, but merely detect or register particulars in their environment. Dretske (2006) argues that there is no such thing as unconscious perception and so would deny that blindsighters perceive. If there is no such thing as unconscious perception, then the qualifying clause in Premise I can be dropped.

Being perceptually directed might be misunderstood as sounding unreasonably active. No such implication is intended. One can be perceptually directed at one's environment even when one has one's eyes closed and is prompted to have a hallucination by an evil scientist.

[9] Premise II does not over-generalize to non-sensory seemings for the same reason. For a discussion of seemings, see Ghijsen 2015.

One might object that the notion of being perceptually directed at one's environment is equivalent to the notion of the environment sensorily seeming a certain way to one. In response, we can say that one could have a notion of being perceptually directed at one's environment while being eliminativist about sensory seemings. This alone shows that the notion of being perceptually directed is distinct from the notion of sensory seemings.

2.1. Support for Premise II: phenomenal states and phenomenal evidence

Premise II is more controversial and so will require more support than Premise I. It posits that phenomenal states provide us with phenomenal evidence. Accounts on which evidence is necessarily factive (Williamson 2000) and disjunctivist accounts (Snowdon 1981, McDowell 1982) are likely to reject it.[10] To give support to this premise, we need to address the question of what the relationship is between phenomenal states and phenomenal evidence.

Since a phenomenal state is a kind of mental state, the thesis that phenomenal states provide phenomenal evidence entails the widely accepted thesis that our phenomenal evidence supervenes on our mental states (together with the theses that only mental states provide phenomenal evidence and that phenomenal evidence exists only if it is provided by something).[11] One might argue that there is a much stronger relation between phenomenal evidence and mental states, namely, identity. But for the sake of the phenomenal evidence argument, supervenience is all that we need.

A different way of understanding the question of what relationship there is between phenomenal states and phenomenal evidence is as a question about their epistemic relation. The key epistemological question is: what is the epistemic bridge that gets us from being in a phenomenal state to having phenomenal evidence? More generally, why is it rational to heed the testimony of our senses, especially given that we may unwittingly be hallucinating? In different ways, these questions ask for the motivation behind Premise II.[12] I will give support to Premise II by arguing that phenomenal states provide us with phenomenal evidence in virtue of being systematically linked (in ways to be explained) to the particulars they are of in the case of an accurate perception. Due to this systematic link it is rational to heed the testimony of our senses.

What is the notion of rationality in play? For present purposes, it will suffice to work with the following understanding: if it is rational to heed the testimony of the senses, then a person who does not heed the testimony of her senses is blameworthy—provided

[10] A disjunctivist could reject Premise II by arguing that if it seems to S as if α is present, then S is in a phenomenal state which provides evidence for the presence of α: in the case of hallucination this amounts to it merely appearing as if α is present, while in the case of perception this amounts to S perceiving that α is present.

[11] See Feldman and Conee 1985, Pryor 2000, and Tucker 2010 for versions of this view and Gupta 2006, White 2006, Wright 2007, DeRose 2011, and McGrath 2013 for critical discussions.

[12] Here and throughout, I understand 'rational' in an epistemic sense. I am not here concerned with practical rationality.

she does not have defeaters. She is, for example, subject to the criticism that she is ignoring relevant information that is available to her.

To get a better grip on the question of why it is rational to heed the testimony of our senses, it will be helpful to consider the shortcomings of internalist conceptions of evidence. Internalist conceptions of evidence go back to at least Russell (1913) and arguably to Descartes (1641, especially *Meditation II*). Russell understood evidence in terms of sense-data, that is, strange particulars that are directly present to the mind. Neo-Russellians and more generally evidential internalists understand perceptual evidence in terms of conscious mental states that can be the very same regardless of the environment of the experiencing subject (e.g. Pollock 1974, Feldman and Conee 1985, Pryor 2000). If our conscious mental states can be the very same regardless of our environment and if these conscious mental states determine our perceptual evidence, then our evidence will be the very same in the good and the bad case—that is, our evidence will be the very same regardless of whether we are accurately perceiving or suffering a hallucination.[13] But if perceptual evidence is the same in the good and the bad case, then it is mysterious why it would be rational to heed the testimony of our senses (see Goldman 1999 for this line of criticism). It is plausible that the reason it is valuable to take how our environment seems to us at face value is that doing so helps us successfully navigate the world. Evidence can play that role, however, only if there is a systematic link between our sensory seemings and the way our environment actually is. Insofar as evidential internalists do not account for such a link, they fail to account for the role of evidence as a guide to the world.

In fairness, it must be noted that at least some evidential internalists take phenomenal evidence as determined simply by how the world sensorily seems to us, where that seeming need not be a guide to how the world actually is.[14] Such internalists are unlikely to be moved by the above line of argument. But the aim was not to argue against evidential internalists. The aim was to motivate the claim that an account of perceptual evidence ought to explain why it is rational to heed the testimony of our senses.

The thesis that evidence is a guide to how the world is puts into focus what phenomenal evidence is evidence for. Evidence is always evidence for something. Phenomenal evidence is evidence for what our experience is of—or would be of, were we perceiving. How should we understand this? Consider again Percy who perceives a white cup on the desk in front of him and Hallie who suffers a hallucination as of a white cup on the desk in front of her. Percy's phenomenal state is of his environment and provides

---

[13] Illusions can be understood as a version of the good or the bad case. For discussion, see Antony 2011. For present purposes, we can remain neutral on how best to classify them. So as to avoid unnecessary complications, I will focus on the uncontroversial good and bad cases: accurate perception and hallucination. In Section 3, I will show how the suggested view applies to illusions.

[14] See e.g. Pollock and Cruz 2004; though note that they talk of justification, rather than evidence. They argue that justification bears no deep connection to truth, but is rather to be understood in internalist procedural terms.

phenomenal evidence that there is a white cup on the desk. Similarly, Hallie's phenomenal state provides phenomenal evidence that there is a white cup on the desk. So Percy and Hallie both have phenomenal evidence in virtue of their environments seeming a certain way to them. In light of this, we can formulate an argument in support of Premise II:

The Rational Support Argument

IIa. If it sensorily seems to a subject S as if α is present, then S is in a phenomenal state that is systematically linked to external, mind-independent particulars of the type under which α falls and that the phenomenal state is of in the good case.

IIb. If S is in a phenomenal state that is systematically linked to external, mind-independent particulars of the type under which α falls and that the phenomenal state is of in the good case, then S is in a phenomenal state that provides phenomenal evidence for the presence of α.

From IIa–IIb: If it sensorily seems to S as if α is present, then S is in a phenomenal state that provides phenomenal evidence for the presence of α.

The conclusion of the rational support argument is Premise II of the basic phenomenal evidence argument, that is, the premise for which we needed further support. If we conjoin this argument for why phenomenal states provide phenomenal evidence with the basic phenomenal evidence argument, we get the following comprehensive phenomenal evidence argument:

The Phenomenal Evidence Argument

I. If a subject S perceives α or suffers an illusion or a hallucination as of α (while not suffering from blindsight or any other form of unconscious perception), then it sensorily seems to S as if α is present.

IIa. If it sensorily seems to a subject S as if α is present, then S is in a phenomenal state that is systematically linked to external, mind-independent particulars of the type under which α falls and that the phenomenal state is of in the good case.

IIb. If S is in a phenomenal state that is systematically linked to external, mind-independent particulars of the type under which α falls and that the phenomenal state is of in the good case, then S is in a phenomenal state that provides phenomenal evidence for the presence of α.

II. If it sensorily seems to S as if α is present, then S is in a phenomenal state that provides phenomenal evidence for the presence of α.

From I–IIb: If S perceives α or suffers an illusion or a hallucination as of α (while not suffering from blindsight or any other form of unconscious perception), then S is in a phenomenal state that provides phenomenal evidence for the presence of α.

We already discussed Premise I. In the rest of this section, I will give support to Premises IIa and IIb.

2.1.1. SUPPORT FOR PREMISE IIA: PHENOMENAL STATES AND PERCEPTUAL
CAPACITIES

To give support to Premise IIa, it will be necessary to show that phenomenal states are systematically linked to external, mind-independent particulars of the type that the phenomenal state is of in the case of perception, and to specify how that systematic linkage is to be understood. Doing so will require drawing on the modest externalist view of phenomenal character developed in Chapter 6. The basic idea of this view is that when we perceive, we employ perceptual capacities by means of which we discriminate and single out particulars in our environment. The relevant particulars are external and mind-independent objects, events, or property-instances. Phenomenal character is understood as constituted by employing perceptual capacities in a sensory mode, that is, modes such as seeing, hearing, touching, smelling, or tasting.[15] As I argued in Chapter 6, if a subject S's environment sensorily seems to contain F particulars to her (regardless of how it in fact is), then S is in a phenomenal state that is constituted by employing perceptual capacities that function to single out F particulars.

How does this view of phenomenal character support Premise IIa of the phenomenal evidence argument? Phenomenal states are systematically linked to what they are of in the good case in the sense that the perceptual capacities employed in the bad case are explanatorily and metaphysically parasitic on their employment in the good case. There is an *explanatory primacy* of the good over the bad case, since one can give an analysis of the perceptual capacities employed in the bad case only by appealing to their role in the good case. Licensing this explanatory primacy there is a *metaphysical primacy* of the good over the bad case. The metaphysical primacy is captured by the asymmetry condition on perceptual capacities from Chapter 2: the employment of a perceptual capacity C_α in cases in which C_α fulfills its function is metaphysically more basic than the employment of C_α in cases in which C_α fails to fulfill its function. As argued there, perceptual capacities function to single out particulars. They do not function to fail to single out particulars. It is compatible with this that they may be employed in hallucination, thereby failing to single out particulars.

To support this, it will be helpful to take a closer look at the notion of function in play. The heart has the function to pump blood. It does not have the function to fail to pump blood—though in the bad case it will fail. One possible way to understand this asymmetry is in terms of evolution: the function of the heart is what it was selected for (Millikan 1984). However, as argued in Chapter 2, it need not be understood in an evolutionary way. Any plausible account of natural function will support the idea that the heart has the function to pump blood rather than the function to fail to pump blood. The same is true of perceptual capacities. An evolutionary account of function would posit that perceptual capacities evolved for the purpose of singling out particulars rather than for the purpose of failing to single out particulars. However, here again, there is no need to explain the asymmetry in evolutionary terms. On any plausible

---

[15] As before, "constituted" is understood in the sense of "at least partially constituted."

account of natural function, we can say that perceptual capacities function to single out particulars rather than function to fail to single out particulars.

Acknowledging the metaphysical primacy of the good case over the bad case is compatible with acknowledging that one could possess a perceptual capacity without ever having used it successfully in perception. So one can employ a perceptual capacity in hallucination without ever having used it in perception. After all, perceptual capacities need not be acquired through perception. They might be innate. Thus, the metaphysical primacy of the good case over the bad case does not imply that we must have successfully used a perceptual capacity in the past to employ it in hallucination.

Now, does the existence of a perceptual capacity require the existence of at least one successful employment of that capacity by someone somewhere? As argued in Chapter 6, while it is possible to possess such a capacity without having been perceptually related to any particulars of the type that the capacity singles out in the good case, it is plausible that any such perceptual capacity is grounded in perception insofar as the existence of the capacity depends on perceptions of the particulars that the capacity singles out.[16] If this is right, then it follows that there cannot exist any such perceptual capacity that is not grounded in perception. It does not, however, follow from this that an individual subject must have had perceptions of the particulars that the capacity singles out to possess the relevant capacity. The argument for the metaphysical priority of the good over the bad case does not depend on resolving the question of whether the existence of a perceptual capacity requires the existence of at least one successful application by someone, somewhere. Depending on what stance one takes on this issue, one must, however, either reject or accept the metaphysical possibility of a world of brains in a vat that can hallucinate. Regardless of what stance one takes on this issue, capacitism allows that a brain in a vat in our world could have hallucinations and so phenomenal evidence.

It is worth highlighting that my argument does not depend on understanding perceptual capacities as discriminatory, selective capacities. They could be understood as concepts or dispositional properties. My argument depends only on the idea that phenomenal states are systematically linked to what they are of in the good case in the sense that the perceptual capacities employed in the bad case are explanatorily and metaphysically parasitic on their employment in the good case.

Summing up: I have argued that phenomenal states are systematically linked to particulars of the type that the relevant phenomenal state is of in the good case, in the sense that the perceptual capacities employed in the bad case are explanatorily and metaphysically parasitic on their employment in the good case. The idea that phenomenal states are constituted by employing such perceptual capacities is what supports Premise IIa of the phenomenal evidence argument.

---

[16] This is not implied by the argument of the chapter. The phenomenal evidence argument requires only a weaker claim, namely, that any perceptual capacity is grounded in how things would come out in the good cases. However, for empiricist reasons independent of the argument of this chapter, it is plausible to assume that such capacities are grounded in actual perceptions and not just possible perceptions. For a discussion of such reasons, see Goodman 1955.

2.1.2. SUPPORT FOR PREMISE IIb: PHENOMENAL EVIDENCE AND SYSTEMATIC LINKAGE

Recall that Premise IIb of the phenomenal evidence argument is as follows: if S is in a phenomenal state that is systematically linked to external, mind-independent particulars of the type under which α falls and that the phenomenal state is of in the good case, then S is in a phenomenal state that provides phenomenal evidence for the presence of α. This premise supports the crucial transition from the metaphysical fact that a phenomenal state is systematically linked to the F particulars it is of in the good case to the epistemic fact that such a phenomenal state provides evidence for the presence of F particulars. Thus, it is the premise that grounds epistemological facts about perception in metaphysical facts about perception.

The truth of Premise IIb depends on two principles. The first is that if phenomenal states are systematically linked to what they are of in the good case in the sense specified, then it is rational to heed their testimony. The second principle is that if it is rational to heed the testimony of phenomenal states, then they provide evidence. I will give support to each principle in turn.

I argued that phenomenal states are systematically linked to particulars of the type that the phenomenal state is of in the good case, in the sense that the perceptual capacities employed in the bad case are explanatorily and metaphysically parasitic on their employment in the good case. This systematic link stems from it being the function of the perceptual capacities employed to single out the relevant particulars. In speaking of it being the function of perceptual capacities to single out the relevant particulars, I do not mean to speak of their actual reliability but rather of how they are to be understood metaphysically. It is the function of a perceptual capacity to single out, say, instances of red. This is so regardless of how often the capacity is employed successfully to single out an instance of red. So this way of understanding why it is rational to heed the testimony of our senses has the advantage of not depending any form of reliabilism. Our senses frequently lead us astray. Nevertheless, they provide us with evidence. Some perceptual capacities may be reliable. However, even if that is the case, it is the systematic linkage to particulars that gives experience its epistemic force. The notion of systematic linkage in play is understood in terms of a metaphysical and explanatory primacy notion, which is not a reliabilist notion. Thus, the epistemic force of perceptual experience does not depend on whatever reliability (if any) perceptual capacities might have.

The second principle states a sufficient condition for something to count as evidence. The principle follows from a substantive but largely uncontroversial view about evidence—namely, that it is a crucial property of evidence that if it is epistemically rational to heed x in the absence of defeaters, then x provides evidence.[17]

---

[17] See Ayer 1972, Kelly 2003, Neta 2003, 2008, Weatherson 2005, and Pryor 2012 for discussions of this property of evidence. An interesting question is what the connection is between the strength of the evidence we have for a proposition and our confidence in that proposition. For discussion of the relation between having evidence for p and having confidence in p, see Neta 2003, 2008 and Silins 2005. Since our

Now, one might object that hopes, fears, and imaginations are, like perceptions, a matter of employing mental capacities. If that is right, why does this account of perceptual evidence not over-generalize to these other mental states?[18] In response, the key idea is that perceptual experiences have epistemic force in virtue of the fact that the perceptual capacities employed have the function to single out particulars in the environment. It is because the capacities constituting perceptual experience function differently than the capacities in play in hoping, fearing, and imagining that perceptual experiences have epistemic force and hopes, fears, and imaginations do not. The fundamental difference between perception, on the one hand, and hopes, fears, and imaginations, on the other, is that perceptual capacities function to single out particulars to which we are perceptually related, while the capacities employed in those other mental states do not have this function.

One might object, further, that beliefs are linked to what they are of in the good case, but it is not rational to treat beliefs as evidence. So why is it rational to treat phenomenal states as evidence but not beliefs? In response, we can concede that many things are in some way linked to what they are of in the good case. It is not rational to treat all those things as evidence. After all, the systematic linkage between phenomenal states and what they are of in the good case was understood in a specific way. The capacities employed in perception link perceptual states with particulars in the environment. Perception is our primordial connection to particulars in our environment. For present purposes, the crucial difference between perception and belief is that perceptual capacities function to single out particulars, while the capacities employed in belief do not necessarily have this function. Of course, some capacities employed in belief do function to single out particulars, for example, the capacities employed in bringing about perceptual beliefs. But perceptual beliefs are a special case in that they are parasitic on perception. Capacities that function to single out particulars may be operative in beliefs that are not perceptual beliefs. Even if that is the case, the capacities that determine beliefs are not systematically linked to what they are of in the good case in the sense that there is an explanatory and metaphysical primacy of their employment in the good case. Therefore, the argument provided for why it is rational to heed the testimony of our senses does not over-generalize to beliefs.

What if we assume for the sake of argument both that beliefs are a kind of phenomenal state and that the capacities that determine beliefs are explanatorily and metaphysically parasitic on their employment in the good case? On these two controversial assumptions, it is plausible that beliefs provide us with evidence.[19] So on these assumptions, the argument provided for why it is rational to heed the testimony

---

concern here is restricted to the questions of what evidence perceptual experience provides us with and why it is rational to heed it, we can bracket this issue for the purposes of this chapter. In Chapter 8, I discuss how the account of evidence developed in this chapter connects to questions about confidence.

[18] Thanks to Alex Byrne and David Chalmers for pressing me on this point.

[19] Indeed, Harman's (1973) coherentist view of justification suggests—albeit for different reasons—that beliefs provide us with justification.

of our senses generalizes to beliefs. It does not, however, over-generalize, and so would not be a problem for capacitism, since beliefs are now understood to have many of the fundamental properties of perceptual states.

2.2. Coda

I have argued that our phenomenal evidence in the bad case is brought about by employing the very same perceptual capacities that in the good case allow us to perceptually navigate our environment. While these capacities are determined by functional relations to the particulars they single out in perception, we can employ the same capacities while failing to single out a relevant particular. So having phenomenal evidence is compatible with our perceptual capacities being employed baselessly. As a consequence, hallucinations provide us with tangible, though misleading, phenomenal evidence.

The notion of phenomenal evidence developed here is externalist in that phenomenal evidence stems from a systematic link to the particulars that perceptual capacities function to single out. It is constituted by employing perceptual capacities and the capacities employed in the bad case are both metaphysically and explanatorily parasitic on their employment in the good case. Despite it being externalist, we can have phenomenal evidence even when we are in the bad case. Thus, the notion of phenomenal evidence is internalist—but only in the sense that the phenomenal evidence of two experiencers in different environments can be the very same. It is not internalist regarding the accessibility of the evidence.[20]

This externalist notion of phenomenal evidence makes room for the idea that having evidence is a matter of being in an epistemic position that is a guide to how the world is, while allowing that we can have evidence even if we happen to have been led astray and so are in a state that is not accurate with regard to our environment. As a consequence, capacitism shows how experience provides us with phenomenal evidence even in the bad case without retreating to introspective evidence.

3. The Factive Evidence Argument

So far I have argued that Percy and Hallie both have phenomenal evidence that is constituted by employing perceptual capacities. How do we explain why Percy has more evidence than Hallie? How do we get from the thesis that perceptual experience is a matter of employing perceptual capacities to the thesis that accurate perceptions yield factive evidence?

Factive perceptual evidence is necessarily determined by the perceived particulars such that the evidence is guaranteed to be an accurate guide to the environment. There are many ways of understanding a factive conception of evidence given this constraint. One way is that such evidence is the set of propositions that one knows at any given

---

[20] See Pryor 2001: 105–8 and Wedgwood 2002 for discussions of different forms of epistemic internalism, including useful distinctions between ways of understanding the access requirement on our evidence.

moment. Another way is that factive evidence is not propositional and does not amount to knowledge. A third way is that factive evidence is propositionally structured without constituting knowledge.[21] We can remain neutral on these options, since we are not concerned here with whether factive perceptual evidence is necessary or sufficient for perceptual knowledge.[22] The question at issue is whether perception provides us with such evidence, not what its relationship is to knowledge.

The fact that factive evidence is necessarily determined by the perceived particulars suffices to distinguish factive from phenomenal evidence. After all, a perceiver and a hallucinator in the very same environment can have different phenomenal evidence. If a perceiver and a hallucinator are, for instance, both sitting in front of a white cup on a desk, the perceiver will have phenomenal evidence that there is a white cup on a desk, while the hallucinator might have phenomenal evidence that there is a green dragon playing the piano—or whatever she may be hallucinating. So in contrast to factive evidence, phenomenal evidence is not necessarily determined by the environment of the experiencing subject.

The argument for the thesis that experience provides us with factive evidence goes as follows:

The Factive Evidence Argument

III.   If a subject S accurately perceives α then S accurately represents α on the basis of perceiving α.

IV.   If S accurately represents α on the basis of perceiving α, then S has factive evidence that is constituted by α.

From III–IV: If S accurately perceives α, then S has factive evidence that is constituted by α.

While the phenomenal evidence argument was premised on the condition of a subject being perceptually directed at her environment, the factive evidence argument is premised on the stronger condition of a subject accurately perceiving her environment.

3.1. Support for Premise III: perceptual content

The truth of Premise III depends on the thesis that perception is representational and moreover on the thesis that perceivers accurately represent their environment on the basis of perceiving it. In this chapter, my argument has so far been neutral on whether experience is representational, but as I argued in Chapter 5, employing perceptual capacities yields perceptual states that have representational content. We can draw on that argument here. The thesis that we accurately represent our environment on the basis of perceiving it implies not only that when we perceive our environment we are

---

[21] If evidence is propositionally structured, then we can say that factive evidence entails what it is evidence for.

[22] In Chapter 9, I argue that factive evidence is sufficient evidence for knowledge. But the argument of this chapter can be accepted without accepting this sufficient evidence requirement on knowledge.

causally related to that environment, but moreover that this causal relation is not deviant. So cases are ruled out in which our experiences are not caused along a normal route by the particulars that we purport to single out.

Consider the following example: we experience a pear as being at location L_1 and coincidentally there is in fact a pear (pear$_1$) at that location. But this pear is behind a mirrored wall. So it could not have caused our experience. However, there is a different pear (pear$_2$) at location L_2 that does cause our experience, albeit in a deviant manner. This pear (pear$_2$) is located such that we see its reflection in the mirror: it is reflected in a way that makes it seem as if it is at location L_1, thereby causing our experience through a deviant causal chain. Since we are not perceptually related to the pear (pear$_1$) at location L_1, we do not accurately represent our environment on the basis of perceiving it—despite our experience being caused by our environment.

For similar reasons, so-called veridical hallucinations do not yield accurate representations of our environment on the basis of that environment. Suppose that we hallucinate a pear at location L_3. As it happens, there is a pear at that very location, which looks just like the one that we are hallucinating. But it is behind a screen, so it could not have caused our experience. Since we are not perceptually related to the pear, our experience is not based on our environment. As these two cases show, we count as accurately perceiving our environment only if we accurately represent our environment on the basis of perceiving it. This is just what Premise III puts forward.

3.2. Support for Premise IV: perceptual content and the factivity of perception

Premise IV has it that if we accurately represent our environment on the basis of perceiving it, then we have factive evidence determined by that environment. Why should we accept this? I argued that phenomenal states provide phenomenal evidence since the perceptual capacities employed in the bad case are systematically linked to their employment in the good case (insofar as perceptual capacities function to discriminate and single out particulars).

The analysis of the rational source of phenomenal evidence in terms of a notion of systematic linkage carries over to an analysis of the rational source of factive evidence. After all, in the case of a perception, there is an ideal link between one's perceptual state and the environment due to one being perceptually related to that environment. Therefore, that perceptual state provides factive evidence. But how should we understand the idea that there is such an ideal link? The truth of Premise V depends jointly on (i) the thesis that we have evidence if we accurately represent our environment on the basis of perceiving it, and (ii) the thesis that such representations yield factive evidence.

The first thesis is neutral on most ways of understanding evidence. For example, we can accept it, if we understand evidence as having the property of being rational to take at face value. After all, it is rational to be guided by an accurate representation of our environment arrived at on the basis of perceiving it. Likewise, we can accept the thesis, if we understand evidence as having the property of being truth-conducive. After all, an accurate representation of our environment arrived at on the basis of perceiving it is truth-conducive, and it is rational to treat truth-conducive representations as evidence. It is fair to say that on any reasonable conception of what having evidence requires, we should hold that we have evidence if we accurately represent our environment on the basis of perceiving it.

Why should we accept the second thesis—that is, the thesis that representations arrived at on the basis of perceiving it yield factive evidence? A simple response is to say that perception is factive and it is reasonable that the evidence provided by perception inherits the factivity of perception. A more substantial response will require showing that perceptual evidence inherits its content from perceptual experience and that perceptual content is constituted by the particulars perceived.

I argued that one has evidence in virtue of being in a perceptual state that is constituted by employing perceptual capacities. While one could say that the evidential state and the perceptual state are distinct, it is more parsimonious to say that the evidential state is itself the perceptual state. Insofar as the perceptual state covaries with its content, such a view posits that any change in content will yield a change in evidence.[23] To suppose otherwise would require having a more complicated view of perceptual evidence and its relation to experience. If perceptual evidence inherits its content from perceptual experience and perceptual content is constituted by the perceived particulars, then, necessarily, an accurate perception will yield evidence that is accurate with respect to that environment.

The thesis that perceptual content is constituted by the particulars perceived can be supported in a number of ways. As I argued in Chapters 3 and 4, if the fact that perceptual capacities function to single out particulars has any semantic significance, then the token content yielded by employing these capacities will be constituted by the particulars perceived (and the capacities employed). According to Fregean particularism, employing perceptual capacities yields a token content that covaries with the environment of the experiencing subject. In the case of an accurate perception, the token content is a singular content. In the case of a hallucination or an illusion, the token content is gappy. These token contents are instances of the same content type: employing perceptual capacities constitutes a content type that perceptions, illusions, and hallucinations with the same phenomenal character have in common.

Fregean particularism provides us with two ways of individuating perceptual states. A perceptual state can be individuated by the content type that is constituted by the perceptual capacities employed. Or it can be individuated by the token content that is constituted by the perceptual capacities employed and the particulars (if any) thereby singled out.

---

[23] One might reject this view by arguing that perceptual evidence merely supervenes on content, such that there could be changes in content without changes in evidence. Any such view would have to account for why there is a difference between perceptual states and perceptual evidence and so would be more complicated than the view suggested. So reasons of parsimony will count against such a view. For a defense of the view that epistemic reasons are mental states, see Turri 2009.

What follows from this for perceptual evidence? Fregean particularism not only puts the notions of phenomenal and factive evidence on a firmer footing, but also integrates them into a unified view of perceptual evidence. Phenomenal evidence is determined by the content type. Factive evidence is determined by the singular token content of a perception. Thus, the factive evidential basis changes as the token content changes—even though one cannot tell. In this sense, factive evidence provides the perceiver with evidence that goes beyond what phenomenal character provides. Capacitism rejects any form of epistemological disjunctivism, since according to capacitism having factive evidence is not reflectively accessible to the perceiver: we do not know that we know in virtue of having factive evidence.[24]

3.3. Coda

To fully support the idea that experience provides us with more evidence in the good than in the bad case, we need to show that we do not have factive evidence in the bad case. It falls out of the argument for why we have factive evidence in the good case that we do not have factive evidence in the bad case. According to Fregean particularism, the token content of an accurate perception is a singular content, but the token content of hallucination is gappy. A gappy token content does not provide evidence, since a gappy content cannot be true. After all, it is defective and so either does not have a truth-value or is necessarily false. It is not rational to heed something that by its very nature could only be false or lacking a truth value. Therefore, gappy content does not provide factive evidence.

4. The Common Rational Source of Phenomenal and Factive Evidence

I have argued that perceptual experience provides us with phenomenal evidence, and that an accurate perception provides us with additional factive evidence. Phenomenal and factive evidence both have their rational source in the perceptual capacities employed in experience. Phenomenal evidence is determined by the content type of an experience, which is in turn constituted by the perceptual capacities employed. Factive evidence is determined by the singular token content of perception, which is in turn constituted by the perceptual capacities employed and the particulars thereby singled out. Insofar as both kinds of evidence have the same rational source, capacitism provides a unified account of the internal and external aspects of perceptual evidence.

As argued in Section 2, phenomenal states provide evidence since they are constituted by employing perceptual capacities that function to single out particulars. As a consequence, they are systematically linked to those particulars. Thus, if a subject is in a phenomenal state that is systematically linked to external and mind-independent F

---

[24] For an alternative context-sensitive view of factive evidence, see Neta 2003.

particulars, then she is in a phenomenal state that provides evidence for the presence of F particulars. After all, if a subject is in a phenomenal state that is constituted by employing perceptual capacities that function to single out F particulars, then the subject is in a phenomenal state that provides evidence for the presence of F particulars.

As I argued in Section 3, an accurate perception provides us moreover with factive evidence. The analysis of the rational source of phenomenal evidence in virtue of a notion of systematic linkage carries over to an analysis of the rational source of factive evidence. After all, in the case of a perception, there is an ideal link between our perceptual state and the environment due to our perceiving it. Therefore, we have additional factive evidence in virtue of accurately representing our environment.

Factive evidence provides additional evidence that is different from phenomenal evidence. It is evidence of a different kind since the systematic linkage to the environment is stronger than the one governing phenomenal evidence. More specifically, it is evidence of a different kind since it is provided by successfully employing perceptual capacities in a particular environment. For any subject S_1 and any subject S_2, if S_1 has all the evidence that S_2 has plus an additional bit of evidence that is factive and thereby of a distinct kind, then S_1 is in a better epistemic position than S_2. So factive evidence provides a rationality boost beyond the rationality boost provided by phenomenal evidence. This explains why Percy is in a better evidential position than Hallie.

As I will argue in more detail in Chapter 8, from the first-person perspective one may not be able to tell the difference between a hallucination, in which one has only phenomenal evidence, and a perception, in which one has both phenomenal and factive evidence. However, we need not think that what is accessible from the first-person perspective dictates what is rational to heed. This principle holds even for phenomenal evidence: a phenomenal state is rational to heed in virtue of being constituted by employing perceptual capacities that function to single out mind-independent particulars. There is no need to have access to all aspects of that phenomenal state.

Now, why not say that in the bad case and the good case, we have the appearance of factive evidence and in the good case we actually have factive evidence? By introducing the idea of the appearance of factive evidence one could avoid introducing a second kind of evidence, namely phenomenal evidence. In response, we can say that any such view would need to explain what the notion of the appearance of factive evidence amounts to. In particular, any such account would need to explain the nature of the content of the appearance of factive evidence, that is, the nature of the content that justifies beliefs formed on the basis of the experience. Arguably, any account of the content of the appearance of factive evidence will either amount to an account of the content of phenomenal evidence, or alternatively, an account of the content of introspective evidence (or something akin to introspective evidence). After all, having the appearance of factive evidence implies that it appears to one that one has factive evidence. In short, any such view will collapse either into a version of the proposed view or into a view on which we only have introspective evidence in the bad case.

5. Coda

In contrast to externalist views such as Williamson's, capacitism shows that we have at least some evidence provided directly through experience in the bad case: we have phenomenal evidence.[25] In contrast to evidential internalist views (cf. Pollock 1974, Feldman and Conee 1985, and Pryor 2000), capacitism shows that we have more evidence in the good than the bad case: we have additional factive evidence. In contrast to disjunctivist views, capacitism shows that there is at least some evidence in common between good and bad cases: in both cases, we have phenomenal evidence. In contrast to epistemological disjunctivism, capacitism shows that we do not know whether we are perceiving rather than hallucinating: we do not know that we know in virtue of having factive evidence. So capacitism provides us with something that neither factive evidentialists nor evidential internalists can supply.

Capacitism has several attractive features. First, it is an externalist view of evidence that nonetheless makes room for phenomenal evidence. Hallucinations provide us with evidence that is neither introspective evidence nor constituted by general content. The view is externalist insofar as the content of factive evidence is a singular token content and insofar as our phenomenal evidence is determined by our phenomenal states, which in turn are individuated externally. Phenomenal states are individuated externally since they are constituted by employing perceptual capacities that are by their very nature linked to the particulars that they are of in the good case. While the content of factive evidence is a singular token content, the content of phenomenal evidence is a content type. No doubt we can articulate a general content or an existentially quantified content to express the content of our phenomenal states. But the fact that we can articulate such content does not imply that the content of phenomenal evidence is such a general content or an existentially quantified content. It is a potentially particularized content type.

Second, capacitism implies that we can have perceptual evidence only if we are in a phenomenal state.[26] I argued that employing perceptual capacities yields phenomenal evidence and, if the environment plays along, also factive evidence. So we can have phenomenal evidence without having factive evidence. However, since we have factive perceptual evidence in virtue of employing perceptual capacities, and since employing such capacities yields a phenomenal state, we cannot have factive perceptual evidence without being in a phenomenal state. If this is right, then monotonicity between factive and phenomenal evidence is guaranteed.[27]

---

[25] According to Williamson, we have only evidence provided by an appearance proposition in the bad case. For discussion of the problems with Williamson's view and knowledge-first views more generally, see Chapter 10.

[26] For a discussion of the role of sensory awareness in perceptual justification, see Bergmann 2006, Glüer-Pagin 2009, Lyons 2009, Hellie 2011, Silins 2011, Johnston 2011, and Smithies 2011.

[27] It is important to note that being in a phenomenal state, as I understand the term, does not necessarily imply that one is in a conscious phenomenal state. On my view, there is no difference in the epistemic force of a phenomenal state depending on whether that phenomenal state is conscious or unconscious.

Third, capacitism provides a unified account of the internal and external elements of perceptual evidence. According to capacitism, phenomenal states are constituted by the perceptual capacities employed. They provide phenomenal evidence, since phenomenal states are systematically linked to particulars of the type that the relevant phenomenal state is of in the good case. This is because the perceptual capacities employed in the bad case are explanatorily and metaphysically parasitic on their employment in the good case. There is an explanatory primacy of the good over the bad case since giving an analysis of the perceptual capacities employed in the bad case requires appealing to their role in the good case. There is a metaphysical primacy of the good over the bad case since perceptual capacities function to single out particulars. The analysis of the rational source of phenomenal evidence in virtue of a notion of systematic linkage carries over to an analysis of the rational source of factive evidence. After all, in the case of a perception, there is an ideal link between one's perceptual state and the environment due to one's being perceptually related to one's environment. The rational source of both kinds of evidence stems from the perceptual capacities employed in experience. In showing that both kinds of evidence have the same rational source, capacitism provides a unified account of the internal and external elements of perceptual evidence.

Fourth, capacitism explains the distinction between the internal and external elements of perceptual evidence in terms of the representational content of perceptual experience. The distinction between phenomenal and factive evidence emerges from two levels of perceptual content. I argued that any perceptual experience can be individuated by a content type or a token content. Phenomenal evidence is determined by the content type, which is in turn constituted by the perceptual capacities employed. Factive evidence is determined by the token content, which is in turn constituted by the perceptual capacities employed and the particulars thereby singled out.

Fifth, capacitism explains why a perceiver is in a better epistemic position than a hallucinator. Perceiving Percy who perceives a white cup on a desk and Hallie who suffers a subjectively indistinguishable hallucination. While perceiving Percy and hallucinating Hallie both have phenomenal evidence for their belief that there is a white cup on the desk, Percy has additional factive evidence. More generally, a perceiver is in a better epistemic position than a hallucinator, since the perceiver has more evidence, where that evidence is a distinct kind of evidence—namely, factive evidence.

Sixth, capacitism is a naturalistic and externalist alternative to reliabilism. According to capacitism, the epistemic power of perceptual experience is explained in terms of metaphysical facts about perceptual experience. By grounding the epistemic force of experience in facts about the metaphysical structure of experience, capacitism is not only an externalist view, but moreover a naturalistic view of the epistemology of perceptual experience.

Indeed, I argue that unconscious perception is a matter of being in a mental state with phenomenal character without having access to that phenomenal character. For a discussion of unconscious perception, see Phillips and Block 2016.

Chapter 8

Justification, Luminosity, and Credences

What is evidence? According to capacitism, evidence and allied notions such as justification and knowledge are to be understood in terms of the mental capacities employed, by means of which the mental state is generated that provides us with evidence. The notion of a capacity is understood to be explanatorily basic. It is because a given subject is employing a mental capacity with a certain nature that her mental states have epistemic force.

Among capacity views there is a distinction to be drawn between normative capacity views, on which mental capacities are understood as virtues or in other normative ways Sosa 1991, 2006, 2007, Zagzebski 1996, Greco 2001, 2010, Bergmann 2006), and capacity views that forgo normative terms (Schellenberg 2013a, 2014b, 2016c). Moreover, there is a distinction to be drawn between reliabilist capacity views, on which mental capacities provide mental states with epistemic force in virtue of their reliability (Sosa 1991, 2006, 2007, Greco 2001, 2010, Burge 2003, Bergmann 2006, Graham 2011), and capacity views that are not grounded in the reliability of mental capacities (Schellenberg 2013a, 2014b, 2016c).

Capacitism can be contrasted with a number of alternative recent epistemological approaches. Dogmatism and evidential internalism treat conscious mental states as explanatorily basic and posit a particular rule for justification, namely, that if it perceptually seems that p, then one has *prima facie* justification for p (Pollock 1974, Pryor 2000, Huemer 2007, among others).[1] The knowledge-first view treats knowledge as explanatorily basic and analyzes justification in terms of a deficiency of knowledge (McDowell 1982, Williamson 2000, Millar 2008, Nagel 2013, Byrne 2014, and Littlejohn 2017, among others). Reliabilism treats the reliability of the perceptual or cognitive system as explanatorily basic and analyzes evidence and justification as a product of this reliable system—be it in virtue of a reliable indicator or a reliable process (Goldman 1979, 1986, Lyons 2009, among others). By contrast, capacity views treat capacities as explanatorily basic and analyze evidence, justification, and knowledge as

---

[1] One could add Feldman and Conee 1985 to this list, however, on their view, as long as a subject's belief fits her total evidence, the belief is propositionally justified by that evidence, so their view need not be committed to seemings.

a product of the capacities employed. So on the first cluster of views, conscious mental states are explanatorily basic, on the second cluster knowledge, on the third reliability, and on the fourth capacities.[2] These options are neither exclusive nor exhaustive. One might think that more than one of these four elements are explanatorily basic, or one might think that what is explanatorily basic is something else entirely. Nevertheless, these four approaches are the main current options.

When I say that conscious mental states, reliability, knowledge, or capacities are explanatorily basic, I do not mean that the relevant views are committed to holding that one cannot give an analysis of these concepts.[3] I mean rather that they are the fundamental elements in terms of which an epistemological account is developed. Most views appeal to conscious mental states and reliability; many appeal to some form of mental capacity. The key question is what the basic elements are in terms of which an epistemological account is developed. On Williamson's view, for example, this basic element is knowledge, rather than conscious mental states, reliability, or methods—even if his view appeals to all three concepts along the way.[4]

Capacitism about the epistemic force of perceptual experience, the capacity view developed in Chapter 7, is distinctly non-normative and non-reliabilist. In this chapter, I will discuss its repercussions for the justification of beliefs and the luminosity of mental states. In light of these discussions, I will explore the implications of the view for familiar problem cases.

1. Evidence and Justification

My focus so far has been on what it is about experience that makes it something that provides us with evidence, not what the relationship is between this evidence and the rational role of beliefs formed on the basis of the experience. I will now address the relationship between evidence and justification. While capacitism has some consequences for the justificatory power of perceptual experience, it does not dictate a particular view about justification. Indeed, it is compatible with a range of views about the relationship between the evidence that experience provides and any beliefs formed on the basis of that evidence.[5] Moreover, it is compatible with a range of views about how and why the evidence provided by perceptual experiences supports beliefs.

For the sake of simplicity and definiteness, I will work with the assumption that having more evidence for a proposition p means that p is better justified. Moreover, for the purposes of this chapter, I will treat the notion of being in a better epistemic position in

---

[2] One could make the case that insofar as on some of the views categorized as capacity views it is essential that the capacities in play are reliable, those views would better be classified as reliabilist views.

[3] Williamson (2000) famously holds that knowledge cannot be analyzed. But one can accept the insights of his account of justification as derivative from knowledge while rejecting his view that knowledge cannot be analyzed.

[4] Williamson's notion of method can be understood as a kind of capacity.

[5] For a discussion of the relationship between evidence and justification, see McGrath and Fantl 2002, 2009.

terms of being better justified, since this is the most straightforward way to think about the quality of an epistemic position.[6] While capacitism is compatible with a range of views about the relationship between the evidence that experience provides and any beliefs formed on the basis of that evidence, it explains in virtue of what one is in a better epistemic position when one perceives than when one hallucinates. When one forms the belief, "that apple is red," on the basis of perceiving a red apple, one's belief is better justified than when one forms the same belief on the basis of hallucinating a red apple. One's evidence in the good case justifies any supported belief to a higher degree than does one's evidence in the bad case.[7]

It is part of the nature of hallucination that one may not be able to tell whether one is in the good case or the bad case and so whether one has factive evidence in addition to phenomenal evidence. If one cannot tell whether one is perceiving or hallucinating, what effect will the difference in evidence have for one's cognitive life? In response, we can say that the difference in evidence will have repercussions for what one is justified in believing. Factive perceptual evidence is evidence of particulars in a perceiver's environment and so justifies singular thoughts about her environment. Phenomenal evidence is not evidence of particulars in a perceiver's environment. More generally, we can say that any perception can give rise to a number of different beliefs, including singular beliefs and general beliefs. The factive evidence provided by my perception will support both singular beliefs and general beliefs. Phenomenal evidence, by contrast, supports—unbeknownst to the experiencing subject—only general beliefs. The point generalizes beyond experience: if you have propositional justification for the singular belief, "that's a red apple," you will also have propositional justification for the general belief it entails: "There is a red apple." That follows from a relatively simple schema for deductive closure. So while one cannot tell whether one is in the good case or the bad case and so cannot tell whether one has factive evidence in addition to phenomenal evidence, it makes an epistemic difference to have factive evidence in addition to phenomenal evidence, in that more of one's beliefs will be justified: while factive evidence supports singular beliefs as well as general beliefs, phenomenal evidence supports only general beliefs.

Another way of expressing the same idea is with regard to the logical role of demonstratives and how we articulate the content of experience. The content type and token content of any subjectively indistinguishable perceptual experiences can be articulated in the very same way in natural language. They had better be. After all, a perception and a hallucination can be subjectively indistinguishable and one should be able to

---

[6] An alternative would be to think of the quality of the epistemic position as an aspect of knowledge distinct from justification. On this way of thinking, one would say that the perceiver and the hallucinator are equally justified, but the perceiver is still in a better epistemic position in virtue of having knowledge, where this difference in epistemic position makes the difference between knowledge and ignorance.

[7] An interesting question is what the connection is between the strength of the evidence we have for a proposition and our confidence in that proposition. For a discussion of the relationship between having evidence for p and having confidence in p, see Neta 2003, 2008, Silins 2005, and Munton 2016.

articulate subjectively indistinguishable experiences in the same way. Consider again a perceptual experience of a red apple. The content type and the singular token content can both be articulated with "that apple is red." The demonstrative "that," however, will play a different logical role in the two cases. In the content type, the demonstrative plays a character role—to use Kaplan's terminology (cf. Kaplan 1989). It purports to refer to whatever particular, if any, there might be, without saying which it happens to be on a given occasion. So in the content type, the demonstrative will refer to whatever (if anything) happens to be available to be singled out. By contrast, in the singular content, the demonstrative plays a content role—in Kaplan's sense of "content." It refers to a specific particular singled out on a given occasion—in the case of a perception, the very thing to which the perceiver is perceptually related. So, unbeknownst to the experiencing subject, the two contents will play different roles in inferences and so have different evidential repercussions for our cognitive lives. In Section 2, I will discuss this set of issues in more detail.

2. Factive Evidence and Luminosity

Capacitism entails that one is not always in a position to know what evidence one has. So capacitism entails that the following principle is false.

> *Evidential Transparency Principle:* For any evidence *E*, whenever one is suitably alert and conceptually sophisticated, one is in a position to know whether one has *E*.

The evidential transparency principle is a particular version of the more general principle that mental states are luminous—assuming that the evidence one has is constituted by the mental state one is in.[8] The idea that evidence is a matter of what mental state one is in does not imply an internalist view of evidence. After all, mental states can be externally individuated. Indeed, capacitism posits that mental states are at least in part externally individuated. Following Williamson, we can specify the principle that mental states are luminous in the following way:

> *Luminosity:* For every mental state *M*, whenever one is suitably alert and conceptually sophisticated, one is in a position to know whether one is in *M*.[9]

The evidential transparency principle is a particular version of luminosity insofar as it posits that subject *S* has evidence *E* because she is in a certain mental state *M* that provides *E*. Capacitism entails that luminosity is false. Now it would put the cart before the horse to reject luminosity so as to uphold capacitism. But as I will show, there are independent reasons to reject the principle.

---

[8] I am taking for granted here that being in a mental state is closed under constitution: what is constituted only by the mental is itself mental. For an argument for the thesis that the evidence one has is a matter of what mental state one is in, see Williamson 2000.

[9] See Williamson 2000: 11 for both principles. For a critical discussion of both principles, see Smithies 2012.

First, let's get clearer about why capacitism entails that one is not always in a position to know what evidence one has. Consider the case in which one has evidence E. If evidence is externally individuated, then one will not always be in a position to know that one has evidence E. Similarly, if one does not have evidence E and evidence is externally individuated, one will not always be in a position to know that one does not have evidence E. To show this, we can formulate the following argument:

The Argument from the Evidence We Have in Perception and Hallucination

1. If one perceives a white cup, then one has factive evidence of that white cup.
2. If one suffers a hallucination as of a white cup, then one does not have factive evidence of a white cup.
3. It is not transparent whether one perceives a white cup or suffers a hallucination as of a white cup.
4. It is not transparent whether or not one has factive evidence of a white cup.
5. If it is not transparent whether or not one has factive evidence of a white cup, then mental states are not luminous.

From 1–5: Therefore, mental states are not luminous.

Premise 1 and Premise 2 are consequences of capacitism. Premise 3 follows from the generally accepted thesis that a perception and hallucination could be subjectively indistinguishable. If Premises 1 through 3 hold, then—given capacitism—one is not always in a position to know what evidence one has.

Now what independent reasons do we have for rejecting the evidential transparency principle and, more generally, luminosity? One such reason is given by the argument from the subjective indistinguishability of perception and hallucination:

The Argument from the Subjective Indistinguishability of Perception and Hallucination

1. If mental states were luminous, it would be luminous to a subject S whether she is perceiving or hallucinating.
2. It is not luminous to S whether she is perceiving or hallucinating.

From 1 & 2: Therefore, mental states are not luminous.

Consider the case in which Hallie is hallucinating that there is a white cup on her desk. It seems to her as if a particular white cup is in front of her—that is, it seems to her as if she is in the good case. That is just what it means for a hallucination to be subjectively indistinguishable from a perception. However, it only seems to her that a particular cup is present. So she does not have factive evidence of the presence of a particular cup, but rather mere phenomenal evidence. She does not know, however, that she does not have factive evidence. After all, if it were accessible to her whether she has factive evidence or only phenomenal evidence, a perception and a hallucination could never be subjectively indistinguishable to her. So it is not transparent to Hallie that she is hallucinating.

An argument analogous to the argument from the subjective indistinguishability of perception and hallucination can be made regarding the perception of qualitatively identical, yet numerically distinct particulars:

The Argument from Perceiving Numerically Distinct but Qualitatively Indistinguishable Objects

1. If mental states were luminous, it would be luminous to a given subject S whether she is perceiving α or β, where α and β are numerically distinct yet qualitatively identical particulars.

2. It is not luminous to S whether she is perceiving α or β.

From 1 & 2: Therefore, mental states are not luminous.

Both arguments show that factive mental states are not luminous. If they were, one would always know whether one is perceiving or hallucinating. Moreover, one would know whether one is perceiving α or β, even if α and β are qualitatively identical and all else is equal. Both are counterintuitive. So capacitism entails that evidence is not luminous. To be clear, the view does not presuppose that one could never have full access to one's evidence, but only that it can be the case that one does not know everything about the specific mental state one is in and thus the specific evidence one has.

A different way of articulating the same point is with regard to the KK principle, that is, the principle that if you know that p is the case then you know that you know that p is the case. While perception yields perceptual knowledge, we do not know when an experience yields knowledge. Luminosity has it that we know what mental state we are in if we are suitably alert and conceptually sophisticated. So luminosity would then entail that, so long as we are suitably alert and conceptually sophisticated, in perception we not only attain the mental state of knowledge but also know that we obtain the mental state of knowledge (since our being in the mental state of knowledge is transparent to us). But this cannot be right. In perception we have mental state M, but we lack knowledge that we have mental state M since we do not know whether we are perceiving or hallucinating. Hence we have a mental state M that is non-transparent. Indeed, we do not know whether we are perceiving or hallucinating, and so when we are perceiving, we do not know that we know. So the KK principle is false.

The more general lesson to be learned from this argument is that one may know things without knowing that one knows them. But even if one does not know what epistemic position one is in, one may nonetheless exploit that epistemic position.[10] After all, one has evidence E, and having that evidence will have repercussions for one's cognitive and epistemic life. The evidence will justify beliefs that would not be justified if one did not have that evidence.

A second independent rationale in support of the thesis that mental states are not luminous is motivated by how best to handle sorites cases. Consider again the following

---

[10] For a recent discussion of related issues, see Greco 2014.

sorites case: we perceive consecutively three subtly distinct shades of red: red_{47}, red_{48}, and red_{49}. We cannot perceptually tell the difference between red_{47} and red_{48}. We cannot perceptually tell the difference between red_{48} and red_{49}. Yet we can perceptually tell the difference between red_{47} and red_{49}. How do we analyze what is going on in such a color sorites case? We do not want to say that perceiving red_{47} and perceiving red_{48} have the same phenomenal character, and that perceiving red_{48} and red_{49} have the same phenomenal character, while perceiving red_{47} has a different phenomenal character from perceiving red_{49}. After all, this would violate Leibniz's law of identity.

How then should we explain how it is possible that we cannot perceptually tell the difference between red_{47} and red_{48}, cannot perceptually tell the difference between red_{48} and red_{49}, yet can perceptually tell the difference between red_{47} and red_{49}? Arguably, the best way to explain how this is possible is in virtue of there being a difference in our phenomenal evidence between red_{47} and red_{48} (as well as between red_{48} and red_{49}) despite the fact that we cannot tell that there is such a difference. An explanation for how we can distinguish between red_{47} and red_{49} draws on the premise that there is a subjectively indiscernible difference between our phenomenal evidence when we perceive red_{47} and red_{48} as well as a subjectively indiscernible difference between our phenomenal evidence when we perceive red_{48} and red_{49}. These two subjectively indiscernible differences add up to a difference that is sufficiently large to tell the difference between our phenomenal evidence when we perceive red_{47} and red_{49}. The idea is that there can be aspects of our phenomenal evidence to which we do not have access. As this case brings out, while it is necessary to reject luminosity if we accept that perceptual states are factive there are reasons to reject the principle even for non-factive mental states.[11] Given that there are reasons to reject luminosity for non-factive mental states, we need not be troubled that we *must* reject it if we recognize that experience provides us with factive evidence.

A third rationale in support of rejecting luminosity is that knowledge of one's mental state relies on introspection, and introspection is well known to be an unreliable guide to one's mental states. We mistake itches for pains, we can fail to notice that we are in pain, and we mistake sensations of hunger for feelings of anger. Given that we can be prey to such dramatic errors, it would be astonishing if we were good at noticing the finer differences between perceptual states.[12]

If these considerations are right, then we can say that while perceiving a cup gives us evidence that the particular cup is present, we do not in virtue of this *know* that we have evidence of this particular cup. In short, we have evidence that it is that cup, without knowing that we have this evidence.

---

[11] Some internalists have understood the accessibility of evidence as an essential part of the very nature of evidence. Indeed, it has been argued that denying the accessibility of evidence amounts to changing the subject (Cohen 1984: 284). It will lead too far astray to address this issue here.

[12] For a more general discussion of the limits and unreliability of introspection, see Pereboom 1994, Goldberg 2000, Bar-On 2004, Schwitzgebel 2008, Fumerton 2009, and Gertler 2011.

3. Identical Twins and Speckled Hens

Having discussed some implications of capacitism for justification and luminosity, I will now explore its application to a range of familiar cases. By thinking through the cases, I will further develop the view, while also displaying its consequences.

> **Identical Twins.**   Ida sees α and knows that there is at least one object β that is qualitatively identical to α. α and β are numerically distinct, yet qualitatively identical particulars. They are identical twins.

Is Ida justified in believing that what she sees is α? Or would this require that she have evidence that she is not seeing β? For our purposes, α and β could be qualitatively identical rubber ducks, coffee cups, or people. To keep issues of personal identity out of the picture, I will focus on inanimate objects. Putting aside issues specific to personal identity, everything said about inanimate objects carries over to persons. Capacitism posits that Ida's experience gives her at least some *prima facie* justification for believing that α is present—even in the absence of evidence that she is not seeing β. After all, she sees α and as a consequence she has phenomenal and factive evidence that α is where she sees it to be.

While one does not need evidence that one is not seeing β to have evidence that one is seeing α, the concern that one might be seeing β can arise when there is positive reason to suspect that what one is seeing could be β. Ida might, for example, be told (falsely) that β was at the very location at which α is now, suggesting that she is in fact not seeing α, but rather β. So she might gain misleading evidence that she is seeing β. In such a case, Ida has a potential defeater of her *prima facie* justification that α is present.

However, even if she has such misleading evidence, she still has factive evidence that α is present. So her evidence in support of her belief that the object in front of her is α is unchanged. Two things change if she has misleading evidence that she could be seeing β. First, she has additional evidence that may affect what overall credence she should invest in the claim that α is present. Second, she has additional evidence in support of her belief that the object is β and so not α. While both changes affect the degree to which she is *ultima facie* justified in believing that the object is α, there is no reason to think that they affect the factive evidence of α she has in virtue of seeing α. So there is no challenge to the claim of *prima facie* justification.[13]

The token content of the perceiver's mental state will differ, depending on which particular she is perceptually related to. According to capacitism, the token content counterfactually varies with the world. So what factive evidence one has is counterfactually sensitive to the world to which one is perceptually related. In W_1 with object α, we have content C_1. If the world changes to W_2 with object β, we have distinct content C_2, however close W_1 and W_2 are. What evidence one has determines what one has justification to believe. So I am arguing that even though we cannot tell whether we are

---

[13] Thanks to Dan Greco for helpful discussions on these issues.

seeing α and not β, we have (unbeknownst to us) evidence for the presence of α when seeing α and so *prima facie* justification for the proposition that α is present.[14]

In the case of seeing identical twins, one is perceptually related to numerically distinct yet qualitatively identical particulars. One's phenomenal evidence is the same, yet one's factive evidence is distinct. What about a case in which one notices a qualitative difference, but it is not obvious what perceptual capacities one is employing to account for the difference in the phenomenal character of one's experience? One such case is that in which one first sees a hen with 48 speckles and then sees a hen with 47 speckles (Chisholm 1942).

> **Spyka and the Speckled Hens.**   At time t_1, Spyka sees a hen with 48 clearly visible speckles. She is aware of the hen and is causally related to all 48 speckles. At time t_2, unbeknownst to Spyka the 48-speckled hen is replaced with a 47-speckled hen. With exception of the 48-speckled hen having one speckle more than the 47-speckled hen, the two hens are qualitatively identical and nothing else changes. So at time t_2, Spyka sees a different hen with 47 clearly visible speckles. She is aware of the hen and is causally related to all the 47 speckles. Spyka does not know that the 48-speckled hen was replaced with the 47-speckled hen and the only change in her phenomenal character between t_1 and t_2 is due to the difference in speckles.

How does Spyka's evidence change between t_1 and t_2? To address this question, let's first take a closer look at the nature of our perceptual state when we see a hen with 48 clearly visible speckles. If Spyka looks at a hen with 48 clearly visible speckles, she is causally related to 48 speckles. Most human perceivers, however, do not have the capacity to subitize 48 speckles, that is, they do not have the capacity to rapidly and accurately judge how many objects there are in a group of 48 objects. The subitizing range for most human perceivers lies at around 4 objects. Of course, they could count the speckles, but that is an entirely different cognitive task from assessing the number of speckles at a glance. The difference between seeing a hen with 3 clearly visible speckles and seeing a hen with 48 speckles will help explain the issue. In the former case, we can be aware that the hen has exactly 3 speckles on the basis of seeing the hen, and so we have phenomenal evidence that the hen has 3 speckles. We can visually discriminate an object that has 3 speckles from one that has 2 speckles or one that has 4 speckles. So we can visually discriminate that there are 3 speckles from relevant alternatives. By contrast, in the case of seeing a hen with 48 speckles, we are not aware that the hen has exactly 48 speckles. After all, we cannot visually discriminate an object that has 48 speckles from relevant alternatives, for instance, an object that has 47 speckles or one that has 49 speckles. So we do not have phenomenal evidence that the hen has exactly 48 speckles.

We are, however, aware that the hen has lots of speckles. Perhaps we are aware that it has more than 30 speckles and less than 80 speckles. To appreciate the subtlety of the

---

[14] For a critical discussion of identical twin cases, see McGrath 2016.

problem, consider the fact that the phenomenal character of Spyka's experience when she sees a hen with 48 speckles may be different from the phenomenal character of her experience when she sees a hen with 47 speckles. I should add immediately that on certain views of phenomenal character, it is possible that the phenomenal character remains exactly the same in the two situations. The important point here is that on all views of phenomenal character, it is possible that one's phenomenal character changes if, for example, one is in Spyka's situation and notices that there is some difference regarding the speckles of the hen one sees at time t_1 and the hen one sees at time t_2. So even if we cannot subitize the number of speckles and even if we cannot say specifically what changed between two scenarios, we can tell that there is some difference in a scenario on the basis of how the scenario looks to us. To be sure, I am not saying that we always notice such a difference, but just that we can notice such a difference. So I am saying only that there *can* be a difference in the phenomenal character of seeing a hen with 48 speckles and seeing a hen with 47 speckles. The fact that there can be such a difference is enough for our purpose.

I will argue that Spyka does not have factive or phenomenal evidence *that* the hen has 48 speckles, but that she nonetheless has factive and phenomenal evidence that the 48-speckled hen is *differently speckled* than the 47-speckled hen. What accounts for the possible difference in phenomenal character between seeing a 47-speckled hen and a 48-speckled hen? If the phenomenal character of experience is grounded in the content of experience, as representationalists have it, then the difference in phenomenal character will be due to a difference in perceptual content. I will here presuppose such a representationalist view of phenomenal character, that is, a view on which the phenomenal character of experience is grounded in the representational content of experience.[15]

Given this presupposition, the question about phenomenal character becomes a question about what we represent when we are perceptually related to a hen with 48 clearly visible speckles. One option might be to say that we represent 48 speckles simply as a consequence of being causally related to the hen and the hen having 48 clearly visible speckles.[16] But this cannot be right. After all, we are causally related to all sorts of things in perception, which we do not represent since we do not have any visual access to them or since we do not notice them: ultraviolet light rays, the microphysical structure of objects, the speck of dust on the floor next to the hen that is visible but which we do not notice. It would be odd to say that we represent all those things.

The condition for representing α must be more constrained than being causally related to α. Two possible constraints are that we represent only what is *detectable* to the perceiver and that we represent only what the perceiver *notices*. In contrast to

---

[15] For a defense of such a view, see Chapter 6. See also Dretske 1995, Tye 1995, Byrne 2001, Chalmers 2006a, Pautz 2010, and Schellenberg 2011b.

[16] For a discussion of such an approach, see McGrath 2013.

ultraviolet light rays and the microphysical structure of objects, the 48 speckles are detectable to Spyka. In contrast to the speck of dust on the floor, Spyka notices the speckles on the hen. More generally, the idea is that a perceiver represents α, only if α satisfies the following three conditions: the perceiver is causally related to α, α is detectable to the perceiver, and the perceiver notices α.

Spyka perceiving the hen with the 48 speckles satisfies all these conditions, yet the fact that Spyka cannot subitize 48 speckles is reason to believe that, nonetheless, Spyka does not represent 48 speckles. As noted, there can, however, be a difference in phenomenal character between seeing a hen with 48 speckles and one with 47 speckles. If there is such a difference in phenomenal character, there will be—assuming a representationalist view of phenomenal character—at least some difference with regard to the content of the experience.

What further constraint could we invoke to account for this difference in perceptual content? To address this question, let's take a closer look at what Spyka discriminates when she sees a hen with 48 speckles and then one with 47 speckles. One kind of perceptual capacity Spyka could be employing is her capacity to discriminate between having 48 speckles and having 47 speckles. Another kind of perceptual capacity Spyka could be employing is her capacity to discriminate between a scenario that includes a hen with 48 speckles and a scenario that includes a hen with 47 speckles. While Spyka cannot subitize 48 speckles and 47 speckles, she can visually tell the difference between the two scenarios, even if the only difference is one speckle on a speckled hen. Due to this, she employs at least some distinct perceptual capacities and this explains why the phenomenal characters of the two experiences differ.

There are several options for specifying just what the difference is in the perceptual capacities that Spyka employs. If what she notices is that there is a speckle on the first hen that is not present on the second hen, then the difference in the perceptual capacities employed will be that she employs the perceptual capacity to single out that speckle when seeing the first hen, but does not employ that perceptual capacity when seeing the second hen.

An alternative option is that she employs the demonstrative concept SO-SPECKLED when seeing the two hens. Demonstrative concepts are individuated by what they single out. Since the hens are speckled differently, the relevant demonstrative concept will be different when she sees the 48-speckled hen compared to when she sees the 47-speckled hen. The difference in the demonstrative concepts employed accounts for the difference in phenomenal character and thus accounts for the difference in phenomenal evidence.

These are just two viable options. There are sure to be many more. Both strategies explain how it can be that Spyka does not have factive or phenomenal evidence that the hen has 48 speckles, but nonetheless can have both factive and phenomenal evidence that the 48-speckled hen is differently speckled than the 47-speckled hen. For our purposes that is all we need.

4. Confidence, Credence, and Evidence

What repercussions do changes in evidence have for the credence we should assign to any beliefs formed on the basis of our experience? To address this question, consider again Percy and Hallie. Percy is perceiving a white cup, while Hallie is unbeknownst to her hallucinating a white cup. Both form the belief "that is a white cup." As I argue, Percy has more evidence than Hallie, since Percy has factive evidence and phenomenal evidence for his belief, while Hallie has only phenomenal evidence. I argue, moreover, that in virtue of having more evidence, Percy's belief is better justified than Hallie's belief: he is more justified in his belief "that is a white cup" since he has factive evidence in addition to phenomenal evidence. We can call the thesis that Percy has more evidence than Hallie *Extra Evidence* and the thesis that Percy's belief is better justified than Hallie's *More Justification*.

One might argue that insofar as Percy and Hallie's evidence can be articulated in the very same way, the evidence they each have will ultimately be the same. Pautz argues for this in his discussion of my view (Pautz 2016). In response, while it is true that Hallie would articulate her evidence with "that cup is white," this does not mean her evidence is "that cup is white." The evidence one has and how one would articulate that evidence are two very different things. There is no reason to think that the verbal expression of an experience is a good guide to the content of the experience and thus the evidence one has. Moreover, if the proposition articulated with the verbal expression of one's evidence were the content of one's evidence that would rule out any externalist account of evidence. Equating the evidence one has with how one would articulate that evidence would not only over-intellectualize the content of experience, it would moreover eradicate any differences in evidence that are not accessed by the experiencing subject. In short, "that cup is white" is not the evidence one has when one suffers a hallucination as of a white cup; it is merely the way one might articulate one's evidence. Pautz writes:

> As for Hallie, Schellenberg's view is that Hallie's total evidence includes "phenomenal evidence" which, she says, can be articulated by saying "that cup is white." So it is very natural to suppose that, on Schellenberg's view, Hallie's phenomenal evidence *also* simply entails Cup, even if that evidence happens to be false.   (Pautz 2016: 920f.)

Cup, according to Pautz, is the proposition "there really is a white cup present" (Pautz 2016: 916). By conflating the evidence one has with how one would articulate that evidence, Pautz is led to claim that on my view:

> *both* Hallie and Percy are in possession of evidence that *entails* Cup. In that case, given standard Bayesianism, Schellenberg's own version of Extra Evidence fails to support her assertion of More Justification, that is, her assertion that Percy's evidence supports the belief in Cup "to a higher degree" than does Hallie's evidence.   (Pautz 2016: 921)

Pautz goes on to say that both Percy and Hallie's evidence has probability 1 conditional on their total evidence.

In response, Hallie does not have evidence that entails Cup, and so there is no Bayesian argument that Hallie has maximal evidence for Cup. Her evidence is determined by a content schema. Indeed, as I have argued, Hallie does not have the evidence "that cup is white," even though she may articulate her evidence in that way when expressing a belief based on her experience. More generally, although one would articulate the evidence in exactly the same way, the evidence in subjectively indistinguishable good and bad cases is different. Given that the experiences are subjectively indistinguishable, it had better be the case that one would articulate them in exactly the same way. Percy does not appreciate his evidence as being factive. Hallie does not appreciate her evidence as being merely phenomenal. Of course, Hallie may falsely believe that there really is a cup present due to it seeming to her that there is a cup. Hallie may falsely believe all sorts of things. Hallie falsely believing that there really is a cup present does not imply that she has evidence that there really is a cup present.

According to capacitism, Percy is in possession of factive evidence that entails Cup and so—at least assuming standard Bayesian principles—Cup has probability 1 on his evidence. But Hallie does not have the factive evidence that Percy possesses, and so Cup does not have probability 1 on her evidence. This is all we need to support the idea that Percy has more evidence than Hallie and that his belief therefore is justified to a higher degree than Hallie's belief "that is a white cup." So contra Pautz, Hallie and Percy have different evidence. Only Percy has evidence that entails Cup, and so only Percy's evidence is such that Cup has probability 1 on it. So Percy's evidence (call it E_p) entails Cup, whereas Hallie's evidence (call it E_h) does not entail Cup. So, we can have both of the following:

1. $Pr(\text{Cup}|E_p) = 1$.
2. $Pr(\text{Cup}|E_h) < 1$.

Now Bayesians model learning via conditionalization, and post-conditionalization, propositions learned must receive probability 1. Standard Bayesianism does not commit one to the idea that the evidence one has is represented by the propositions on which one conditionalizes. It is important to separate the question of how to properly model "learning" from how to individuate a subject's evidence. Bayesians need not identify the evidence a subject has with the propositions to which they assign maximal credence (or to those on which they have conditionalized or "learned"). Indeed, Bayesians are free to count uncertain claims as part of an agent's evidence.[17] So Bayesians are free to say that the experiencing subject is less than certain in the proposition p which encodes the content of her hallucination—so long as she has not updated on p via conditionalization. So Extra Evidence supports More Justification and, moreover, nothing in my view precludes me from appealing to standard Bayesianism to support More Justification. Once one departs from standard Bayesianism and allows alternatives

---

[17] See Joyce 2005 for a helpful discussion of these issues. For a discussion of the relationship between having evidence for p and having confidence in p, see also Neta 2003, 2008, and Silins 2005.

to strict conditionalization to model the learning process (e.g. Jeffrey conditionalization), then it is no longer required that all "learned" propositions have probability 1. This is an attractive alternative that I am sympathetic to. However, as I hope to have shown, capacitism is compatible even with standard Bayesianism.[18]

One question waiting in the wings is how evidence bears on the rationality of mental states other than beliefs, such as credences. Neta raises this issue in response to my capacity view by imagining a case in which one is first perceiving a white cup (cup$_1$) and then starts hallucinating a cup. Neta asks, "What implications does this new hallucination have for the rationality of Percy's states of comparative confidence, or for the rationality of his degrees of confidence?" (Neta 2016: 913). In response, the subject in this case has phenomenal and factive evidence for the presence of cup$_1$ and phenomenal evidence for the cup he is hallucinating. In contrast to Neta, I see no reason for thinking that Percy's evidence for the presence of cup$_1$ changes after he has started to hallucinate an additional cup—while still perceiving cup$_1$. After all, he does not know he is hallucinating an additional cup. So he has no reason to doubt his overall epistemic standing. Moreover, there are good reasons to treat separately the fact that he is veridically perceiving cup$_1$ while hallucinating an additional cup. We do not have to treat these two aspects of his current mental state as interfering with one another.

Percy's rational confidence in cup$_1$ being present is 1 (before and after he starts hallucinating the second cup), but his rational confidence in an additional cup being present is lower. After all, he is hallucinating rather than perceiving that additional cup. I see no reason to think that hallucinating an additional cup should lower his rational confidence in the presence of cup$_1$. This approach goes hand in hand with arguing that the rationality of his degree of confidence will change as his environment changes. In that sense, I am following the standard externalist approach about rationality in holding that the amount of rational confidence one has can change due to external factors.[19]

5. Brains in Vats, Matrixes, and the New Evil Demon Scenario

What evidence do we have in cases in which we are not just hallucinating, but are dramatically deceived? To address this question, it will be helpful to consider the new evil demon scenario (Lehrer and Cohen 1983, Cohen 1984).

Matt and the New Evil Demon. Matt finds himself inadvertently entrapped in a matrix. The matrix looks just like the real world to Matt, but it is in fact a

---

[18] Thanks to Branden Fitelson for a helpful email exchange on these issues.

[19] For a more detailed discussion of this set of issues, see Schellenberg 2016c. For an argument that we have no good grip on what counts as evidence for p that does not enter into determining one's rational level of confidence that p, see Neta 2008.

computer-generated world in which he is unwittingly entrapped. Matt is programmed to have a sensory state as of a white cup. Matt has a counterpart in the real world. Matt's counterpart is called Max. Max sees a white cup. So Matt has the same sensory experience as Max. But Max perceives what Matt merely seems to see while being trapped in a matrix.

While Max's evidence is truth-conducive, Matt's evidence is not. Indeed, Matt's experiences are systematically misleading. There are two central questions. Is capacitism compatible with Matrix Matt having evidence? And what evidence does Matt have when, unbeknownst to him, the new evil demon presents him with false experiences?

Capacitism is compatible with accepting that the victim of the new evil demon has evidence. After all, the idea that phenomenal states are systematically linked to what they are of in the good case requires only that there is the possibility of getting things right in the good case. That is compatible with there not being any actual good cases.[20] Given that the possession of perceptual capacities is not understood phylogenetically or ontogenetically, there is no reason to require that an experiencing subject has a history of employing a perceptual capacity successfully in perception to employ the capacity in the bad case. There is no reason to think that the victim of the new evil demon does not have properly functioning capacities while being presented with false experiences. He is simply unlucky. Insofar as the mere possibility of good cases is sufficient, capacitism is compatible with the victim having evidence.

In light of this response to the first question, we can now address the question of what evidence a victim has who suffers perceptual experiences at the hands of a new evil demon. The victim of the demon has phenomenal evidence but no factive evidence beyond the propositions one might still know in a new evil demon scenario, such as, "I think, therefore I am." He has no factive evidence beyond such propositions, since he does not perceive external mind-independent particulars and so will fail to single out any such particulars when employing perceptual capacities. So while Matrix Matt has the same sensory state as his counterpart in the real world, he does not have the same evidence. Matt has only phenomenal evidence, whereas Max has both phenomenal and factive evidence.

Now there are ways of understanding the new evil demon scenario on which it is stipulated that the person trapped in the matrix has the very same evidence as his counterpart in the real world who is in the good case. I am rejecting any such stipulation. I am rather following the common interpretation of the new evil demon scenario on which the person in the matrix and his counterpart have the same sensory experience. Having the same sensory experience is compatible with having different evidence. After all, having the same sensory experience is compatible with being in mental states with different content if the relationship between the phenomenal character and the content of a mental state is not identity but rather supervenience. If the phenomenal

---

[20] For a more detailed discussion of this issue, see Chapter 6, Section 4.

character of a mental state supervenes on the content of the mental state, there can be differences in content that are not reflected in phenomenal character.[21] Moreover, if the content of one's mental state determines one's evidence, then a view on which the phenomenal character of a mental state supervenes on the content of the mental state will allow that two beings whose experiences have the same phenomenal character could fail to have the same evidence.

So capacitism respects the key internalist intuition that mental duplicates will have the same evidence. However, according to capacitism, Matt in the matrix and his counterpart Max in the real world could never be mental duplicates. After all, Matt is in the bad case and Max is in the good case. So Matt fails to single out any particulars, while Max singles out the particulars he purports to single out. As a consequence, the content of Matt's experiential state differs from the content of Max's mental state. Therefore, Matt and his counterpart could never have exactly the same mental state and so could never have exactly the same overall evidence. While they have the same phenomenal evidence, Max has additional factive evidence. This externalist response to the new evil demon problem differs from traditional externalist responses (see Sosa 1991, Goldman 1993, Bergmann 2006) insofar as it rejects the claim that Matt and his counterpart could have the very same evidence, while accepting that the content of one's mental state determines one's evidence.

Can an envatted brain hallucinate?

Brain in a Vat.   Brian is a disembodied brain in a vat. He is hooked up to a sophisticated computer program that produces electrical impulses that stimulate the brain in the way that embodied brains are stimulated as a result of perceiving particulars in the environment. So the computer program simulates experiences of the outside world.

An envatted brain cannot perceive; it does not have the sensory organs to do so. But it could possess perceptual capacities, despite never being able to use them accurately. After all, perceptual capacities are not tied to the proper functioning of sense organs or even their existence. As long as the envatted brain has perceptual capacities that function to single out particulars, then there is no reason to think that the envatted brain could not have hallucinations. Insofar as the brain in a vat can hallucinate, it has phenomenal evidence.[22]

Naturally, the brain in a vat could employ its capacities successfully only if it were connected to the necessary sensory organs. But the fact that it cannot employ its perceptual capacity successfully in its current envatted state does not have any repercussion for the fact that perceptual capacities have a certain function. Even if a being is not in a position to be perceptually related to its environment, the perceptual capacities that this being possesses do not cease to have the function of singling out particulars.

---

[21] For a defense of such a weak representationalist view, see my 2010. See also Chapters 4 and 5.
[22] For a discussion of brains in vats, see Brueckner 1986.

So brains in a vat are analyzed in the same way as the subject who suffers at the hands of an evil demon.

A somewhat different case is one in which one suffers a veridical hallucination.

Veridical Hallucinations. Vernon suffers a veridical hallucination as of a white cup. He hallucinates a white cup at location L_1 and as it so happens, there is a white cup behind a screen just where he hallucinates a white cup to be. Since the actual white cup is behind a screen, he could not be perceptually related to it. So the cup at L_1 is not causally relevant in bringing about his hallucination. On the basis of his hallucination, he forms the belief that there is a white cup at L_1.[23]

Capacitism provides a way to do justice to internalist and externalist intuitions about this case. According to capacitism, Vernon employs the very same perceptual capacities that he would employ, were he perceiving a white cup. As a consequence, he is in a mental state with content that provides him with phenomenal evidence that there is a white cup at L_1. So capacitism can explain why he is not blameworthy for his belief that there is a white cup at L_1. Not only is Vernon excused in believing that there is a cup at L_1, since he has phenomenal evidence that there is a cup at L_1 and since phenomenal evidence justifies general propositions, Vernon has some justification for his belief. But Vernon does not have factive evidence, since he is not perceptually related to the white cup at L_1. Since his evidence is merely phenomenal, he is not justified in believing the singular proposition "that is a white cup."

6. Time-Slice Epistemology and Swampman

One issue we have not yet discussed in detail is how the history of a perceiver affects the epistemic force of her perceptual experience. To address this question, recall Davidson's Swampman scenario (Davidson 1987: 443f.).

Swampman. Donald Davidson goes hiking in a swamp and is struck and killed by a lightning bolt. Simultaneously, a second lightning bolt spontaneously rearranges molecules such that they take on exactly the same form that Davidson's body had at the moment of his death. The resulting Swampman behaves exactly like the original author of "Radical Interpretation." His brain is structurally identical to that which Davidson had at the moment of his death. Swampman walks out of the swamp, returns to Davidson's office at Berkeley, and writes the same essays Davidson would have written. Swampman has no causal history.

Does Swampman possess perceptual capacities? Do his perceptual experiences provide him with phenomenal and factive evidence? According to the view developed here,

---

[23] This case differs from Bonjour's (1980) Norman case, since there is no assumption that Vernon arrives at his hallucination by way of a reliable process. By contrast, clairvoyant Norman arrives at his beliefs by way of a reliable process that is not, however, based on any evidence or reasons.

no past experiences are necessary to possess perceptual capacities. Since possessing perceptual capacities does not depend on a history of proper usage—or any usage for that matter—and since perceptual capacities are not understood in an evolutionary way, there is no reason to think that Swampman could not possess the perceptual capacities in play. After all, the condition for their possession is understood counterfactually: if one possesses the capacity to single out red, then one would be able to single out an instance of red, were one related to such an instance. Since Swampman possesses the relevant perceptual capacities, he can through perception gain phenomenal and factive evidence about the swampy world around him.

Insofar as the history of employing a perceptual capacity is in no way relevant for the epistemic force of the mental state generated by employing the relevant capacity, capacitism is a kind of time-slice epistemology. Discussions of time-slice epistemology have focused on what it is rationally permissible or obligatory for agents to do (see e.g. Moss 2015: 172). The focus here is not on the epistemic norms governing subjects' actions, but rather on the epistemic force of subjects' mental states. Applied to this issue, time-slice epistemology is committed to the following principle:

> *Time-Slice Principle:*   The epistemic force of a subject S's mental state M at time t_1 is determined exclusively by history-independent properties of M at t_1.

Applied to capacitism, the point is that the history of a subject is not relevant for the epistemic force of her mental states. Moreover, the history of employing a mental capacity is not relevant for the epistemic force of the mental states generated by employing those capacities.

7. Coda

Perceptions guide our actions and provide us with evidence of the world around us. Hallucinations can mislead us: they may prompt us to act in ways that do not mesh with the world around us and they may lead us to form false beliefs about that world. Capacitism provides an account of evidence that does justice to these two facts. It shows in virtue of what hallucinations mislead us. Moreover, it shows in virtue of what we are in a better epistemic position when we perceive than when we hallucinate. Phenomenal evidence and factive evidence are both world-directed due to being constituted by capacities that are world-directed. While factive evidence cannot by its very nature be false, phenomenal evidence can be false. This discrepancy between phenomenal and factive evidence can be fruitfully exploited in analyzing a range of familiar cases. As I aim to have shown, capacitism respects our intuitions about these cases.

Chapter 9

Perceptual Knowledge and Gettier Cases

In this chapter, I will exploit the resources of capacitism to offer a view of perceptual knowledge that is externalist but neither disjunctivist nor reliabilist. I will show how this view helps handle perceptual Gettier cases. As I will argue, while factive evidence is sufficient evidence for knowledge, phenomenal evidence is not.

To recap: the basic idea of capacitism is that in perception, hallucination, and illusion we employ perceptual capacities that function to discriminate and single out particulars in our environment. Perceptual states have epistemic force due to the nature of these perceptual capacities. Employing such perceptual capacities in perception, hallucination, and illusion yields a weak type of evidence that I call phenomenal evidence. Employing such capacities in perception provides us, moreover, with a second strong type of evidence that I call factive evidence.

The standard analysis of Gettier cases is that the Gettiered subject has a true belief and sufficient evidence for knowledge, but still lacks knowledge. On my view, this analysis is too simplistic. The distinction between phenomenal and factive evidence gives us the resources to say that the Gettiered subject has mere phenomenal evidence; since she does not have factive evidence, she fails to have sufficient evidence for knowledge. Thus, capacitism offers a way of handling perceptual Gettier cases without appeal to any factor beyond that of evidence.

To keep the discussion tractable, I will focus on perceptual knowledge and perceptual Gettier cases. The lessons I wish to draw reach beyond perception, however. Toward the end of the chapter, I will consider the extent to which my account generalizes to non-perceptual cases.

1. A Sufficient Evidence Requirement for Knowledge

To develop a sufficient evidence requirement for knowledge, let's discuss the relation between phenomenal evidence, factive evidence, and perceptual knowledge. Phenomenal evidence is not sufficient evidence for knowledge. After all, having mere phenomenal evidence is compatible with suffering a hallucination. In hallucination, the subject has a justified mental state (such as a belief) that falls short of knowledge. Factive evidence, on the other hand, is sufficient evidence for knowledge. After all, factive evidence is infallible: the token content of perception that determines factive evidence is determined by and covariant with the perceiver's environment and thus guaranteed to be accurate.[1] So regardless of whether one thinks of sufficient evidence for knowledge in terms of safety guarantees or in terms of low fallibility, then one should agree that factive evidence is sufficient evidence for knowledge.

If factive evidence is sufficient evidence for knowledge, then we gain perceptual knowledge by successfully employing perceptual capacities. Insofar as capacities are mental tools by means of which we relate to our environment, the states constituted by employing such capacities are mental states. Moreover, insofar as successfully employing capacities yields perceptual knowledge, capacitism entails that knowledge is a mental state. In this way, capacitism gives an explanation of what it means for knowledge to be a mental state: knowledge is a mental state in virtue of being constituted by employing mental capacities.[2]

Orthodoxy has it that sufficient evidence is a necessary condition for knowledge: for subject S to have perceptual knowledge that p, S must have sufficient evidence for p. Note that this is weaker than the sufficient evidence requirement for knowledge articulated above: that requirement states a sufficient condition for knowledge (not a mere necessary condition). I will follow orthodoxy and assume that sufficient evidence is necessary for knowledge. Given this assumption and given the analysis so far, we are now in a position to formulate the following necessary and jointly sufficient conditions for a subject to have perceptual knowledge:

Subject S has perceptual knowledge that p if and only if p is true, S employed a capacity to single out what she purports to single out, and S's mental state has the content it has in virtue of S having successfully employed her capacity to single out what she purports to single out.

This analysis of perceptual knowledge does not rely on any belief condition on knowledge: one can know that p without believing that p. The standard view is that one cannot know that p without believing that p. Omitting a belief condition on knowledge is attractive for at least two reasons. First, it allows that we can gain knowledge about a particular α simply in virtue of perceiving α. While any perceptual belief will be grounded in perception, we can perceive α without forming any beliefs about α. A second reason for giving up a belief condition on perceptual knowledge is that an experiential state that falls short of knowledge does not amount to a belief. If we fail to perceive what it seems to us we are perceiving and so fail to acquire knowledge, this does not entail that we believe what it seems to us we are perceiving. We may be hallucinating without forming any beliefs based on our hallucination.[3]

---

[1] For a detailed discussion of the accuracy conditions of perceptual content, see Chapter 4, Section 3.5.

[2] For the idea that knowledge is a mental state, see Williamson 2000 and Nagel 2013.

[3] For alternative arguments that we can know without believing, see Pritchard 2012 and Turri 2010. The arguments provided here need to be modified only slightly to accommodate a belief condition on knowledge. If we add a belief condition on knowledge, the necessary and jointly sufficient conditions for S to have perceptual knowledge that p would be: S has perceptual knowledge that p if and only if p is true, S employed a capacity to single out what she purports to single out, S believes that p, and her belief has the content it has in virtue of S having successfully employed her capacity to single out what she purports to single out.

If an experiential state that falls short of knowledge is not a belief, how then should we think of this mental state? In response, we can think of it as a justified mental state. A justified mental state may be belief, but it need not be.

Justified mental states can be true or false: hallucinations, illusions, and perceptual Gettier cases yield justified mental states that fall short of knowledge. Perception yields knowledge states. Both kinds of states are constituted by employing perceptual capacities. The relevant difference between justified mental states that fall short of knowledge and knowledge states is that the latter but not the former are ones in which capacities are employed such that they fulfill their function. Any additional difference between knowledge and justified mental states can be traced back to this difference.

2. Perceptual Gettier Cases: Phenomenal Evidence without Factive Evidence

So far I have sketched a conception of knowledge on which factive evidence constitutes sufficient evidence for knowledge while phenomenal evidence does not. I am now in a position to discuss the consequences of capacitism for perceptual Gettier cases. I will argue that the subject in a perceptual Gettier case lacks sufficient evidence for knowledge. This allows me to explain why she lacks knowledge, without appealing to anything beyond a sufficient evidence requirement. Consider the following case:

> **Robot Dog.**   James is relaxing on a bench in a park and sees what he takes to be a dog in a nearby field. On the basis of his perception, he believes, "there is a dog in the field." As it happens, James is in fact seeing a robot that looks like a dog. The robot is so well constructed that it could not be distinguished from an actual dog—at least not from where James sits. James does not know that such robot dogs exist. So if that was a full description of the case, James's belief "there is a dog in the field" would be false. However, coincidentally there is a real dog in the same field, concealed from James's view. So James's belief "there is a dog in the field" happens to be true.[4]

What should we make of this case? The standard approach is to say that James's belief "there is a dog in the field" is both true and supported by sufficient evidence for knowledge. The motivation for this approach is that there is in fact a dog in the field, and the belief was based on ordinary perceptual processes—albeit on grounds of perceiving a robot dog rather than the actual dog in the field. So on this approach, James has sufficient evidence for knowledge, but nonetheless lacks knowledge. The reasoning for why he has sufficient evidence for knowledge seems to stem from the internalist

---

[4] See Ichikawa and Steup 2012, Section 4. This case is structurally the same as Chisholm's (1966: 23, fn. 22) sheep-shaped rock case.

idea that James is doing just the same thing from his own perspective as a successful perceiver would be doing in a simple case of seeing a dog in the field (with no robots or other complications).

Capacitism has a different verdict of this case. Since James is not perceptually related to a dog, he does not discriminate and single out a dog (despite it seeming to him that he is doing just that). As a consequence, he does not have factive evidence of a dog. The fact that unbeknownst to James there happens to be a dog in the field does not mean that James has factive evidence of that dog. After all, he did not discriminate and single out that dog. Despite lacking factive evidence, James has a justified true belief. His belief is true due to the presence of the dog in the field. His belief is justified since he employs his capacity to single out a dog and in virtue of this, he is in a mental state that is intentionally directed at a dog. Being in this mental state provides him with some evidence for his belief that there is a dog in the field. It provides him with phenomenal evidence. Thus we can acknowledge that James's belief "there is a dog in the field" is a justified true belief: the belief is true since there is a dog in the field and the belief is justified since it is supported by James's phenomenal evidence.

In short, James has phenomenal evidence but fails to have factive evidence that there is a dog in the field. Since phenomenal evidence is not sufficient evidence for knowledge, James lacks sufficient evidence to know that there is a dog in the field.

More generally, we can say that the Gettiered subject's mental state is constituted by employing mental capacities that fail to fulfill their function. As a consequence, her belief has some justification (due to the subject having phenomenal evidence), but lacks knowledge-level justification (due to the subject failing to have factive evidence).

According to capacitism, we gain knowledge of our environment if we single out particulars in our environment by employing perceptual capacities that function to single out those very particulars. So when we employ the capacity to discriminate and single out a particular at location L_1 in our environment and we in fact discriminate and single out that particular at L_1, we gain factive evidence and thus perceptual knowledge of the particular at L_1.

In a Gettier case, the particular at L_1 is not in fact the particular that the subject purports to single out. So in this case, the subject employs capacities that fail to discriminate and single out the particular at L_1. That is the case even if it seems to the subject that she is successfully discriminating and singling out that particular at L_1. Moreover that is the case even if there is a particular at location L_2 that the subject could have successfully singled out but did not in fact successfully single out, as in the robot dog case where there is a real dog a few feet away from the robot, and in Chisholm's original case of the sheep-shaped rock with a real sheep hidden behind it.

Perceptual knowledge differs from mere justified true mental states in that the capacities employed in knowledge in fact succeed in serving their natural function. In mere justified true mental states, the capacities are employed while failing to single out what the subject purports to single out.

Now, one might argue that insofar as employing perceptual capacities yields knowledge, these capacities should simply be analyzed as capacities to know.[5] But such a view would put the cart before the horse. It is unclear what the explanatory gain would be of analyzing knowledge in terms of capacities to know. Arguably, any such account would be circular.

According to capacitism, the perceptual capacities in play are not analyzed as capacities to know: one neither employs the capacity to know when one is in the bad case, nor when one is in the good case. Perceptual capacities are analyzed rather in terms of their natural function, namely their function to discriminate and single out particulars in the environment. So capacitism grounds the epistemic force of experience in the metaphysical properties of experience. Every epistemic property has a ground. If a mental state has an epistemic property there is a meaningful question what grounds that property. As I argue, the ground of the epistemic force of perceptual states lies in the function of perceptual capacities to discriminate and single out particulars in the environment—the perceptual capacities that constitute the perceptual states.

Now, insofar as one can employ capacities to single out particulars or employ them while failing to single out the particular one purports to single out, they are fallible. Indeed, they yield states that are either accurate or defective (and thus guaranteed to be false). In this respect, the view here differs fundamentally from Williamson's (2000) view. According to Williamson, the methods employed in gaining evidence are infallible and the mental state yielded is always factive.[6]

As I argued in Chapter 8, according to capacitism, a mental state can be justified by a perception or a perceptual experience that falls short of perception, as is the case in a hallucination, an illusion, or a misperception. In any case in which perceptual capacities are employed, a phenomenal state is constituted that at the very least provides phenomenal evidence. Insofar as perceptions, hallucinations, and illusions each provide the experiencing subject with at least some evidence, and so justification for any belief she might form, capacitism entails that justification is common to both cases of knowledge and mental states that fall short of knowledge (such as mere beliefs).

While capacities are fallible, this does not mean that the good case and the bad case are on a par. As I argued in Chapter 7, any employment of capacities in the bad case is derivative from their employment in the good case. Since perceptual capacities function to single out particulars, their employment yields states that are prone to yield factive evidence and knowledge, even though the environment does not always play along. After all, both the good and the bad case are brought about by employing perceptual capacities. We get at how the world is via perception in a particular way, namely by employing perceptual capacities. And even when we fail to get at how the world is (and

---

[5] See Miracchi 2015 for such a view.

[6] In a similar vein as Williamson, Millar (2008) argues that abilities are infallible and yield mental states that are factive. I am here assuming that Williamson's notion of method and Millar's notion of ability can be treated as analogous to my notion of capacity. For a more detailed discussion of the difference between capacitism and knowledge-first views, see Chapter 10, Section 1.

so are in the bad case), we are employing perceptual capacities by means of which we aim to get at how the world is. In this way, capacitism provides an explanation of perceptual justification and the way justification is, on the one hand, necessary for knowledge, but why mere justified mental states are nevertheless metaphysically and epistemically dependent on mental states that amount to knowledge.

So with the knowledge-first view, capacitism explains the bad case in terms of the good case. But against the knowledge-first view (and any other disjunctivist view), capacitism has it that there is a metaphysically substantial common element between the good and the bad case, namely the capacities employed. This common element explains how it is that we have at least some justification in the bad case. In virtue of this, capacitism is a unified account of knowledge, on the one hand, and justified mental states that fall short of knowledge, on the other.

3. Separating the Barns from the Sheep and the Clocks

Now let's get back to perceptual Gettier cases. Perceptual Gettier cases are similar to hallucinations in that in both cases capacities are employed without fulfilling their function. In contrast to hallucinations, however, there is an external, mind-independent ground for employing the capacity elsewhere in the environment. But the relevant perceptual capacity is not directed toward the right particular. As I have argued, when a true mental state is justified, this is due to the relevant subject employing capacities that function to single out what seems to be present. In perceptual Gettier cases, the subject fails to have knowledge despite having a justified true mental state since she is not appropriately related to what it seems to her to be present. She fails to have knowledge since the capacities she employs do not single out what they function to single out and it seems to her she is singling out.

There is at least one case that has traditionally been understood to be a Gettier case that would not count as a Gettier case according to capacitism, namely Ginet's and Goldman's barn façade county case (Goldman 1976: 772f.).[7] But this is a good outcome. To show why let's first consider the case.

> **Barn Façade County.**   Henry is driving down the road in barn façade county. The county is peppered with barn façades: from the road they look just like barns, but they are in fact structures that only look like barns when seen from the road. Viewed from any other angle, one would immediately be able to tell that they are mere façades. Henry is looking at the one and only barn in barn façade county and forms the belief "that is a barn." His belief is justified and true.

The standard verdict of this case is to say that since the truth of the belief is a result of luck, Henry does not know that what he sees is a barn. Henry's belief is a result of luck since it is false in most of the closest non-actual cases.

---

[7] Goldman credits Ginet with this example, though Ginet never put it in writing.

The verdict of capacitism is different and arguably more plausible: Henry employs his capacity to single out the barn he sees, and since he is perceptually related to that very barn, he has both phenomenal and factive evidence of the barn. In virtue of having factive perceptual evidence, he has perceptual knowledge. After all, he sees a real barn. One might argue that while Henry has perceptual knowledge, he lacks a more sophisticated kind of knowledge. Taking that route would follow Sosa's analysis of the case (Sosa 2007: 96, fn. 1).[8] Sosa argues that Henry has animal knowledge but lacks reflective knowledge. We can remain neutral here on whether Henry lacks such reflective knowledge and whether we should distinguish more primitive from more sophisticated kinds of knowledge.

Either way, even though Henry has factive evidence and so sufficient evidence for perceptual knowledge, one might argue that the sheer existence of the barn façade entails that it is unreasonable for him to believe that there is a barn, despite the fact that Henry is unaware that he is in barn façade county. But even if we grant this, it will not affect what factive perceptual evidence he has regarding the barn. It will affect only what he ends up being justified in believing, all things considered.[9] Being in barn façade county might affect the degree to which Henry is *ultima facie* justified in believing that there is a barn in front of him, but given capacitism, there is no reason to think that it will affect the factive evidence he has of the barn in virtue of seeing the barn. So there is no challenge to Henry's *prima facie* justification for the presence of the barn that he gains in virtue of seeing the barn.

Once Henry learns that he is in barn façade county the situation changes. If Henry gains the information that he is in barn façade county, then he gains new evidence. But even though he gains evidence that he is in barn façade county, this does not entail that his perceptual evidence is weakened.[10] After all, even if he has defeaters they are not undercutting defeaters, but rather mere rebutting defeaters. So although Henry may have such defeaters, it will not affect what evidence he has regarding the barn. It will affect only what he ends up being justified in believing, all things considered. So even in this case, while gaining information that he is in barn façade county might affect the degree to which Henry is *ultima facie* justified in believing that there is a barn in front of him, there is no reason to think that gaining this information will affect the factive evidence he has of the barn in virtue of seeing the barn. Once Henry knows that he is in barn façade county, he has good reason to be suspicious of what he learns

---

[8] See Sylvan (forthcoming) for an alternative analysis, on which Henry could have knowledge of the barn he sees.

[9] Lackey (2007 and 2009) distinguishes between knowing that *p* and deserving credit for truly believing that *p*. This allows her to argue that *S* can know that *p* without deserving credit for truly believing that *p*. If one assumes that successfully employing perceptual capacities is not something one deserves credit for, then one could say that Henry knows that there is a barn in front of him, while denying that he deserves credit for truly believing that there is a barn in front of him. This would allow one to distinguish Henry's epistemic situation from that of someone who sees a barn in a county in which there are no fake barns. Alternatively, one could argue that successfully employing perceptual capacities is something for which one does deserve credit.

[10] See Lasonen-Aarnio 2010 for a similar view. Lasonen-Aarnio argues that one can know even if one's belief is unreasonable.

through perception. Nonetheless, he has factive perceptual evidence of the barn he is seeing in virtue of seeing the barn. And in virtue of having factive perceptual evidence, he has perceptual knowledge of the barn. In short, perceptual evidence is so powerful that Henry has perceptual factive evidence regardless of whether he is consciously aware of being in barn façade county.

The fake barn case should be sharply distinguished from Russell's broken clock case (Russell 1948: 154).

> **Broken Clock.**   Sophie glances at a clock. The small hand points to the 3 and the long hand points to the 12. She forms the justified true belief that it is 3 p.m. But unbeknownst to Sophie the clock is stuck on 3 p.m. and she just glanced at it during one of the two moments in the day when it coincidentally showed the right time.

In this case, Sophie has factive evidence that the small hand points to the 3, while the long hand points to the 12, and so perceptually knows that the small hand points to the 3, while the long hand points to the 12. On that basis she forms the inferred justified true belief that it is 3 p.m., but her inference is subject to defeat (after all, the clock is broken), and is in any case no longer a perceptual matter. She does not know that it is 3 p.m., since that is not the kind of knowledge that one can gain via perception.

So I am suggesting that we move beyond the taxonomy of "Gettier cases," and separate out such cases as the robot dog case (perceptual Gettier case), the fake barn case (successful perception), and the broken clock case (inferential Gettier case). Once the topic of inferential Gettier cases comes into view, the worry arises that my view is specially designed for perceptual Gettier cases, insofar as it is based on an understanding of the nature of perceptual experience in terms of singling out particulars, which is not apt for inference, memory, testimony, or other bases for knowledge. So one might object that there is a unified phenomenon of "Gettier cases" across perception and these other bases for knowledge which calls for a unified solution, when my account is only apt for perceptual cases.

I have two very different responses to this worry. First, there are reasons to doubt that there is a unified phenomenon of Gettier cases. From an epistemic perspective, perception may have special features (as may inference, memory, and testimony). The robot dog and broken clock cases, for example, have in common that there is justified true belief without knowledge, but they differ in many other details, such as whether one even lays one's eyes on the relevant particular. Both cases need to be resolved, but it is not obvious that they need to be—or ought to be—resolved in the same way.

The second response to the worry is more ambitious. There are reasons to think that the underlying account of epistemic force I offer generalizes in unifying ways. On my account, perceptual experience has evidential force because of the systematic linkage between perceptual capacities and the good case of successful perception. The natural generalization of this view of evidential force to, say, inference would be that inferred beliefs preserve evidential force because of the systematic linkage between inferential capacities and the good case of successful inference. On this view, the broken clock case might then be analyzed as an inferential bad case in which the environment was not playing along, with the result being that Sophie only winds up with phenomenal inferential evidence that it is 3 p.m. and not with factive inferential evidence that it is 3 p.m.[11]

4. Coda

I have offered a distinctive externalist view of perceptual knowledge and shown how it helps handle perceptual Gettier cases. I argued that employing perceptual capacities yields a mental state that provides us with phenomenal evidence, and employing such capacities in the good case provides us with additional knowledge-worthy factive evidence. In perceptual Gettier cases, the subject only has phenomenal evidence, and so lacks sufficient evidence for knowledge. This approach is distinctive in three respects. It groups perceptual Gettier cases in with hallucinations. It analyzes perceptual Gettier cases in terms of a lack of sufficient evidence (rather than through invoking some sort of fourth condition on knowledge beyond truth, justification, and belief). It analyzes perceptual Gettier cases differently than fake barn cases and broken clock cases.

[11] It would lead too far astray to work through such a generalized account of knowledge here. I will reserve that for another occasion. For discussion, see Schellenberg 2017.

Chapter 10

Capacitism and Alternative Views

It will be helpful to discuss the key differences between capacitism and related alternative views: knowledge-first epistemology, reliabilism, and virtue epistemology.

1. Capacitism and Knowledge-First Epistemology

As Williamson develops knowledge-first epistemology, knowledge is a mental state and evidence is a known proposition or a set of such propositions (Williamson 2000). On Williamson's knowledge-first view, there are two kinds of facts that can figure as the truthmakers of the content of experiential states: facts about the experience and facts about the environment in which one is experiencing. In perception, we have factive perceptual evidence about the environment. In hallucination, we have factive introspective evidence, that is, known propositions about how things seem to us.[1] Such an approach restricts the evidence we can gain through perceptual experience to factive evidence. However, this factive evidence includes not just perceptual evidence, but also introspective evidence: the evidence we gain through perceptual experience is either factive with regard to our environment or with regard to our experience.

Like the knowledge-first view, capacitism holds that knowledge is a mental state and that we have some evidence in the bad case, but that we have more evidence in the good case. There are five key differences between the two views.

One key difference is that the fundamental explanatory notion of capacitism is capacities rather than knowledge. A second and related difference is that the knowledge-first view is disjunctivist, and recognizes no epistemically relevant common element between the good case and the bad case. As I argued in Chapter 7, capacitism is not disjunctivist, and recognizes an epistemically relevant and metaphysically substantial common element between the good case and the bad case, namely the capacities employed.

A third key difference is that according to capacitism, we have at least some evidence in common between the good and the bad case—namely, we have phenomenal evidence. So while capacitism and the knowledge-first view both have it that we have some evidence in the bad case, but that we have more evidence in the good case,

---

[1] For a discussion of introspective evidence, see Chapter 7, Section 1: "Perceptual Evidence and Introspective Evidence."

according to capacitism the evidence we have in the bad case is evidence that we also have in the good case. Thus capacitism is non-disjunctivist with regard to the content, the metaphysics, and the epistemology of perception.

A fourth key difference is that on the knowledge-first view, the methods employed in gaining evidence are infallible: evidence always receives probability 1, and thus the mental state yielded is factive. According to capacitism, the methods employed in gaining evidence are not infallible and while the mental state yielded is factive in the good case, it is not factive in the bad case.

Finally, a fifth key difference concerns the nature of the evidence we have in the bad case. Given that according to the knowledge-first view evidence is a known proposition, there is no room for evidence provided directly through experience in the bad case. After all, in the bad case there are no true propositions provided directly through experience: we have only introspective evidence in the bad case. So the view posits that we do not get evidence directly through our experience when we hallucinate, but only through introspection. On the knowledge-first view, Percy has factive perceptual evidence and factive introspective evidence, while Hallie has only factive introspective evidence.

According to capacitism, by contrast, Percy has phenomenal and factive perceptual evidence, while Hallie has phenomenal perceptual evidence. Phenomenal evidence is not introspective evidence. It is evidence provided directly through experience. So by contrast to the knowledge-first view, capacitism makes room for experience providing us with evidence directly even in the bad case without retreating to introspective evidence. This is an important advantage of capacitism over Williamson's version of the knowledge-first view for three reasons.

First, introspection is a sophisticated intellectual ability, yet even subjects who lack this ability can gain evidence through hallucination. By relying on subjects attending to how things seem to them, Williamson's knowledge-first view over-intellectualizes the way we get evidence in the bad case.

A second and more pressing over-intellectualization worry with Williamson's knowledge-first view concerns Williamson's claim that the evidence we have in the bad case is an appearance proposition, such as the proposition "it seems to me that the tiger looks dangerous." The problem with this view is that appearance propositions involve appearance concepts and being in a mental state characterized by such a proposition requires self-reference. Non-rational animals do not possess appearance concepts nor are they capable of self-reference. Nonetheless, they can hallucinate and, plausibly, thereby gain evidence.

Capacitism does not face these two over-intellectualization problems, since we have phenomenal evidence in the bad case in virtue of being in a phenomenal state: there is no need to introspect or attend to our experience to have phenomenal evidence. On the view developed, we can have phenomenal evidence even if we have no ability to refer to ourselves and do not possess appearance concepts.

The third reason why it is more attractive to say that experience provides us with phenomenal evidence directly even in the bad case without retreating to introspective evidence concerns the source of the evidence. According to the knowledge-first view, the source of our evidence in the good case is perceptual experience; the source of our evidence in the bad case is introspection. So the source of our evidence differs at least in part in the good and the bad case. According to capacitism, by contrast, the source of both factive and phenomenal evidence is our perceptual experience. Thus, capacitism provides a unified account of the source of perceptual evidence.

In short, I am following the knowledge-first approach in arguing that we have a kind of evidence in the good case that we do not have in the bad case. In contrast to Williamson's view, however, capacitism does not identify evidence with knowledge and makes room for a phenomenal conception of evidence. We should not and need not retreat to the idea that experience provides us only with introspective evidence in the bad case. Any such retreat would not do justice to the epistemic force of experience.

2. Capacitism and Reliabilism

Capacitism makes room for an externalist account of the epistemic role of perceptual experience that neither depends on nor entail reliabilism (Goldman 1979). A reliabilist might argue that phenomenal states provide us with evidence since they are constituted by reliable perceptual capacities. According to capacitism, however, the epistemic force of perceptual experience neither stems from perceptual capacities being reliable nor from the reliability of conditions underwriting one's having the capacity. Reliability simply plays no role in my account. This is a good thing, since perception is not a particularly reliable faculty. According to capacitism, phenomenal states provide us with evidence since phenomenal states are systematically linked to the particulars that the relevant perceptual capacities function to single out. If a subject's environment sensorily seems to contain F particulars, then she is in a phenomenal state that is constituted by employing perceptual capacities that function to single out F particulars. Such a phenomenal state provides evidence for the presence of F particulars.

So the notion of systematic linkage in play is understood not in terms of reliability but in terms of a metaphysical and explanatory primacy of employing perceptual capacities in perception. In speaking of it being the function of perceptual capacities to single out the relevant particulars, I do not mean to speak of their reliability but rather of how they are to be understood metaphysically. In other words, I am not speaking of their actual track-record, whatever that might be, but their metaphysical nature (what they are). Perceptual states provide evidence in virtue of the metaphysical nature and function of the capacities that constitute perceptual states. Now, the perceptual capacities employed in perception may happen to be reliable. However, even so it is the metaphysical and explanatory primacy of the good over the bad case that gives experience its epistemic force.

Part of what is at issue in whether or not one invokes reliability is what one can say about Davidson's Swampman, in which an atom-for-atom duplicate of a human being forms spontaneously when lightning strikes a swamp. Intuitively one wants to say that

Swampman's experience can provide him with evidence. Capacitism can say this. After all, given the notion of capacity in play, Swampman's perceptual capacities function to single out particulars just as ours do. Just as Swampman's heart has the function to pump blood, his perceptual capacities have the function to single out particulars. This is the case even though Swampman himself has no evolutionary history. So, I can vindicate the intuitive response that Swampman has evidence even though he has no past interactions with anything and lacks ancestors. Standard versions of reliabilism, however, are forced to deny that Swampman has evidence.

3. Capacitism and Virtue Epistemology

Virtue epistemologists hold that you deserve credit for what you know, since what you know is due to your intellectual virtues. To know is, for example, to believe truly because you believe virtuously. More specifically, the idea is that knowledge is a true belief that is not accidentally true, but rather true due to the subject's capacities (or dispositions, competences, abilities, or virtues).[2] As Greco (2004: 111) puts it: "To say that someone knows is to say that his believing the truth can be credited to him. It is to say that the person got things right due to his own abilities, efforts and actions, rather than due to dumb luck, or blind chance, or something else." There are at least two versions of virtue epistemology. For reliabilist virtue epistemologists, the reliability of the relevant capacities is key in analyzing the epistemic force of mental states (Sosa 1980, 2007, 2010 and Greco 2009, 2012). For responsibilist virtue epistemologists, the responsibility by means of which the relevant capacities are exercised is key in analyzing the epistemic force of mental states (Zagzebski 1996).

Sosa (2007) develops his version of virtue epistemology within the framework of his AAA-model of assessment. Performances can be assessed for accuracy (truth), adroitness (manifesting intellectual competence), and aptness (being true in virtue of being competent). Knowledge is identified with apt belief. This provides a way to say that knowledge is non-accidentally true belief, while allowing that one might know, even if one might easily have been wrong.

Capacitism shares with virtue epistemology the guiding idea of explaining knowledge in terms of a mental activity that has certain distinctive properties in the good case. Moreover, like virtue epistemology, capacitism is a kind of anti-luck theory in that it rejects the JTB+ approach of analyzing knowledge in terms of a combination of independent epistemic properties: justification, truth, belief, and some further condition.

There are six key differences between capacitism and virtue epistemology. One key difference is that while virtue epistemologists treat knowledge as a particularly successful or valuable case of belief, according to capacitism, knowledge is the primary

[2] For ease of presentation, I will refer to the relevant virtues as capacities. It is important to note, that different virtue epistemologists use different terms and that these differences may not be mere terminological differences.

case. In this respect, capacitism follows knowledge-first views. According to capacitism, we know in virtue of successfully employing capacities that function to single out particulars in our environment. By contrast, if we fail to employ those very same capacities successfully, we do not have sufficient evidence for knowledge. When we fail to employ the capacities successfully, we may not be in a belief state. So in contrast to the virtue epistemological approach, knowledge is not analyzed as a particularly successful or valuable case of belief.

A second key difference between capacitism and virtue epistemology concerns whether the relevant capacities (the successful employment of which generates knowledge) are themselves to be understood in normative or naturalistic terms. For the virtue epistemologist, capacities are understood normatively, as intellectual virtues. While reliabilist virtue epistemologists can allow that some performances have aims due to having biological functions, the relevant capacities are nonetheless understood normatively. According to capacitism, capacities are not understood normatively but rather naturalistically, in terms of their natural function.[3]

The third key difference concerns the relation between employing capacities and mental states. According to virtue epistemology, the relevant capacities are capacities to believe truly. Thus, they are by their nature imbued with rich epistemic properties. Employing them does not constitute mental states, rather the mental states are manifestations of exercising the relevant capacities. According to capacitism, by contrast, the relevant capacities are low-level mental capacities, such as the capacity to discriminate and single out instances of red. Employing such capacities constitutes the relevant mental states.

A fourth key difference is that on standard virtue epistemologist views, a subject can exercise a capacity in the appropriate environment and nevertheless fail (Sosa 2015). A subject might form a false belief, even though the belief is the output of a capacity employed in an appropriate environment.

According to capacitism, such competent failure is not possible. When the subject is perceptually related to a mind-independent particular, she is in the good case. She could not employ perceptual capacities and nevertheless fail to refer to the particulars present. After all, she is perceptually related to those particulars and employing perceptual capacities that function to single out particulars of the type to which she is perceptually related.

A fifth key difference concerns the analysis of knowledge. According to virtue epistemology, a subject S knows that p if and only if p is true, S believes that p, S exercised a capacity to believe truly in believing that p, and S believes truly due to having formed her belief in virtue of exercising the capacity to believe truly. Responsibilist and reliabilist versions of virtue epistemology differ in how they understand the "in virtue of"

---

[3] For an argument that natural functions need not be understood in normative terms, see Broome 2013. The only sense in which such natural functions could be arguably have a normative element is if such a function grounds the possibility of malfunction. But on standard notions of normativity that would not be sufficient to qualify as having a normative element.

relation. Among reliabilist interpretations, we can distinguish further between views that understand the "in virtue of" relation causally (Sosa 2007: 95ff.) and those that understand it dispositionally (Sosa 2010, 2015). According to capacitism, by contrast, S knows that p if and only if p is true, S employed a capacity to single out what she purports to single out, and the content of S's mental state p has the content it has in virtue of S having employed her capacity, and in virtue of employing this capacity to successfully single out what she purports to single out. So the capacity employed that brings about knowledge that p is not the capacity to believe truly that p or the capacity to know that p. It is the capacity to discriminate and single out a particular α in the environment. Employing this capacity will constitute a factive mental state if and only if one is perceptually related to α while employing the capacity to discriminate and single out α (thereby discriminating and singling out α). So by employing this capacity successfully one knows that α is present.

It will be helpful to show how these differences play out for Gettier cases. Consider the case in which p is true, but S does not know p despite having some evidence in support of p. The virtue epistemologist argues that while p is true, S believes that p, and S exercised a capacity to believe truly in believing that p, S does not believe truly due to S having formed her belief by exercising the capacity to believe truly. More simply, S fails to know, since her belief is not due to her capacity in the right way. As Sosa puts it, S does not believe aptly. As argued in Chapter 9, capacitism analyzes the Gettier case as follows: p is true and S employed a capacity to single out what she purports to single out, but the content of S's mental state does not have the content it has in virtue of S having employed her capacity and in virtue of employing this capacity to successfully single out what she purports to single out.

The sixth key difference holds only with regard to reliabilist virtue epistemology. Most versions of virtue epistemology currently on the table develop the notion of capacities in reliabilist terms (e.g. Sosa 1980, 2007, 2010 and Greco 2009, 2012). Insofar as the reliabilist virtue epistemologist grounds the epistemic force that virtues provide in their reliability, their view is subject to all the well-known problems of reliabilism.[4] Moreover, the reliabilist virtue epistemologist is, like the standard reliabilist, forced to deny that Swampman has evidence. Since capacitism is distinctly non-normative and non-reliabilist it avoids these problems.

Despite these differences, however, capacitism is compatible with a broadly virtue-based epistemology. Indeed, by adopting key features of capacitism, such as the asymmetry principle, virtue epistemologists could give up their reliabilist commitments and thereby avoid a host of problems. Moreover, while Sosa and other virtue epistemologists do not appeal to the difference between phenomenal and factive evidence, nothing in their view precludes them from incorporating two kinds of evidence.

[4] For example, Lehrer's (1990) Truetemp counterexample: Mr. Truetemp has, unbeknownst to him, a temperature-detecting device implanted in his head that regularly produces accurate beliefs about the ambient temperature.

4. Coda

Capacitism shows how the epistemic force of experience is grounded in metaphysical facts about experience. Perceptual states have epistemic force due to the nature of the perceptual capacities that bring them about. Neither the capacities nor the metaphysical and explanatory primacy notions in play need be understood in terms of reliability, or in normative ways. Putting this together, capacitism is an externalist view that does not invoke reliability, remains steadfastly naturalistic, and recognizes a metaphysically substantial common element shared by perception, hallucination, and illusion.

References

Allen, K. 2013. "Blur." *Philosophical Studies* 162: 257–73.

Almäng, J. 2013. "The Causal Self-Referential Theory of Perception Revisited." *Dialectica* 67: 29–53.

Alston, W. 1986. "Internalism and Externalism in Epistemology." *Philosophical Topics* 4: 179–221.

Antony, L. 2011. "The Openness of Illusions." *Philosophical Issues* 21: 25–44.

Aristotle. 1984. *The Complete Works of Aristotle*, ed. J. Barnes. Princeton: Princeton University Press.

Armstrong, D. 1989. *Universals: An Opinionated Introduction.* Boulder, CO: Westview Press.

Austin, J. L. 1946. "Other Minds." *Supplement to the Proceedings of the Aristotelian Society* 20: 148–87.

Austin, J. L. 1970. "Ifs and Cans." *Philosophical Papers*, 2nd edn. London: Oxford University Press.

Averill, E. W. 2005. "Toward a Projectivist Account of Color." *The Journal of Philosophy* 102: 217–34.

Ayala, F. 1970. "Teleological Explanations in Evolutionary Biology." *Philosophy of Science* 37: 1–15.

Ayer, A. J. 1972. *Probability and Evidence.* New York: Columbia University Press.

Bach, K. 1987/1994. *Thought and Reference.* Oxford: Oxford University Press (revised with postscript 1994).

Bach, K. 2007. "Searle Against the World: How Can Experiences Find their Objects." *John Searle's Philosophy of Language: Force, Meaning, and Mind*, ed. S. L. Tsohatzidis. Cambridge: Cambridge University Press.

Barcan Marcus, R. 1961. "Modalities and Intentional Languages." *Synthese* 13: 303–22.

Bar-On, D. 2004. "Externalism and Self-Knowledge: Content, Use, and Expression." *Noûs* 38: 430–55.

Barrett, H. C., and Kurzban, R. 2006. "Modularity in Cognition: Framing the Debate." *Psychological Review* 113: 628–47.

Barsalou, L. W. 1999. "Perceptual Symbol Systems." *Behavioral and Brain Sciences* 22: 577–660.

Batty, C. 2010. "A Representational Account of Olfactory Experience." *Canadian Journal of Philosophy* 40: 511–38.

Batty, C. 2011. "Smelling Lessons." *Philosophical Studies* 153: 161–74.

Bayne, T. 2010. "Perception and the Reach of Phenomenal Content." *The Philosophical Quarterly* 236: 385–404.

Beck, O. forthcoming. "Rethinking Naïve Realism." *Philosophical Studies.*

Bengson, J. 2015. "The Intellectual Given." *Mind* 124: 707–60.

Bengson, J., Grube, E., and Korman, D. 2011. "A New Framework for Conceptualism." *Noûs* 45: 167–89.

Bergmann, M. 2006. *Justification without Awareness.* Oxford: Oxford University Press.

Berger, J. 2015. "The Sensory Content of Perceptual Experience." *Pacific Philosophical Quarterly* 96: 446–68.

Block, N. 1978. "Troubles with Functionalism." *Minnesota Studies in the Philosophy of Science* 9: 261–325.

Block, N. 1990. "Inverted Earth." *Philosophical Perspectives* 4, ed. J. Tomberlin. Northridge: Ridgeview Publishing Company.

Block, N. 2003. "Mental Paint." *Reflections and Replies: Essays on the Philosophy of Tyler Burge*, ed. M. Hahn and B. Ramberg. Cambridge, MA: MIT Press.

Block, N. 2007. "Consciousness, Accessibility, and the Mesh between Psychology and Neuroscience." *Behavioral and Brain Sciences* 30: 481–548.

Block, N. 2014. "Seeing-As in the Light of Vision Science." *Philosophy and Phenomenological Research* 89: 560–72.

Boghossian, P., and Velleman, J. D. 1989. "Colour as a Secondary Quality." *Mind* 98: 81–103.

Bonjour, L. 1980. "Externalist Theories of Empirical Knowledge." *Midwest Studies in Philosophy* 5: 53–73.

Brandom, R. 1994. *Making It Explicit*. Cambridge, MA: Harvard University Press.

Braun, D. 1993. "Empty Names." *Noûs* 27: 449–69.

Brewer, B. 1999. *Perception and Reason*. Oxford: Oxford University Press.

Brewer, B. 2006. "Perception and Content." *The European Journal of Philosophy* 14: 165–81.

Brewer, B. 2007. "Perception and its Object." *Philosophical Studies* 132: 87–97.

Brewer, B. 2011. *Perception and its Objects*. Oxford: Oxford University Press.

Broad, C. D. 1923. *Scientific Thought*. London: Kegan Paul.

Brogaard, B. 2015. "Perceptual Reports." *Oxford Handbook of the Philosophy of Perception*, ed. M. Matthen. Oxford: Oxford University Press.

Broome, J. 2013. *Rationality through Reasoning*. Oxford: Wiley-Blackwell.

Brueckner, A. 1986. "Brains in a Vat." *The Journal of Philosophy* 83: 148–67.

Burge, T. 1977/2007. "Belief *De Re*" with Postscript. *Foundations of Mind*. Oxford: Oxford University Press.

Burge, T. 1979. "Individualism and the Mental." *Midwest Studies in Philosophy* 4: 73–121.

Burge, T. 1991. "Vision and Intentional Content." *John Searle and his Critics*, ed. E. LePore and R. van Gulick. Oxford: Blackwell.

Burge, T. 2003. "Perceptual Entitlement." *Philosophy and Phenomenological Research* 67: 503–48.

Burge, T. 2010. *Origins of Objectivity*. Oxford: Oxford University Press.

Burge, T. 2014. "Perception, Where Mind Begins." *Philosophy* 89: 385–403.

Burnston, D., and Cohen, J. 2012. "Perception of Features and Perception of Objects." *The Croatian Journal of Philosophy* 36: 283–314.

Byrne, A. 2001. "Intentionalism Defended." *The Philosophical Review* 110: 199–240.

Byrne, A. 2009. "Experience and Content." *Philosophical Quarterly* 59: 429–51.

Byrne, A. 2014. "Perception and Evidence." *Philosophical Studies* 170: 101–13.

Byrne, A., and Hilbert, D. 2003. "Color Realism and Color Science." *Behavioral and Brain Sciences* 26: 3–21.

Byrne, A., and Logue, H. 2008. "Either/Or." *Disjunctivism: Perception, Action, Knowledge*, ed. F. E. Macpherson and A. Haddock. Oxford: Oxford University Press.

Campbell, J. 2002. *Reference and Consciousness*. Oxford: Oxford University Press.

Campbell. J. 2009. "Consciousness and Reference." *Oxford Handbook of Philosophy of Mind*, ed. B. McLaughlin and A. Beckermann. Oxford: Oxford University Press.

Campbell, J. 2010. "Demonstrative Reference, the Relational View of Experience and the Proximality Principle." *New Essays on Singular Thought*, ed. R. Jeshion. Oxford: Oxford University Press.

Carruthers, P. 2006. *The Architecture of the Mind*. Oxford: Oxford University Press.

Cartwright, N. 1994. *Nature's Capacities and Their Measurement*. Oxford: Oxford University Press.

Caston, V. 2002. "Aristotle on Consciousness." *Mind* 111: 751–815.

Chalmers, D. 1996. *The Conscious Mind*. Oxford: Oxford University Press.

Chalmers, D. 2004. "The Representational Character of Experience." *The Future of Philosophy*, ed. B. Leiter. Oxford: Oxford University Press.

Chalmers, D. 2006a. "Perception and the Fall from Eden." *Perceptual Experience*, ed. T. Gendler and J. Hawthorne. Oxford: Clarendon Press.

Chalmers, D. 2006b. "Two-Dimensional Semantics." *Oxford Handbook of the Philosophy of Language*, ed. E. LePore and B. Smith. Oxford: Oxford University Press.

Chisholm, R. 1942. "The Problem of the Speckled Hen." *Mind* 51: 363–73.

Chisholm, R. 1957. *Perceiving: A Philosophical Study*. Ithaca, NY: Cornell University Press.

Chisholm, R. 1966. *A Theory of Knowledge*. Englewood Cliffs, NJ: Prentice-Hall.

Chomsky, N. 1995. "Language and Nature." *Mind* 104: 1–61.

Chowdhury, S. A., and DeAngelis, G. C. 2008. "Fine Discrimination Training Alters the Causal Contribution of Macaque Area MT to Depth Perception." *Neuron* 60: 367–77.

Chudnoff, E. 2012. "Awareness of Abstract Objects." *Noûs* 47: 1–24.

Cohen, J. 2010. "Perception and Computation." *Philosophical Issues* 20: 96–124.

Cohen, S. 1984. "Justification and Truth." *Philosophical Studies* 46: 279–96.

Cohen, S. 2002. "Basic Knowledge and the Problem of Easy Knowledge." *Philosophy and Phenomenological Research* 65: 309–29.

Coltheart, M. 1999. "Modularity and Cognition." *Trends in Cognitive Sciences* 3: 115–20.

Comesaña, J. 2010. "Evidentialist Reliabilism." *Noûs* 44: 571–600.

Conee, E., and Feldman, R. 2008. "Evidence." *Epistemology: New Essays*, ed. Q. Smith. Oxford: Oxford University Press.

Correia, F. 2010. "Grounding and Truth-Functions." *Logique et analyse* 53: 251–79.

Crane, T. 1998. "Intentionality as the Mark of the Mental." *Contemporary Issues in the Philosophy of Mind*, ed. A. O'Hear. Cambridge: Cambridge University Press.

Crane, T. 2006. "Is there a Perceptual Relation?" *Perceptual Experience*, ed. T. Gendler and J. Hawthorne. Oxford: Oxford University Press.

Crane, T. 2009. "Is Perception a Propositional Attitude?" *Philosophical Quarterly* 59: 452–69.

Crane, T. 2011. "The Singularity of Singular Thought." *Aristotelian Society Supplementary Volume* 85: 21–43.

Craver, C. 2007. *Explaining the Brain: Mechanisms and the Mosaic Unity of Neuroscience*. Oxford: Oxford University Press.

Craver, C., and Darden, L. 2013. *In Search of Mechanisms: Discoveries across the Life Sciences*. Chicago: University of Chicago Press.

Cummins, R. 1985. *The Nature of Psychological Explanation*. Cambridge, MA: MIT Press.

Davidson, D. 1970. "Mental Events." Reprinted in his *Essays on Actions and Events*. Oxford: Clarendon Press (1980).

Davidson, D. 1987. "Knowing One's Own Mind." *Proceedings and Addresses of the American Philosophical Association* 60: 441–58.

Davies, M. 1992. "Perceptual Content and Local Supervenience." *Proceedings of the Aristotelian Society* 92: 21–45.

de Lafuente, V., and Romo, R. 2005. "Neuronal Correlates of Subjective Sensory Experience." *Nature Neuroscience* 8: 1698–703.

Dennett, D. C. 1991. *Consciousness Explained*. Boston: Little, Brown & Co.

DeRose, K. 2009. *The Case for Contextualism*. Oxford: Oxford University Press.

DeRose, K. 2011. "Questioning Evidentialism." *Evidentialism and its Discontents*, ed. T. Dougherty. Oxford: Oxford University Press.

DeRose, K., and Grandy, R. 1999. "Conditional Assertions and 'Biscuit' Conditionals." *Noûs* 33: 405–20.

DeRoy, O. 2014. "Multimodal Unity and Multimodal Binding." *Sensory Integration and the Unity of Consciousness*, ed. C. Hill and D. Bennett. Cambridge, MA: MIT Press.

DeRoy, O., Chen, Y. C., and Spence, C. 2014. "Multisensory Constraints on Awareness." *Philosophical Transactions of the Royal Society B: Biological Sciences* 369: 20130207.

Descartes, R. 1641. "Meditations on First Philosophy." Trans. J. Cottingham. *The Philosophical Writings of Descartes*, vol. 2, ed. J. Cottingham, R. Stoothoff, and D. Murdoch. Cambridge: Cambridge University Press (1986).

de Vignemont, F. 2014. "A Multimodal Conception of Bodily Awareness." *Mind* 123: 989–1020.

Devitt, M. 1981. *Designation*. New York: Columbia University Press.

Donnellan, K. 1966. "Reference and Definite Descriptions." *The Philosophical Review* 75: 281–304.

Dorsch, F. 2013. "Experience and Introspection." *Hallucination*, ed. F. Macpherson and D. Platchias. Cambridge, MA: MIT Press.

Dove, G. O. 2009. "Beyond Perceptual Symbols: A Call for Representational Pluralism." *Cognition* 110: 412–31.

Drayson, Z. 2014. "The Personal/Subpersonal Distinction." *Philosophy Compass* 9: 338–46.

Dretske, F. 1969. *Seeing and Knowing*. Chicago: The University of Chicago Press.

Dretske, F. 1981. *Knowledge and the Flow of Information*. Cambridge, MA: MIT Press.

Dretske, F. 1995. *Naturalizing the Mind*. Cambridge, MA: MIT Press.

Dretske, F. 2000. "The Mind's Awareness of Itself." *Perception, Knowledge, and Belief*. Cambridge: Cambridge University Press.

Dretske, F. 2006. "Perception without Awareness." *Perceptual Experience*, ed. T. Gendler and J. Hawthorne. Oxford: Oxford University Press.

Egan, A. 2006. "Appearance Properties?" *Noûs* 40: 495–521.

Egan, F. 1992. "Individualism, Computation, and Perceptual Content." *Mind* 101: 443–59.

Evans, G. 1982. *The Varieties of Reference*, ed. J. McDowell. Oxford: Oxford University Press.

Evans, J. St B. T., and Frankish, K. 2009. *In Two Minds: Dual Processes and Beyond*. Oxford: Oxford University Press.

Everett, A. 2003. "Empty Names and 'Gappy' Propositions." *Philosophical Studies* 116: 1–36.

Fara, D. G. 2001. "Phenomenal Continua and the Sorites." *Mind* 110: 905–35. Published under the name "Delia Graff."

Feldman, R., and Conee, E. 1985. "Evidentialism." *Philosophical Studies* 48: 15–34.

Ffytche, D. H. 2008. "The Hodology of Hallucinations." *Cortex* 44: 1067–83.

Ffytche, D. H., and Howard, R. J. 1999. "The Perceptual Consequences of Visual Loss. 'Positive' Pathologies of Vision." *Brain* 122: 1247–60.

Fine, K. 2001. "The Question of Realism." *Philosophers' Imprint* 1: 1–30.

Fish, W. 2009. *Perception, Hallucination, and Illusion*. Oxford: Oxford University Press.

Fodor, J. 1975. *The Language of Thought*. Cambridge, MA: Harvard University Press.

Fodor, J. 1983. *The Modularity of Mind: An Essay on Faculty Psychology*. Cambridge, MA: MIT Press.

Fodor, J. 1987. *Psychosemantics: The Problem of Meaning in the Philosophy of Mind*. Cambridge, MA: MIT Press.

Fodor, J. 1990. "A Theory of Content, I & II." *A Theory of Content and Other Essays*, ed. J. Fodor, Cambridge, MA: MIT Press.

Fodor, J. 1998. *Concepts: Where Cognitive Science Went Wrong*. New York: Oxford University Press.

Fodor, J. 2008. *LOT2: The Language of Thought Revisited*. Oxford: Oxford University Press.

Fodor, J. 1990. *A Theory of Content and Other Essays*. Cambridge, MA: MIT Press.

Fontenelle (1683) *Nouveaux Dialogues des morts*.

Frankish, K. 2009. "Systems and Levels: Dual-System Theories and the Personal–Subpersonal Distinction." *In Two Minds: Dual Processes and Beyond*, ed. J. St B. T. Evans and K. Frankish. Oxford: Oxford University Press.

Frankish, K. 2011. "Cognitive Capacities, Mental Modules, and Neural Regions." *Philosophy, Psychiatry, & Psychology* 18: 279–82.

Frege, G. 1879. *Begriffsschrift: Eine der Arithmetischen nachgebildete Formelsprache des reinen Denkens*. Halle: L. Nebert.

French, C. 2014. "Naive Realist Perspectives on Seeing Blurrily." *Ratio* 27: 393–413.

French, C. 2016. "Idiosyncratic Perception." *Philosophical Quarterly* 66: 391–99.

Fulkerson, M. 2011. "The Unity of Haptic Touch." *Philosophical Psychology* 24: 493–516.

Fumerton, R. 2009. "Luminous Enough for a Cognitive Home." *Philosophical Studies* 142: 67–76.

Ganson, T., Bronner, B., and Kerr, A. 2014. "Burge's Defense of Perceptual Content." *Philosophy and Phenomenological Research* 88: 556–73.

García-Carpintero, M. 2010. "Fictional Singular Imaginings." *New Essays on Singular Thought*, ed. R. Jeshion. Oxford: Oxford University Press.

Genone, J. 2014. "Appearance and Illusion." *Mind* 123: 339–76.

Gertler, B. 2011. *Self-Knowledge*. London: Routledge.

Ghijsen, H. 2015. "Grounding Perceptual Dogmatism: What Are Perceptual Seemings?" *Southern Journal of Philosophy* 53: 196–215.

Glick, E. 2012. "Abilities and Know-How Attributions." *Knowledge Ascriptions*, ed. J. Brown and M. Gerken. Oxford: Oxford University Press.

Glüer-Pagin, K. 2009. "In Defence of a Doxastic Account of Experience." *Mind and Language* 24: 297–327.

Godfrey-Smith, P. 2008. "Reduction in Real Life." *Being Reduced*, ed. J. Hohwy and J. Kallestrup. Oxford: Oxford University Press.

Goff, P. 2018. "Conscious Thought and the Cognitive Fine-Tuning Problem." *Philosophical Quarterly* 68: 98–122.

Goldberg, S. 2000. "Externalism and Authoritative Knowledge of Content: A New Incompatibilist Strategy." *Philosophical Studies* 100: 51–79.

Goldman, A. 1976. "Discrimination and Perceptual Knowledge." *The Journal of Philosophy* 73: 771–91.

Goldman, A. 1979. "What is Justified Belief?" *Knowledge and Justification*, ed. G. Pappas. Dordrecht: Reidel.

Goldman, A. 1986. *Epistemology and Cognition*. Cambridge, MA: Harvard University Press.

Goldman, A. 1993. "Epistemic Folkways and Scientific Epistemology." *Philosophical Issues* 3: 271–85.

Goldman, A. 1999. "Internalism Exposed." *The Journal of Philosophy* 96: 271–93.

Goldman, A. 2011. "Toward a Synthesis of Reliabilism and Evidentialism?" *Evidentialism and its Discontents*, ed. T. Doughterty. Oxford: Oxford University Press.

Gomes, A., and French, C. 2016. "On the Particularity of Experience." *Philosophical Studies* 173: 451–60.

Goodman, N. 1955. *Fact, Fiction, and Forecast*. Cambridge, MA: Harvard University Press.

Graham, P. 2011. "Epistemic Entitlement." *Noûs* 46: 449–82.

Greco, D. 2014. "Could KK be OK?" *The Journal of Philosophy* 111: 169–97.

Greco, J. 2001. "Virtues and Rules in Epistemology." *Virtue Epistemology: Essays on Epistemic Virtue and Responsibility*, ed. A. Fairweather and L. Zagzebski. Oxford: Oxford University Press.

Greco, J. 2004. "Knowledge as Credit for True Belief." *Intellectual Virtue: Perspectives from Ethics and Epistemology*, ed. M. DePaul and L. Zagzebski. Oxford: Oxford University Press.

Greco, J. 2009. "Knowledge and Success from Ability." *Philosophical Studies* 142: 17–26.

Greco, J. 2010. *Achieving Knowledge: A Virtue-Theoretic Account of Epistemic Normativity*. Cambridge: Cambridge University Press.

Greco, J. 2012. "A (Different) Virtue Epistemology." *Philosophy and Phenomenological Research* 85: 1–26.

Green, E. J. 2017. "Attentive Visual Reference." *Mind and Language* 32: 3–38.

Grice, H. P. 1961. "The Causal Theory of Perception." *Proceedings of the Aristotelian Society* 35: 121–68.

Gross, S., and Flombaum, J. 2017. "Does Perceptual Consciousness Overflow Cognitive Access? The Challenge from Probabilistic, Hierarchical Processes." *Mind & Language* 32: 358–91.

Gupta, A. 2006. *Empiricism and Experience*. Oxford: Oxford University Press.

Gupta, A. 2012. "An Account of Conscious Experience." *Analytic Philosophy* 53: 1–29.

Hardin, C. L. 1988/1993. *Color for Philosophers*. Indianapolis: Hackett.

Hardin, C. L. 2003. "A Reflectance Doth Not a Color Make." *The Journal of Philosophy* 100: 191–202.

Hardin, C. L. 2008. "Color Qualities and the Physical World." *The Case for Qualia*, ed. E. Wright. Cambridge, MA: MIT Press.

Harman, G. 1973. *Thought*. Princeton: Princeton University Press.

Harman, G. 1990. "The Intrinsic Quality of Experience." *Philosophical Perspectives* 4, ed. J. Tomberlin. Northridge: Ridgeview Publishing Company.

Hawthorne, J. 2003. *Knowledge and Lotteries*. Oxford: Oxford University Press.

Hawthorne, J., and Manley, D. 2012. *The Reference Book*. Oxford: Oxford University Press.

Heck, R. 2000. "Nonconceptual Content and the Space of Reasons." *The Philosophical Review* 109: 483–523.

Hellie, B. 2011. "There it is." *Philosophical Issues* 21: 110–64.

Hill, C. 2006. "Perceptual Consciousness: How it Opens Directly onto the World, Preferring the World to Itself." *Self-Representational Approaches to Consciousness*, ed. U. Kriegel and K. Williford. Cambridge, MA: MIT Press.

Hill, C. 2009. *Consciousness*. Cambridge: Cambridge University Press.

Hinton, J. M. 1973. *Experiences*. Oxford: Oxford University Press.

Hopkins, R. 1998. *Picture, Image and Experience: A Philosophical Inquiry*. Cambridge: Cambridge University Press.

Horgan, T., and Tienson, J. 2002. "The Intentionality of Phenomenology and the Phenomenology of Intentionality." *Philosophy of Mind: Classical and Contemporary Readings*, ed. D. Chalmers. Oxford: Oxford University Press.

Howell, R. H. J. 2016. "Perception from the First-Person Perspective." *European Journal of Philosophy* 24: 187–213.

Huemer, M. 2007. "Compassionate Phenomenal Conservatism." *Philosophy and Phenomenological Research* 74: 30–55.

Hyman, J. 1992. "The Causal Theory of Perception." *Philosophical Quarterly* 42: 277–96.

Ichikawa, J., and Steup, M. 2012. "The Analysis of Knowledge." *The Stanford Encyclopedia of Philosophy*: <http://plato.stanford.edu/entries/knowledge-analysis/> <accessed 8/17/15>.

Ivanov, I. 2011. "Pains and Sounds." *Journal of Consciousness Studies* 18: 143–63.

Jackson, F. 1977. *Perception: A Representative Theory*. Cambridge: Cambridge University Press.

Jackson, F. 1982. "Epiphenomenal Qualia." *Philosophical Quarterly* 32: 127–36.

Jackson, F. 1986. "What Mary Didn't Know." *Journal of Philosophy* 83: 291–95.

Jagnow, R. 2012. "Representationalism and the Perspectival Character of Perceptual Experience." *Philosophical Studies* 157: 227–49.

Jeshion, R. 2010. "Singular Thought: Acquaintance, Semantic Instrumentalism, and Cognitivism." *New Essays on Singular Thought*, ed. R. Jeshion. Oxford: Oxford University Press.

Johnston, M. 1992. "How to Speak of the Colors." *Philosophical Studies* 68: 221–63.

Johnston, M. 2004. "The Obscure Object of Hallucination." *Philosophical Studies* 120: 113–83.

Johnston, M. 2011. "On a Neglected Epistemic Virtue." *Philosophical Issues* 21: 165–218.

Johnston, M. 2014. "The Problem with the Content View." *Does Perception Have Content?*, ed. B. Brogaard. Oxford: Oxford University Press.

Joyce, J. 2005. "How Probabilities Reflect Evidence." *Philosophical Perspectives* 19: 153–78.

Julesz, B. 1981. "A Theory of Preattentive Texture Discrimination Based on First-Order Statistics of Textons." *Biological Cybernetics* 41: 131–8.

Kahnt, T., Grueschow, M., Speck, O., and Haynes, J. 2011. "Perceptual Learning and Decision-Making in Human Medial Frontal Cortex." *Neuron* 70: 549–59.

Kant, I. 1781. *Kritik der reinen Vernunft. Critique of Pure Reason*, trans. N. K. Smith. New York: St Martin's Press (1965).

Kaplan, D. 1989. "Demonstratives" and "Afterthoughts." *Themes From Kaplan*, ed. J. Almog, J. Perry, and H. Wettstein. Oxford: Oxford University Press.

Kelly, T. 2003. "Epistemic Rationality as Instrumental Rationality: A Critique." *Philosophy and Phenomenological Research* 66: 612–40.

Kind, A. 2003. "What's so Transparent about Transparency?" *Philosophical Studies* 115: 225–44.

King, J. C. 2007. *The Nature and Structure of Content*. Oxford: Oxford University Press.

King, J. C. 2015. "Acquaintance, Singular Thought, and Propositional Constituency." *Philosophical Studies* 172: 543–60.

Koch, C., Massimini, M., Boly, M., and Tononi, G. 2016. "Neural Correlates of Consciousness: Progress and Problems." *Nature Reviews Neuroscience* 17: 307–21.

Kriegel, U. 2009. *Subjective Consciousness: A Self-Representational Theory*. Oxford: Oxford University Press.

Kriegel, U. 2011. "The Veil of Abstracta." *Philosophical Issues* 21: 245–67.

Kripke, S. 1972. *Naming and Necessity*. Cambridge, MA: Harvard University Press.

Krummenacher, J., Grubert, A., et al. 2010. "Inter-Trial and Redundant-Signals Effects in Visual Search and Discrimination Tasks: Separable Pre-Attentive and Post-Selective Effects." *Vision Research* 50: 1382–95.

Lackey, J. 2007. "Why we don't Deserve Credit for Everything we Know." *Synthese* 158: 345–61.

Lackey, J. 2009. "Knowledge and Credit." *Philosophical Studies* 142: 27–42.

Lasonen-Aarnio, M. 2010. "Unreasonable Knowledge." *Philosophical Perspectives* 24: 1–21.

Law, C. T., and Gold, J. I. 2008. "Neural Correlates of Perceptual Learning in a Sensory-Motor, but not a Sensory, Cortical Area." *Nature Neuroscience* 11: 505–13.

Lehrer, K. 1990. *Theory of Knowledge*. Boulder, CO: Westview Press.

Lehrer, K., and Cohen, S. 1983. "Justification, Truth, and Coherence." *Synthese* 55: 191–207.

Levine, J. 1983. "Materialism and Qualia: The Explanatory Gap." *Pacific Philosophical Quarterly* 64: 354–61.

Lewis, D. 1966. "An Argument for the Identity Theory." *Journal of Philosophy* 63: 17–25.

Lewis, D. 1973. *Counterfactuals*. Oxford: Blackwell.

Lewis, D. 1980. "Veridical Hallucination and Prosthetic Vision." *Australasian Journal of Philosophy* 58: 239–49.

Lewis, D. 1997. "Finkish Dispositions." *Philosophical Quarterly* 47: 143–58.

Li, S., Mayhew, S. D., and Kourtzi, Z. 2009. "Learning Shapes the Representation of Behavioral Choice in the Human Brain." *Neuron* 62: 441–52.

Li, W., Piech, V., and Gilbert, C. D. 2004. "Perceptual Learning and Top-Down Influences in Primary Visual Cortex." *Nature Neuroscience* 7: 651–57.

Littlejohn, C. 2017. "How and Why Knowledge is First." *Knowledge-First Epistemology*, ed. A. Carter, E. Gordon, and B. Jarvis. Oxford: Oxford University Press.

Loar, B. 2003. "Transparent Experience and the Availability of Qualia." *New Philosophical Perspectives*, ed. Q. Smith and A. Jokic. Oxford: Oxford University Press.

Lloyd, D. 2011. "Through a Glass Darkly: Schizophrenia and Functional Brain Imaging." *Philosophy, Psychiatry and Psychology* 18: 257–74.

Locke, J. 1690. *An Essay Concerning Human Understanding*. London: Thomas Bassett.

Logue, H. 2012. "Why Naive Realism?" *Proceedings of the Aristotelian Society* 112: 211–37.

Logue, H. 2014. "Experiential Content and Naïve Realism: A Reconciliation." *Does Perception Have Content?*, ed. B. Brogaard. Oxford: Oxford University Press.

Luna, R., Hernández, A., Brody, C. D., and Romo, R. 2005. "Neural Codes for Perceptual Discrimination in Primary Somatosensory Cortex." *Nature Neuroscience* 8: 1210–19.

Lycan, W. G. 1996. *Consciousness and Experience*. Cambridge, MA: MIT Press.

Lyons, J. 2009. *Perception and Basic Beliefs: Zombies, Modules, and the Problem of the External World*. Oxford: Oxford University Press.

McDowell, J. 1982. "Criteria, Defeasibility, and Knowledge." *Proceedings of the British Academy* 68: 455–79.

McDowell, J. 1984. "*De Re* Senses." *The Philosophical Quarterly* 34: 283–94.

McDowell, J. 1994. *Mind and World*. Cambridge, MA: Harvard University Press.

McDowell, J. 2013. "Perceptual Experience: Both Relational and Contentful." *European Journal of Philosophy* 21: 144–57.

McGinn, C. 1982. *The Character of Mind*. Oxford: Oxford University Press.

McGrath, M. 2013. "Dogmatism, Underminers and Skepticism." *Philosophy and Phenomenological Research* 86: 533–62.

McGrath, M. 2016. "Schellenberg on the Epistemic Force of Experience." *Philosophical Studies* 173: 897–905.

McGrath, M., and Fantl, J. 2002. "Evidence, Pragmatics, and Justification." *The Philosophical Review* 111: 67–94.

McGrath, M., and Fantl, J. 2009. *Knowledge in an Uncertain World*. Oxford: Oxford University Press.

McLaughlin, B. 2007. "Type Materialism for Phenomenal Consciousness." *Blackwell Companion to Consciousness*, ed. M. Velmans and S. Schneider. Oxford: Blackwell Publishing.

Mach, E. 1959. *The Analysis of Sensations, and the Relation of the Physical to the Psychical*. New York: Dover Publications Inc.

Machery, E. 2007. "Concept Empiricism: A Methodological Critique." *Cognition* 104: 19–46.

Macpherson, F. 2003. "Novel Colors and the Content of Experience." *Pacific Philosophical Quarterly* 84: 43–66.

Macpherson, F. 2006. "Ambiguous Figures and the Content of Experience." *Noûs* 40: 82–117.

Macpherson, F. 2011. "Individuating the Senses." *The Senses: Classical and Contemporary Readings*, ed. F. Macpherson. Oxford: Oxford University Press.

Macpherson, F. 2012. "Cognitive Penetration of Colour Experience: Rethinking the Issue in Light of an Indirect Mechanism." *Philosophy and Phenomenological Research* 84: 24–62.

Macpherson, F., and Batty, C. 2016. "Redefining Illusion and Hallucination in Light of New Cases." *Philosophical Issues* 26: 263–96.

Malik, J. and Perona, P. 1990. "Preattentive Texture Discrimination with Early Vision Mechanisms Effects." *Journal of the Optical Society of America* 7: 923–32.

Manzotti, R. 2011. "The Spread Mind: Is Consciousness Situated?" *Teorema: International Journal of Philosophy* 30: 55–78.

Martin, C. B. 1996. "Dispositions and Conditionals." *The Philosophical Quarterly* 44: 1–8.

Martin, M. G. F. 1998. "Setting Things Before the Mind." *Royal Institute of Philosophy Supplement* 43: 157–79.

Martin, M. G. F. 2002a. "The Transparency of Experience." *Mind and Language* 17: 376–425.

Martin, M. G. F. 2002b. "Particular Thoughts and Singular Thoughts." *Logic, Thought and Language*, ed. A. O'Hear. Cambridge: Cambridge University Press.

Martin, M. G. F. 2004. "The Limits of Self-Awareness." *Philosophical Studies* 103: 37–89.

Martin, M. G. F. 2010. "What's in a Look?" *Perceiving the World*, ed. B. Nanay. Oxford: Oxford University Press.

Marušić, B. 2016. "Asymmetry Arguments." *Philosophical Studies* 173: 1081–102.

Matthen, M. 2015. "The Individuation of the Senses." *Oxford Handbook of the Philosophy of Perception*, ed. M. Matthen. Oxford: Oxford University Press.

Maund, J. B. 1995. *Colors: Their Nature and Representation*. Cambridge: Cambridge University Press.

Maund, J. B. 2006. "The Illusion Theory of Colour: An Anti-Realist Theory." *Dialectica* 60: 245–68.

Maund, J. B. 2011. "Color Eliminativism." *Primary and Secondary Qualities: The Historical and Ongoing Debates*, ed. L. Nolan. Oxford: Oxford University Press.

Mehta, N. 2014. "The Limited Role of Particulars in Phenomenal Experience." *The Journal of Philosophy* 111: 311–31.

Mehta, N., and Ganson, T. 2016. "On the Generality of Experience: A Reply to French and Gomes." *Philosophical Studies* 173: 3223–9.

Mendelovici, A. 2013. "Reliable Misrepresentation and Tracking Theories of Mental Representation." *Philosophical Studies* 165: 421–43.

Metzger, W. 1930. "Optische Untersuchungen am Ganzfeld." *Psychologische Forschungen* 13: 6–29.

Millar, A. 1991. *Reasons and Experiences*. Oxford: Clarendon Press.

Millar, A. 2007. "What the Disjunctivist Is Right about." *Philosophy and Phenomenological Research* 74: 176–99.

Millar, A. 2008. "Perceptual-Recognitional Abilities and Perceptual Knowledge." *Disjunctivism: Perception, Action, Knowledge*, ed. A. Haddock and F. Macpherson. Oxford: Oxford University Press.

Millar, B. 2016. "Frege's Puzzle for Perception." *Philosophy and Phenomenological Research* 93: 368–92.

Millikan, R. G. 1984. *Language, Thought and Other Biological Categories*. Cambridge, MA: MIT Press.

Millikan, R. G. 1989. "In Defense of Proper Functions." *Philosophy of Science* 56: 288–302.

Miracchi, L. 2015. "Competence to Know." *Philosophical Studies* 172: 29–56.

Mizrahi, V. 2009. "Is Color Composition Phenomenal?" *Color Perception: Physiology, Processes and Analysis*, ed. D. Skusevich and P. Matikas. Hauppage: Nova Science Publishers.

Montague, M. 2011. "The Phenomenology of Particularity." *Cognitive Phenomenology*, ed. T. Bayne and M. Montague. Oxford: Oxford University Press.

Moore, G. E. 1925. "A Defence of Common Sense." *Contemporary British Philosophy*, ed. J. H. Muirhead. London: George Allen and Unwin. (Reprinted in G. E. Moore, *Philosophical Papers*, 1959. New York: Macmillan.)

Moore, G. E. 1953. *Some Main Problems of Philosophy*. London: George Allen and Unwin.

Morrison, J. 2013. "Anti-Atomism about Color Representation." *Noûs* 47: 94–122.

Moss, S. 2015. "Time-Slice Epistemology and Action Under Indeterminacy." *Oxford Studies in Epistemology*, ed. J. Hawthorne and T. Gendler. Oxford: Oxford University Press.

Munton, J. 2016. "Visual Confidences and Direct Perceptual Justification." *Philosophical Topics* 44: 301–26.

Nagel, J. 2013. "Knowledge as a Mental State." *Oxford Studies in Epistemology* 4: 273–308.

Nanay, B. 2010. "A Modal Theory of Content." *Journal of Philosophy* 107: 412–31.

Nanay, B. 2012. "Perceiving Tropes." *Erkenntnis* 77: 1–14.

Nanay, B. 2013. "The Representationalism versus Relationalism Debate: Explanatory Contextualism about Perception." *European Journal of Philosophy* 23: 321–36.

Nanay, B. 2014. "Empirical Problems with Anti-Representationalism." *Does Perception have Content?*, ed. B. Brogaard. Oxford: Oxford University Press.

Neander, K. 1991. "Functions as Selected Effects." *Philosophy of Science* 58: 168–84.

Neander, K. 1998. "The Division of Phenomenal Labor: A Problem for Representational Theories of Consciousness." *Philosophical Perspectives* 12, ed. J. E. Tomberlin. Atascadero, CA: Ridgeview Publishing.

Neta, R. 2003. "Contextualism and the Problem of the External World." *Philosophy and Phenomenological Research* 66: 1–31.

Neta, R. 2008. "What Evidence Do You Have?" *British Journal for the Philosophy of Science* 59: 89–119.

Neta, R. 2016. "Perceptual Evidence and the Capacity View." *Philosophical Studies* 173: 907–14.

Nickel, B. 2007. "Against Intentionalism." *Philosophical Studies* 136: 279–304.

Noë, A. 2004. *Action in Perception*. Cambridge, MA: MIT Press.

Nudds, M. 2001. "Experiencing the Production of Sounds." *European Journal of Philosophy* 9: 210–29.

O'Callaghan, C. 2010. *Sounds: A Philosophical Theory*. Oxford: Oxford University Press.

Orlandi, N. 2010. "Are Sensory Properties Represented in Perceptual Experience?" *Philosophical Psychology* 23: 721–40.

Orlandi, N. 2014. *The Innocent Eye: Why Vision is not a Cognitive Process*. New York: Oxford University Press.

Panksepp, J., and Panksepp, J. B. 2001. "A Continuing Critique of Evolutionary Psychology: Seven Sins for Seven Sinners, Plus or Minus Two." *Evolution and Cognition* 7: 56–80.

Papineau, D. 2014. "Sensory Experience and Representational Properties." *Proceedings of the Aristotelian Society* 114: 1–33.

Papineau, D. 2016. "Against Representationalism about Conscious Sensory Experience." *International Journal of Philosophical Studies* 24: 324–47.

Parsons, T. 1980. *Nonexistent Objects*. New Haven: Yale University Press.

Pasnau, R. 2016. "Therapeutic Reflections on our Bipolar History of Perception." *Analytic Philosophy* 57: 253–84.

Paul, L. 2010. "The Puzzles of Material Constitution." *Philosophy Compass* 5: 579–90.

Pautz, A. 2007. "Intentionalism and Perceptual Presence." *Philosophical Perspectives* 21, ed. J. Hawthorne. Northridge: Ridgeview Publishing Company.

Pautz, A. 2010. "Why Explain Visual Experience in Terms of Content?" *Perceiving the World*, ed. B. Nanay. Oxford: Oxford University Press.

Pautz, A. 2016. "What is my Evidence that here is a Cup?" *Philosophical Studies* 173: 915–27.

Peacocke, C. 1983. *Sense and Content: Experience, Thought, and their Relations*. Oxford: Oxford University Press.

Peacocke, C. 1992. *A Study of Concepts*. Cambridge, MA: MIT Press.

Peacocke, C. 1998. "Nonconceptual Content Defended." *Philosophy and Phenomenological Research* 63: 381–8.

Peacocke, C. 2009. "Objectivity." *Mind* 118: 739–69.

Pereboom, D. 1994. "Bats, Brain Scientists, and the Limitations of Introspection." *Philosophy and Phenomenological Research* 54: 315–29.

Phillips, I. 2013. "Hallucinating Silence." *Hallucination*, ed. F. Macpherson and D. Platchias. Cambridge, MA: MIT Press.

Phillips, I., and Block, N. 2016. "Debate on Unconscious Perception." *Current Controversies in Philosophy of Perception*, ed. B. Nanay. London: Routledge.

Plantinga, A. 1993. *Warrant and Proper Function*. Oxford: Oxford University Press.

Pollock, J. 1974. *Experience and Justification*. Princeton: Princeton University Press.

Pollock, J., and Cruz, J. 2004. "The Chimerical Appeal of Epistemic Externalism." *The Externalist Challenge*, ed. R. Schantz. Berlin: De Gruyter.

Price, H. H. 1932. *Perception*. London: Methuen.

Prinz, J. 2002. *Furnishing the Mind: Concepts and their Perceptual Basis*. Cambridge, MA: MIT Press.

Pritchard, D. 2010. "Relevant Alternatives, Perceptual Knowledge, and Discrimination." *Noûs* 44: 245–68.

Pritchard, D. 2012. *Epistemological Disjunctivism*. Oxford: Oxford University Press.

Pryor, J. 2000. "The Skeptic and the Dogmatist." *Noûs* 34: 517–49.

Pryor, J. 2001. "Highlights of Recent Epistemology." *British Journal for the Philosophy of Science* 52: 95–124.

Pryor, J. 2012. "When Warrant Transmits." *Wittgenstein, Epistemology and Mind: Themes from the Philosophy of Crispin Wright*, ed. A. Coliva. Oxford: Oxford University Press.

Putnam, H. 1975. "The Meaning of Meaning." Reprinted in his *Philosophical Papers*, vol. 1: *Mind, Language, and Reality*. Cambridge: Cambridge University Press.

Pylyshyn, Z. W. 2007. *Things and Places: How the Mind Connects with the World*. Cambridge, MA: MIT Press.

Pylyshyn, Z. W., and Storm, R. W. 1988. "Tracking Multiple Independent Targets: Evidence for a Parallel Tracking Mechanism." *Spatial Vision* 3: 179–97.

Raleigh, T. 2014. "A New Approach to 'Perfect' Hallucinations." *Journal of Consciousness Studies* 21: 81–110.

Raleigh, T. 2015. "Phenomenology Without Representation." *European Journal of Philosophy* 23: 1209–37.

Recanati, F. 1993. *Direct Reference: From Language to Thought*. London: Blackwell.

Recanati, F. 2010. "Singular Thought: In Defence of Acquaintance." *New Essays on Singular Thought*, ed. R. Jeshion. Oxford: Oxford University Press.

Reid, T. 1764. *An Inquiry into the Human Mind: On the Principles of Common Sense*. *The Works of Thomas Reid*, ed. W. Hamilton. Edinburgh: Maclachlan and Stewart (1863).

Rescorla, M. 2014. "Perceptual Constancies and Perceptual Modes of Presentation." *Philosophy and Phenomenological Research* 88: 468–76.

Robinson, H. 1994. *Perception*. London: Routledge.

Robinson, W. 2004. *Understanding Phenomenal Consciousness*. Cambridge: Cambridge University Press.

Rosen, G. 2010. "Metaphysical Dependence: Grounding and Reduction." *Modality: Metaphysics, Logic, and Epistemology*, ed. B. Hale and A. Hoffmann. Oxford: Oxford University Press.

Russell, B. 1911. "Knowledge by Acquaintance and Knowledge by Description." *Proceedings of the Aristotelian Society* 11: 108–28.

Russell, B. 1913. *Theory of Knowledge*. London: Routledge.

Russell, B. 1948. *Human Knowledge: Its Scope and Limits*. New York: Simon and Schuster.

Sagi, D., and Julesz, B. 1985. "Detection versus Discrimination of Visual Orientation." *Perception* 14: 619–28.

Schaffer, J. 2005. "Contrastive Knowledge." *Oxford Studies in Epistemology*, ed. T. S. Gendler and J. Hawthorne. Oxford: Oxford University Press.

Schaffer, J. 2009. "On What Grounds What." *Metametaphysics: New Essays on the Foundations of Ontology*, ed. D. Chalmers, D. Manley, and R. Wasserman. Oxford: Oxford University Press.

Schellenberg, S. 2006. *Perception in Perspective*. Doctoral Dissertation. University of Pittsburgh.

Schellenberg, S. 2007. "Action and Self-Location in Perception." *Mind* 116: 603–32.

Schellenberg, S. 2008. "The Situation-Dependency of Perception." *The Journal of Philosophy* 105: 55–84.

Schellenberg, S. 2010. "The Particularity and Phenomenology of Perceptual Experience." *Philosophical Studies* 149: 19–48.

Schellenberg, S. 2011a. "Perceptual Content Defended." *Noûs* 45: 714–50.

Schellenberg, S. 2011b. "Ontological Minimalism about Phenomenology." *Philosophy and Phenomenological Research* 83: 1–40.

Schellenberg, S. 2012. "Sameness of Fregean Sense." *Synthese*, special volume edited by R. Briggs, 189: 163–75.

Schellenberg, S. 2013a. "Experience and Evidence." *Mind* 122: 699–747.

Schellenberg, S. 2013b. "Externalism and the Gappy Content of Hallucination." *Hallucination*, ed. F. E. Macpherson and D. Platchias. Cambridge, MA: MIT Press.

Schellenberg, S. 2014a. "The Relational and Representational Character of Perceptual Experience." *Does Perception have Content?*, ed. B. Brogaard. Oxford: Oxford University Press.

Schellenberg, S. 2014b. "The Epistemic Force of Perceptual Experience." With a response by Alex Byrne, *Philosophical Studies* 170: 87–100.

Schellenberg, S. 2016a. "Perceptual Particularity." *Philosophy and Phenomenological Research* 93: 25–54.

Schellenberg, S. 2016b. "Phenomenal Evidence and Factive Evidence." Symposium with comments by Matt McGrath, Ram Neta, and Adam Pautz, *Philosophical Studies* 173: 875–96.

Schellenberg, S. 2016c. "Phenomenal Evidence and Factive Evidence Defended: Replies to McGrath, Neta, and Pautz." *Philosophical Studies* 173: 929–46.

Schellenberg, S. 2017. "Perceptual Capacities, Knowledge, and Gettier Cases." *Explaining Knowledge: New Essays on the Gettier Problem*, ed. R. Borges, C. de Almeida, and P. Klein. Oxford: Oxford University Press.

Schroer, R. 2002. "Seeing It All Clearly: The Real Story on Blurry Vision." *American Philosophical Quarterly* 39: 297–301.

Schwenkler, J., and Briscoe, R. 2015. "Conscious Vision in Action." *Cognitive Science* 39: 1435–67.

Schwitzgebel, E. 2008. "The Unreliability of Introspection." *The Philosophical Review* 117: 245–73.

Scott, L. S., Pascalis, O., and Nelson, C. A. 2007. "A Domain-General Theory of the Development of Perceptual Discrimination." *Current Directions in Psychological Science* 16: 197–201.

Searle, J. 1983. *Intentionality: An Essay in the Philosophy of Mind*. Cambridge: Cambridge University Press.

Segal, G. 1996. "The Modularity of Theory of Mind." *Theories of Theories of Mind*, ed. P. Carruthers and P. K. Smith. Cambridge: Cambridge University Press.

Shoemaker, S. 1982. "The Inverted Spectrum." *The Journal of Philosophy* 79: 357–81.

Shoemaker, S. 1994. "Phenomenal Character." *Noûs* 28: 21–38.

Siegel, S. 2006. "Subject and Object in the Contents of Visual Experience." *Philosophical Review* 115: 355–88.

Siegel, S. 2010. "Do Visual Experiences have Content?" *Perceiving the World*, ed. B. Nanay. Oxford: Oxford University Press.

Siegel, S. 2011. *The Contents of Visual Experience*. Oxford: Oxford University Press.

Siewert, C. 1998. *The Significance of Consciousness*. Princeton: Princeton University Press.

Silins, N. 2005. "Deception and Evidence." *Philosophical Perspective* 19: 375–404.

Silins, N. 2011. "Seeing Through the 'Veil of Perception'." *Mind* 120: 329–67.

Silva, A. and Bickle, J. 2009. "Science of Research and the Search for Molecular Mechanisms of Cognition." *Oxford Handbook of Philosophy and Neuroscience*, ed. J. Bickle. Oxford: Oxford University Press.

Smith, A. D. 2002. *The Problem of Perception*. Cambridge, MA: Harvard University Press.

Smith, A. D. 2008. "Translucent Experiences." *Philosophical Studies* 140: 197–212.

Smith, B. 2007. "The Objectivity of Taste and Tasting." *Questions of Taste: The Philosophy of Wine*, ed. B. Smith. Oxford: Oxford University Press.

Smithies, D. 2011. "What is the Role of Consciousness in Demonstrative Thought." *The Journal of Philosophy* 108: 5–34.

Smithies, D. 2012. "Mentalism and Epistemic Transparency." *Australasian Journal of Philosophy* 90: 723–41.

Snowdon, P. 1981. "Perception, Vision and Causation." *Proceedings of the Aristotelian Society* 81: 175–92.

Snowdon, P. 1992. "How to Interpret Direct Perception." *The Contents of Experience*, ed. T. Crane. Cambridge: Cambridge University Press.

Sosa, E. 1980. "The Raft and the Pyramid: Coherence versus Foundations in the Theory of Knowledge." *Midwest Studies in Philosophy* 5: 3–25.

Sosa, E. 1991. *Knowledge in Perspective*. Cambridge: Cambridge University Press.

Sosa, E. 2006. "Internal Foundations or External Virtues?" *Philosophical Studies* 131: 769–33.

Sosa, E. 2007. *A Virtue Epistemology: Apt Belief and Reflective Knowledge*. New York: Oxford University Press.

Sosa, E. 2010. "How Competence Matters in Epistemology." *Philosophical Perspectives* 24: 465–75.

Sosa, E. 2015. *Judgment and Agency*. Oxford: Oxford University Press.

Soteriou, M. 2000. "The Particularity of Visual Perception." *European Journal of Philosophy* 8: 173–89.

Soteriou, M. 2005. "The Subjective View of Experience and its Objective Commitments." *Proceedings of the Aristotelian Society* 105: 177–90.

Soteriou, M. 2013. *The Mind's Construction*. Oxford: Oxford University Press.

Speaks, J. 2005. "Is there a Problem about Non-Conceptual Content?" *The Philosophical Review* 113: 359–98.

Speaks, J. 2006. "Is Mental Content Prior to Linguistic Meaning?" *Noûs* 40: 428–67.

Speaks, J. 2009. "Transparency, Intentionalism, and the Nature of Perceptual Content." *Philosophy and Phenomenological Research* 79: 539–73.

Speaks, J. 2011. "Frege's Puzzle and Descriptive Enrichment." *Philosophy and Phenomenological Research* 83: 267–82.

Speaks, J. 2014. *Transparency and Availability: An Essay in the Philosophy of Perception*. Oxford: Oxford University Press.

Stanley, J. 2005. *Knowledge and Practical Interests*. Oxford: Oxford University Press.

Stazicker, J. 2016. "The Visual Presence of Determinable Properties." *Phenomenal Presence*, ed. F. E. Macpherson, F. Dorsch, and M. Nida-Rümelin. Oxford: Oxford University Press.

Stevens, S. S. 1939. "Psychology and the Science of Science." *Psychological Bulletin* 36: 221–63.

Stoljar, D. 2004. "The Argument from Diaphanousness." *New Essays in the Philosophy of Language and Mind. Supplemental volume of The Canadian Journal of Philosophy*, ed. M. Ezcurdia, R. Stainton, and C. Viger. Calgary: University of Calgary Press.

Strawson, P. F. 1979. "Perception and its Objects." *Perception and Identity*, ed. G. F. MacDonald. London: Macmillan.

Strevens, M. 2004. "The Causal and Unification Accounts of Explanation Unified—Causally." *Noûs* 38: 154–79.

Sundström, P. 2013. "Are Colors Visually Complex?" *Johanssonian Investigations: Essays in Honour of Ingvar Johansson on his Seventieth Birthday*, ed. C. Svennerlind, J. Almäng, and R. Ingthorsson. Frankfurt: Ontos Verlag.

Sylvan, K. forthcoming. "Knowledge as a Non-Normative Relation." *Philosophy and Phenomenological Research*.

Thompson, B. J. 2009. "Senses for Senses." *Australasian Journal of Philosophy* 87: 99–117.

To, M. P., Gilchrist, I. D., et al. 2011. "Discrimination of Natural Scenes in Central and Peripheral Vision." *Vision Research* 51: 1686–98.

Toribio, J. 2002. "Modularity, Relativism, and Neural Constructivism." *Cognitive Science Quarterly* 2: 93–106.

Travis, C. 2004. "Silence of the Senses." *Mind* 113: 57–94.

Tucker, C. 2010. "Why Open-Minded People Should Endorse Dogmatism." *Philosophical Perspectives* 24: 529–45.

Turri, J. 2009. "The Ontology of Epistemic Reasons." *Noûs* 43: 490–512.

Turri, J. 2010. "Does Perceiving Entail Knowing?" *Theoria* 76: 197–206.

Tye, M. 1995. *Ten Problems of Consciousness: A Representational Theory of the Phenomenal Mind*. Cambridge, MA: MIT Press.

Tye, M. 2000. *Consciousness, Color and Content*. Cambridge, MA: MIT Press.

Tye, M. 2002. "Representationalism and the Transparency of Experience." *Noûs* 36: 137–51.

Tye, M. 2007. "Intentionalism and the Argument from no Common Content." *Philosophical Perspectives* 21, ed. J. Hawthorne. Northridge: Ridgeview Publishing Company.

Tye, M. 2009. *Consciousness Revisited: Materialism Without Phenomenal Concepts*. Cambridge, MA: MIT Press.

Unger, P. 1979. "There are no Ordinary Things." *Synthese* 41: 117–54.

van Inwagen, P. 1990. *Material Beings*. Ithaca, NY: Cornell University Press.

Vihvelin, K. 2013. *Causes, Laws, and Free Will: Why Determinism Doesn't Matter*. Oxford: Oxford University Press.

Wackermann, J., Pütz, P., and Allefeld, C. 2008. "Ganzfeld-Induced Hallucinatory Experience, its Phenomenology and Cerebral Electrophysiology." *Cortex* 44: 1364–78.

Watson, A., and Robson, J. 1981. "Discrimination at Threshold: Labelled Detectors in Human Vision." *Vision Research* 21: 1115–22.

Watzl, S. 2014. "Perceptual Guidance." *Ratio* 27: 369–505.

Weatherson, B. 2005. "Scepticism, Rationalism, and Empiricism." *Oxford Studies in Epistemology* 1, ed. T. Gendler and J. Hawthorne. Oxford: Oxford University Press.

Wedgwood, R. 2002. "Internalism Explained." *Philosophy and Phenomenological Research* 65: 349–69.

White, R. 2006. "Problems for Dogmatism." *Philosophical Studies* 131: 525–57.

Whittle, A. 2010. "Dispositional Abilities." *Philosophers' Imprint* 10: 1–23.

Williams, D. C. 1953. "The Elements of Being." *Review of Metaphysics* 7: 3–18 and 171–92.

Williamson, T. 2000. *Knowledge and Its Limits*. Oxford: Oxford University Press.

Williamson, T. 2006. "Can Cognition be Factorized into Internal and External Components?" *Contemporary Debates in Cognitive Science*, ed. R. Stainton. Oxford: Blackwell.

Wilson, K. 2013. "Reid's Direct Realism and Visible Figure." *The Philosophical Quarterly* 63: 783–803.

Wright, C. 2007. "The Perils of Dogmatism." *Themes from G. E. Moore: New Essays in Epistemology and Ethics*, ed. S. Nuccetelli and G. Seay. Oxford: Oxford University Press.

Wright, L. 1973. "Functions." *The Philosophical Review* 82: 139–68.

Wu, W. 2014. "Against Division: Consciousness, Information, and Visual Stream." *Mind and Language* 29: 383–406.

Wu, W. and Cho, R. 2013. "Mechanisms of Auditory Verbal Hallucination in Schizophrenia." *Frontiers in Psychiatry 4: 155.*

Zagzebski, L. 1996. *Virtues of the Mind.* Cambridge: Cambridge University Press.

Index

Printed and bound by CPI Group (UK) Ltd, Croydon, CR0 4YY